Bill 'Swan
winning w
songs and
his youth
South Wales. Bill was forced to give
up any idea he had of a 'career' as a
cricketer when a stint at agricultural
college was curtailed because of illness,
and so began his hobby of writing.
After backpacking through three continents and working in the wine
industry, his writing hobby blossomed into a career.

His first collection of short stories, *Beckom Pop. 64*, was published
in 1988; his second, *Old Yanconian Daze*, in 1995; and his third,
Looking for Dad, in 1998. During 1999, Bill released *Australia*, a CD
of his songs and stories. That was followed in 2002 by *A Drover's
Wife* and *Glory, Glory — A Tribute to the Royal Flying Doctor Service* in
2008. He has written soundtrack songs and music for the television
documentaries, *The Last Mail from Birdsville — The Story of Tom
Kruse, Source to Sea — The Story of the Murray Riverboats* and the
German travel documentaries *Traumzeit auf dem Stuart Highway*
and *Clinic Flights (Tilpa & Marble Bar)*.

Bill runs writing workshops in schools and communities and is a
teacher of short story writing within the Adelaide Institute of TAFE's
Professional Writing Unit. He has won and judged many nationwide
short story writing and songwriting competitions and short film
awards.

Great Australian CWA Stories is part of Bill's very successful
series of 'Great Australian' stories including: *New Great Australian
Flying Doctor Stories* (2010), *The ABC Book of Great Aussie Stories
for Young People* (2010),*Great Australian Stories — Outback Towns
and Pubs* (2009), *More Great Australian Flying Doctor Stories*, (2007),
Great Australian Railway Stories (2005), *Great Australian Droving
Stories* (2003) *Great Australian Shearing Stories* (2001) and *Great
Australian Flying Doctor Stories* (1999). Bill's story of *Goldie* was
published in 2008.

More information about the author can be found on
www.billswampymarsh.com

Great Australian
CWA
STORIES

Great Australian
CWA
STORIES

Bill 'Swampy' Marsh

ABC
Books

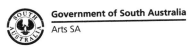

Government of South Australia
Arts SA

The writing of this book was assisted by the South Australian Government through Arts SA.

The ABC 'Wave' device is a trademark of the Australian Broadcasting Corporation and is used under licence by HarperCollins*Publishers* Australia.

First published in Australia in 2011
by HarperCollins*Publishers* Australia Pty Limited
ABN 36 009 913 517
harpercollins.com.au

HarperCollins*Publishers*
Level 13, 201 Elizabeth Street, Sydney NSW 2000, Australia
31 View Road, Glenfield, Auckland 0627, New Zealand
1–A Hamilton House, Connaught Place, New Delhi — 110 001, India
77–85 Fulham Palace Road, London W6 8JB, United Kingdom
2 Bloor Street East, 20th floor, Toronto, Ontario M4W 1A8, Canada
10 East 53rd Street, New York NY 10022, USA

National Library of Australia Cataloguing-in-Publication data:

Marsh, Bill, 1950–
Great Australian Country Women's Association Stories —/ Bill 'Swampy' Marsh.
ISBN: 9780733324352 (pbk.)
Series: Great Australian stories.
Country life—Australia—Anecdotes.
Australia—Social life and customs.
Other Authors/Contributors: Australian Broadcasting Corporation.
305.9630994

Cover designed by Jane Waterhouse, HarperCollins Design Studio
Cover image © James Elsby/Newspix
Author photo by Chris Carter
May by Alicia Freile, Tango Media
Typeset in 10/15pt ITC Bookman by Kirby Jones
Printed and bound in Australia by Griffin Press
70gsm Classic used by HarperCollins*Publishers* is a natural, recyclable product made from wood grown in sustainable forests. The manufacturing processes conform to the environmental regulations in the country of origin, Finland.

5 4 3   12 13 14

Dedicated to all the wonderful women of the CWA.

Recipes from CWA NSW taken from *The Coronation Cookery Book*, first published 1937 and the *21st Birthday Cookery Book of the CWA Tasmania*, first published 1957. Many thanks to both for allowing me to use the recipes and household hints in this book.

Contents

Introduction   1
Conversion Tables   4
Household Hints   6

Entrees and Savouries   11–14

Judy Anicomatis — Darwin, Northern Territory   15
Elaine Armstrong — Oura, New South Wales   19
Valerie Asche — Darwin, Northern Territory   22
Melinda Beckett — Boulder and Metropolitan, Western Australia   25
Jean Black — Casterton, Victoria   30
Jessie Black — Barmoya, Queensland   34

Soups   36–38

Kit Bright — Moss Vale, New South Wales   39
Lillian Burgess — Palmerston, Northern Territory   42
Roddy Calvert — Tennant Creek, Northern Territory   44
Eva Campbell — Camden, New South Wales   47
Bette Chapman — Palmerston, Northern Territory   51
Helen Christie — Rochester, Victoria   53

Meat   55–61

Elizabeth Clark — Cressy, Tasmania   62
Faye Clark — Molong, New South Wales   65
Carol Clay — Packenham, Victoria   69
Mavis Cooper, OBE — Jamestown, South Australia   73
Rosalie Crocker — Bordertown, South Australia   77
Alice Davies — Bencubbin, Western Australia   80

Poultry   84–87

Mary Edwards — Arno Bay, South Australia 88
Nikki Egginton — Quairading, Western Australia 92
Maude Ellis — Darwin, Northern Territory 95
Coral Elsden — Keppoch, South Australia 98
Valerie Fisher AO, OBE —Barnawartha, Victoria 102
Dulcie French — West Ulverstone, Tasmania 108

Fish 111–114

Nancy Fuchs — Darwin, Northern Territory 115
Judy Fulton — Broadford-Mount Piper, Victoria 120
Lorraine Greenfield — Branch of the Air, South Australia 123
Margaret Hampel — Loxton, South Australia 126
Lynette Harris — Carlisle River, Victoria 129
Shauna Hartig — Alice Springs, Northern Territory 133

Sauces 137–139

Jo Hawkins — Perth Belles, Western Australia 140
Jill Hayes — Huonville, Tasmania 144
Eulie Henderson — Port Germein and Adelaide, South Australia 148
Janet Henderson — Nelson Bay, New South Wales 152
Alma Herrmann — Murrami, New South Wales 156
Jennie Hill — Miles, Queensland 159

Pickles and Chutneys 162–163

Joyce Hughes — West Hobart, Tasmania 164
Gloria Hyatt — Glenreagh, New South Wales 165
Nicola Kelliher — Wandering, Western Australia 168
Heather Kerr — Oaklands, New South Wales 173
Joan Kesson — Lucaston, Tasmania 176
Maria Keys — Condamine-Arubial, Queensland 179

Scones, Buns, Pikelets, Tea Cakes and Loaves 183–187

Jane Kidd — Croydon, Queensland 188
Barbara Kregor — Wattle Hill, Tasmania 192
Marie Lally AM — Lock, South Australia 195
Janette Mason — Tatura, Victoria 200
Val Maynard — Cobden, Victoria 203
Joyce McDonald — Myrtleford, Victoria 206

Large Cakes 212–215

Wendy Meyer — Kaniva, Victoria	216
Mavis Mincherton — Wongan Hills, Western Australia	221
Heather Mitchell — Happy Valley, South Australia	224
Anne Morris — Mt Isa, Queensland	227
Shirley Morrisby — Howrah, Tasmania	230
Lynne Robinson — Wollar, New South Wales	233

Small Cakes 236–238

Yvonne Scarrabelotti — Kyogle, New South Wales	239
Geraldine Scott — Wrattonbully, South Australia	242
Ruth Shanks — Dubbo, New South Wales	245
Mary Shattock — Booborowie, South Australia	248
Pam Simcoe — Lisarow-Ourimbah, New South Wales	252
Vera Stephenson — Spalding, South Australia	257

Biscuits and Cookies 261–263

June Thiedeke — Goovigen, Queensland	264
Pam Vallett — Fairfield, New South Wales	267
Dorothy Walker — Eromanga, Queensland	271
Helen Wall — Caniambo, Victoria	274
Joan Wallwork — Hamilton, Victoria	278
Janette Williams — Trundle, New South Wales	282

Confectionery and Homemade Sweets 284–287

Evelyn Wilson — Darwin, Northern Territory	288
Dawn Worrall — Para Hills, South Australia	292
Gloria Wright — Cloncurry, Queensland	296
Robyn Wright — Moruya, New South Wales	299

Darwin
Palmerston

Western
Australia

Bencubbin
Wongan Hills
Perth Belles
Quairading
Boulder and Metropolitan
Wandering

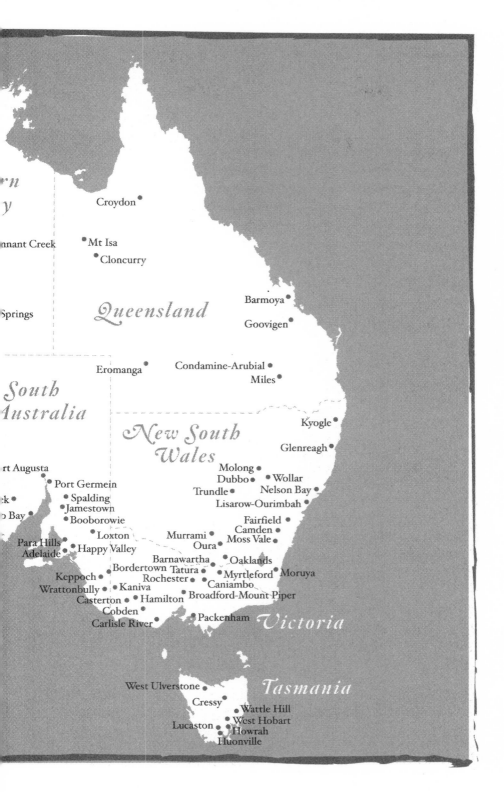

rn
y

Croydon

nnant Creek   Mt Isa
                       Cloncurry

Springs   *Queensland*   Barmoya

                                                 Goovigen

                          Eromanga   Condamine-Arubial
South   Miles
Australia
                          New South   Kyogle
                              Wales   Glenreagh

rt Augusta   Molong
                                   Dubbo   Wollar
         Port Germein   Trundle   Nelson Bay
         Spalding   Lisarow-Ourimbah
         Jamestown
         Booborowie   Fairfield
                    Loxton   Camden
Para Hills   Murrami   Moss Vale
Adelaide   Happy Valley   Oura
                        Barnawartha   Oaklands
         Keppoch   Bordertown Tatura   Myrtleford   Moruya
Wrattonbully   Kaniva Rochester   Caniambo
         Casterton   Hamilton Broadford-Mount Piper
            Cobden
         Carlisle River   Packenham *Victoria*

                                              Tasmania
            West Ulverstone
                        Cressy
                              Wattle Hill
            Lucaston   West Hobart
                          Howrah
                       Huonville

Introduction

I began the journey of this book back in 2008. Having lived in the few rural towns in New South Wales I was well aware of the importance of the Country Women's Association (CWA). In fact, they were the backbone of many of these communities. Whenever there was a footy or cricket match, the CWA ladies were always there selling sandwiches, tea, cakes, scones and, of course, there was the inevitable raffle. Whenever there was a fire or a flood they'd be right at hand helping out wherever they could. If someone was going through a hard time they'd be the first at the door offering support. They catered at weddings and funerals. They ran our annual CWA Ball.

To interview as many members of the CWA as possible I've travelled as much of this beautiful land as economically possible. Thanks largely to Arts SA, who helped with travel expenses, and also with a contribution from ABC Books, there were the memorable road trips from Adelaide into western and central New South Wales then, later on, across a surprisingly 'lush' Hay Plain to Sydney. There was the journey through eastern South Australia and Victoria, and on to Melbourne. I was able to visit Tasmania and on one of my story-collection excursions sit beside a mirror-flat Lake Pedder on a perfect autumnal day. There was the trip up into the Northern Territory, to Darwin, where the weather and hospitality warmed my spirit. In fact, wherever I went I was spoilt rotten.

Unfortunately, since my childhood, CWA memberships have fallen. But one thing I was unaware of is the vast areas where they still offer help. This is definitely not just a 'tea and scones' association. As one member told me, 'You'd be surprised just how many people don't realise all the good work that CWA does. That's because it's not in the nature of my generation and perhaps the one behind me to get up on our soap boxes and shout out, "Look at us. We're doing this. We're doing that." We just go about what we do and we do it quietly.'

And she was right. I was surprised: whether it be sending out pamper packs to women who may be suffering hard times on the land or to women and their children who need medical and educational assistance throughout the Pacific Islands, and beyond. It could be the gift of a small electric piano to a retirement village that sparked the residents' memories of the old songs. Maybe it's the taking of arts and crafts to women in the outback. There's their support for the Victims of Chernobyl National Relief Fund. Their political lobbying on social issues such as rural health, agricultural management practices, getting toilets in shopping plazas. Anything. Bush fire relief. Flood relief. The homeless. The list goes on. Anywhere there's an area of need, CWA will try their best to help. And remember that it is a voluntary organisation.

So other than hoping that the stories in this book will be enjoyable to read I also hope that they might encourage more women to join CWA, so that the association's great work can continue. I know that some of the younger people see CWA as an older woman's group, but it's not. It goes far deeper than that. It's also a philosophy of life. As one of the younger members, Eva Campbell, an ex-Mayor of Camden in New South Wales, said, 'Maybe my involvement is a direct reflection of my personal values, which are also the values that are so strongly upheld by the CWA; where a broad knowledge of life skills is important and your worth is not measured by how much money you can earn but by how much difference you can make.'

As is mentioned in the CWA's 'Collect' prayer over the page:

CWA's 'Collect' prayer

Let us, o Lord, achieve the nobler purpose,
for which we live, that others may be blest.
Save us from pettiness and all self-seeking;
Teach us to seek, to find, to give our best,
Let us be genuine with one another,
And to see in each the best we can find.
So many lives depend on ours for brightness,
Lord, keep us brave, and help us to be kind.

Conversions
CWA Tasmania
All conversions are approximate

The measurements given here are imperial. Note that imperial cup and spoon measures are different from modern Australian and US cup measures (e.g. 1 imperial cup = 285ml, 1 Australian cup = 250 ml and 1 US cup = 237 ml). An imperial tablespoon is equivalent to 3 teaspoons while a modern Australian tablespoon is equivalent to 4 teaspoons.

Imperial	Millilitres	Fluid ounces (UK)
1 tablespoon	15 ml	½ fl oz
¼ cup	70 ml	2¾ oz
⅓ cup	95 ml	3½ fl oz
½ cup	140 ml	5 fl oz
¾ cup	215 ml	7½ fl oz
1 cup	285 ml	10 fl oz

Fluid ounces (UK)	Millilitres
1 fl oz	30 ml
2 fl oz	60 ml
3 fl oz	85 ml
4 fl oz	115 ml
5 fl oz (1 gill)	140 ml
10 fl oz (½ pint)	285 ml
15 fl oz (¾ pint)	425 ml
20 fl oz (1 pint)	570 ml
1½ pint	850 ml
2 pint (1 quart)	1.1 litre

Ounces	Grams
½ oz	15 g
1 oz	30 g
2 oz	60 g
3 oz	85 g
4 oz (¼ lb)	110 g
5 oz	140 g
6 oz	170 g
7 oz	200 g
8 oz (½ lb)	225 g
16 oz (1 lb)	450 g
2 lb	900 g

Inches	Centimetres
½ inch	1 cm
1 in	2.5 cm
2 in	5 cm
4 in	10 cm
6 in	15 cm
8 in	20 cm
10 in	25 cm
12 in	30 cm

Fahrenheit	Celsius
300°F	150°C
320°F	160°C
340°F	170°C
360°F	180°C
375°F	190°C
390°F	200°C
410°F	210°C
420°F	220°C

Household Hints
Cooking Hints

1) When poaching eggs use the very freshest. Also, a few drops of lemon juice in the water in which the eggs are being poached will keep the eggs from separating. When boiling for savoury eggs or salads, stale eggs will be much easier to peel.

2) A paper bag tied on the mouth of mincer will prevent crumbs scattering when putting stale bread through.

3) To remove egg stains from spoons and forks, stand them in separated milk in an aluminium saucepan till clean.

4) When cooking rice, add a few drops of lemon juice as it will improve the flavour and the grains will keep separate.

5) When whipping cream, add 3 or 4 drops of lemon juice to each cup of cream to make it stiff and firm.

6) Do not grate chocolate. It is far easier to stand it in the oven for a few minutes, as it will become quite soft and can be easily beaten up with butter, eggs etc.

7) If eggs are placed in cold water 2 hours before using they will beat easier and make cakes lighter.

8) If you grease the cup in which you measure treacle, syrup or honey, every drop will run out and there will be no waste.

9) When making scones, put the milk and butter in the saucepan over the fire until the butter is melted, then add to the flour.

10) Test the purity of milk with a steel knitting needle. If the liquid runs off the needle quickly then water has been added, while pure milk will cling to the needle, dropping off slowly.

11) When making white sauce and milk is scarce, save the water that the potatoes have been boiled in and add some butter and half the quantity of milk and proceed as usual.

12) Mustard mixed with milk to which a pinch of salt has been added will not harden in the pot.

13) To make more butter, take ¼ lb of butter and ¼ pint of fresh milk. Warm the milk to blood heat (no hotter) and add a little salt. Have the butter slightly warmed, but not melted. Beat butter briskly, adding milk gradually until the butter will not absorb any more milk. Let stand a few minutes. Result: half a pound of good butter.

14) A tablespoon of gelatine added to a cake will equal three eggs. Dissolve the gelatine in a little cold water for a few minutes then add enough boiling water to make a cupful. Whip mixture with an egg beater until it is light and then add to other ingredients.

15) If you happen to run short of eggs when making a cake, a mixture of warm milk and golden syrup will serve the same purpose. Use one tablespoon of syrup to every half pint of milk. This quantity is equivalent to three eggs.

16) Golden syrup used in a pudding will serve the purpose of sugar, eggs and milk and will keep the pudding moist.

17) When picnicking and you wish to take a bottle of milk, add a good pinch of bicarbonate of soda and it will keep fresh all day when corked. This applies also to home use where there is no ice chest.

18) When you have no lemons and wish to make a lemon sago, boil sago in water, add a packet of lemon jelly crystals and a little lemon essence and sugar to taste. Serve with cream or custard.

19) When making junket, dissolve the tablet in vanilla essence instead of water. It is nicer.

20) Grated potatoes are an excellent substitute for suet in boiled puddings. Use 4 oz of potato to half a pound of flour.

21) When mashing potatoes use hot milk instead of cold and add a little baking powder — about a teaspoonful to a large pot — and beat well. It will make them fluffy and they go further.

22) If sugar is added to mint while chopping on the board, the mint will be easier to chop and finer. Sugar will not drop to bottom of jug when served.

23) For additional flavour take a tip from the Hungarians and add a few caraway seeds to any brown stew; about a small half teaspoonful to 2 lb meat.

24) To pasteurise cream, heat cream for ½ hour at 180 degrees. Add boracic at the rate of 1 teaspoon to a pint of cream. Stir in and heat for 3 minutes longer. Have bottles heated, corks boiling and sealing wax ready. Pour straight into bottles, cork and seal at once, while very hot.

General Hints

1) Boils. Cut up finely a whole root of garlic and cover with a flask of rum. Let stand a day or so then take a wineglass every morning, first thing. As it is extremely unpalatable, have a cup of tea ready to drink.

2) Brass door steps. If you have been away for a holiday and your door steps have become discoloured, clean with vinegar first. It cleans in a jiffy.

3) Burnt saucepans should not be cleaned with soda. Cover the burnt area with salt water, leave several hours, then bring slowly to the boil. If stains are very stubborn put the pan in the sun for a few days.

4) For all chrome furniture or glass-topped tables, clean with methylated spirits. Polish with a dry cloth. Tile can also be cleaned effectively this way.

5) Chilblains. A paste of whiting (finely ground chalk) and water applied will give ease almost at once. Seldom needed twice.

6) Dusters soaked in kerosene and hung out to dry before using will keep polished furniture in good condition.

7) Save your egg shells when cooking. Soak in water and use to water your pot plants. Excellent.

8) Soak dirty clothing in Epsom salts. Works wonders.

9) Floor polish: 6 oz beeswax, 4 large cups water, 1 pint mineral turps, 1 tablespoon ammonia. Put the wax in water, over heat, when melted, take off, add turps and ammonia and stir well.

10) Black grease marks on garments can be removed by first rubbing the spot (garment must be dry) with dripping, then wash in soap and water.

11) Wipe out the inside of a handbag with a cloth dipped in eau de cologne, to remove grease and powder marks.

12) Homemade soap. Dissolve 1 lb of caustic soda in 3 pints of water. Take 6½ lb fat, tallow or lard, and heat until liquid. Let it cool. When lukewarm add the caustic solution, stirring for 2 minutes. Pour into a mould — a wooden box is satisfactory — lined with a moistened cloth and stand in a warm place for 24 hours. Remove block of soap, cut into bars or blocks and allow to harden for about a month. The above quantities make 12 lb soap.
    Do not use aluminium or galvanised utensils for soap making and the fat used must be free from salt. Always wear gloves and protective clothing when using caustic soda.

13) Coughs and colds. A teaspoon of honey in hot milk for troublesome coughs. Honey and lemon juice for colds.

14) Frosted glass. A simple method of making imitation frosted glass is to dissolve 2 oz of Epsom salts in a teacupful of warm beer. When the mixture is cold, apply to the glass with soft muslin.

15) Ironing sheet. Starch the ironing sheet and it will always remain straight. It will be even better when ironing large articles if tapes are sewn to each corner and tied to table legs.

16) Knitted jumpers, renovation. When the sleeves of your knitted jumpers or cardigans are getting thin, unpick around the armhole and reverse the sleeve in opposite armhole. The thin part comes on the inside of each, thus lengthening the life of the sleeve.

17) Nylon stockings. If you have several good nylon stockings, put them all into a pot, boil them in water for a few minutes with ½ teaspoon salt, then let them stay in the water till cold. Rinse and hang out. They will all be the same shade when dry.

18) Stained bath. To restore to its pristine whiteness, take 4 tablespoons flour, 4 tablespoons vinegar and 8 tablespoons of peroxide. Mix to a paste and spread over bath. Leave for a few hours. Wash off with cold water.

19) Keeping flowers. Eucalyptus in the water will lengthen the life of any cut flowers. Salt will kill the odour of stocks, heliotrope and mignonette and will preserve wild flowers. Sugar in the water helps keep delphiniums and marigolds, as alum does for hydrangeas.

20) Blades of a mincing machine become blunt after time, but if two or three small pieces of bath brick are ground through the machine they will sharpen them.

21) White felt hat, to clean. Rub with fine emery paper all over, using a circular movement. Coat with a generous layer of black magnesia. Leave for 24 hours then brush well.

22) To clean white tennis shoes and wear them right away, use methylated spirits instead of water to mix the cleaner. Will dry in minutes.

23) To clean windows mix equal parts water, kerosene, methylated spirit and ammonia (shake well). Also helps to keep flies away.

24) Bee stings. Apply a thick slice of raw onion. Renew every 10 minutes until pain is removed. The acid of the onion draws out the poison and prevents injured parts from swelling.

Entrees and Savouries

Anchovy Squares
CWA NSW

Cut some squares of toast, butter and spread with a thick layer of anchovy. Blanch some almonds and cut them thinly, but diagonally, so as to obtain as large a piece as possible. Arrange them on top of the paste and place under the grill for a few moments to toast the almonds.

Brains (Savoury)
CWA NSW

1 set of sheep's brains, soaked in water
Salt and pepper
½ cup white sauce (see p138)
Browned breadcrumbs
4 oz savoury short-pastry
Rice

SHORT PASTRY
4 oz flour
2 oz butter or dripping
¼ egg yolk
¼ dessertspoonful lemon juice
¾ tablespoon cold water
¼ tablespoon sugar

To make pastry, sift flour, add butter and mix in with knife or the fingertips then add yolk of egg, lemon juice, sugar and water beaten together. Knead slightly and roll up, only roll out once.

Line some boat-shaped moulds with short-pastry. Prick the centres or place a piece of greaseproof paper in each and fill with rice. Bake in a moderate (180°C) oven for about 10 minutes. Remove paper and rice and return the pastry cases to the oven for another five minutes to dry. Skin the soaked brains then cook them. Make the sauce and add chopped brains. Place the mix in the boat-shaped moulds to serve.

Cawnpore Cutlets

CWA NSW

1 cup cold boiled rice

1 cup minced meat

1 dessertspoon curry
   powder

1 dessertspoon
   Worcester sauce

1 well-beaten egg

1 teaspoon parsley
   (finely chopped)

1 teaspoon onion
   (finely chopped)

1 teaspoon butter

½ teaspoon salt

⅛ teaspoon pepper

Put all the ingredients into saucepan and cook 5 minutes, stirring all the time. Turn on to plate to cool. Form into cutlet shapes, glaze with egg, cover with breadcrumbs and fry in boiling fat till golden brown.

Cheese Fingers

Mrs W. Young, CWA Tas

Cut bread into ½ inch thick fingers and soak each finger in melted butter. Grate cheese thickly on top and heat well in oven until the cheese melts into bread. Serve hot.

Corn Fritters

CWA NSW

2 cups corn

1 teaspoon salt

Pepper

1 egg

1 teaspoon melted fat

2 cups flour

2 teaspoons baking
   powder

½ cup milk

Chop the corn very fine and add salt. Combine pepper, well-beaten egg, melted fat, flour, baking powder and milk. Add chopped corn and deep fry fritters for 2 to 3 minutes.

Hors d'oeuvres Allemandes

CWA NSW

Frankfurter sausages
Vinegar
French dressing

Hard-boiled eggs
Pimento

Cook frankfurter sausages for five minutes in boiling water to which enough sharp vinegar has been added to make it slightly acid. Drain, cool, peel and cut into inch sections. Marinate these in French dressing for an hour then place slices of hard-cooked egg on a plate and stand the sausage sections upright on the egg slices. Top each with a disc of pimento.

Macaroni Cheese

Mrs J. L. Creed, CWA Tas

3 pints water
4 oz macaroni
3 oz grated cheese
1½ oz butter
1 oz flour
½ teaspoon salt

Very little cayenne
1 pint milk
2 tablespoons tomato
   sauce
Fine breadcrumbs

Boil water, add macaroni, cook for ½ hour, strain and put into pie dish. Grate cheese. Melt the butter in saucepan, stir in flour, salt, cayenne. Mix till smooth, add milk and nearly all the cheese, stir over the fire till boiling then add tomato sauce. Pour over macaroni and mix well. Sprinkle breadcrumbs on top with rest of cheese. Bake till golden brown.

Oyster Rolls

C. Blackwell, Campbell Town, CWA Tas

½ lb streaky bacon
2 dozen bearded oysters
Cayenne
Lemon juice

Cut rind from bacon and cut each rasher into about 4 pieces. Place a bearded oyster in each strip, add squeeze of lemon juice and pinch of cayenne. Roll up, skewer and cook in hot (200°C) oven between two enamel plates for about 12 minutes.

Potato Balls

CWA NSW

1½ lb potatoes
1 dessertspoon butter
4 tablespoons finely
   grated cheese
1 egg yolk

Cayenne
Salt
1 beaten egg
Soft breadcrumbs

Boil potatoes and dry them off. Mash them and add the butter, cheese, egg yolk and seasoning. Spread on plate till cold. Take small portions and roll into balls. Dip in beaten egg then coat with breadcrumbs. Place in a basket and deep fry in boiling fat till golden brown. Do not attempt to fry too many at one time or the temperature of the fat will be reduced. Drain on kitchen paper.

Prawn Cocktail

CWA NSW

1 tablespoon strained
   lemon juice
1 tablespoonful tomato
   catsup (ketchup)
½ teaspoon piquant
   sauce

½ teaspoon grated
   horseradish
9 shelled prawns
A few drops of
   Tabasco sauce

Mix the strained lemon juice, catsup, piquant sauce and grated horseradish well together. Add the prawns, season with a few drops of Tabasco. Serve very cold in cocktail glass, garnished with a slice of lemon.

Savoury Patties

Mrs F. J. Moyle, Zeehan, CWA Tas

8 oz puff pastry
Parsley
½ pint white sauce see (page 138 for recipe)
8 oz shrimps, oysters, scallops, crayfish or asparagus

Roll out pastry to ¼–½ inch thick, cut in strips as for cream horns. Wind around cream horn tins. Cook in hot oven first then reduce heat for drying out. When cold fill with savoury filling in white sauce. Garnish with tips of parsley. If asparagus is used, garnish with small asparagus tips.

Judy Anicomatis
Darwin, Northern Territory

I was actually born in Victoria but then, when I was eight months old, my parents decided to leave the sheep and wheat farm we were on and head north. There were just the five of us at that stage. I was the youngest, then I had a sister who was twelve months older than me, a brother who was twelve months older than her and, of course, there was my mother and father. My father loved the outback and he was very keen on prospecting so we went up to Murray Downs Station, near Barrow Creek. Barrow Creek's nearly three hundred kilometres north of Alice Springs, just in behind the Aboriginal settlement of Ali Curung.

That's where I grew up, and we lived on Murray Downs right up until I was nine years old and, for our education, we did School of the Air through Alice Springs. I remember it well because during the first few years we had a transceiver that was operated by a pedal machine and we had to pedal the machine to keep the electricity going while we were doing our lessons. Then later on we got a generator, which helped a bit, and after that they changed it all over to electricity. That would've been in about the early 1950s and over that time we had a few more add-ons to our family. After me, my mother had twins girls and then there were two more girls and another boy, which made us a family of eight children: one boy, six girls and another boy.

My parents owned the property — well, the bank did really — and as I said, other than a great love of the outback, my father had a great interest in mining and prospecting. In fact I've even got the paper clippings of when he went on a couple of expeditions to find Lasseter's Reef. He wasn't successful, of course.

So then we lived on Murray Downs until I was almost nine which was when we had the big drought. Then after the big drought hit us, we moved off Murray Downs and we drifted further north. We're in about 1956 or '57 now. So we went from a big drought in the middle of Australia and we moved up to a lush plantation property about eight miles out of Bachelor, near where the Rum Jungle mine was. The farm we lived on was called Banyan Farm and we grew pineapples and bananas. I think it was named after a huge banyan tree that was there.

By that stage there were a couple more add-ons because, while we were on Murray Downs Station, my parents had adopted a couple of part-Aboriginal boys and so they also came along with us. That made ten of us kids in all and so when there was a sudden influx of us Browns into the local Bachelor school — Brown being my maiden name — they had to build on a couple more classrooms and employ a couple more teachers. So then we stayed on at Banyan Farm until we moved to Darwin River, which is where the Darwin River water supply dam is today. But back then they had the quarry there and they mined the blue metal for the Bachelor RAAF airport. We lived there as caretakers, to look after the infrastructure, and even though none of us had a licence, to get to school we drove on the back road to the mine site then we left the car there and we caught the bus that the men went to and fro from work on. Then after I finished my schooling I moved to Darwin and I worked as a tracer with a mapping company, and I met my husband through mutual friends and I got married very young. By that stage I was eighteen and I had a family straight away.

But CWA has been in my family for quite a while. When we moved up to the Northern Territory my mother joined what was known as the Airwaves Group. The Airwaves Group ran along the same lines as did School of the Air, in as much as the meetings and that were held over the radio, and it also came out of Alice Springs. Then when we moved to Banyan Farm my mother became a member of the Bachelor Branch of CWA, and I remember how envious I was because these women always seemed to be getting together and having cups of teas and doing crafts. I'd say it was probably because of that influence that I became quite good at handiwork myself and while I was in my second year of high school I remember how it gave me great pleasure when, one day, the CWA ladies actually asked me to come and teach them to smock; smocking being a form of embroidery work that's done on pleats. It's mostly done on children's clothing to improve the look of a gathered garment. Basically, you gather it into a pleat and then you sew fancy stitches on it. It's called smocking. There's some over there on the trading table.

Then I joined CWA in Darwin when my two girls were quite small. How that came about was that a couple of mutual friends had children at the kindy that my two girls went to and they were CWA members and I thought, Oh that's what I want to do. I've always wanted to do that. So I went along to a meeting and I'm still here today, twenty-six years later on.

But it's funny how CWA has run through the family and, in particular, the influence it's had on my two girls. In those days, the youngest one would've been about three years old and the oldest one was six, and I'd always take them along to the meetings and craft days with me. Back then we used to get together in each other's houses. There was no problem with that. The children were no trouble. Sometimes I even used to take them along to our conferences and whatever.

So the girls were always around CWA and this just goes to show how observant children are because, one day they had some friends over at our place and I was busy doing something or other in the bedroom and I came out of the bedroom, and there they all were — they'd set the room up with the tables and chairs, exactly how we did it at our CWA meetings and they were pretending to have cups of teas and eat cake and sandwiches just like we did at our meetings. And I sort of stood there and I watched and I got the shock of my life when one of them said, 'So Mrs Fuchs how was your day today?' Nancy Fuchs is one of our past presidents. And the next one replies, 'Well, to be honest Mrs Anicomatis it hasn't been one of my better days. I went looking for some cotton thread and I just could not find the exact colour I was after.'

I nearly died. There they were, these young girls playing CWAs and they were taking us off to a tee, even right down to using our names. And when I told the other CWA ladies, they just couldn't believe it either. So yes, it's out of the mouths of babes, I suppose.

Elaine Armstrong
Oura, New South Wales

I belong to the Oura Branch of the Riverina Group of CWA. A lot of people think you say Cowra or Nowra but, no, it's Oura. Though, actually, I'm a Wollongong girl, from the coast. I was teaching there and my husband was in real estate and then, when he turned fifty, he said, 'Let's sell up and go farming.'

So at that age we sold up in Wollongong and we looked around and eventually we came to Oura. Oura's only a small village, really, on the eastern side of Wagga Wagga. There's only about a hundred houses in the town and its surrounding area. There's not even anything like a bank but there's a timber yard and that has a small canteen where you can buy bread and milk and things like that. So we bought some property there.

My husband came off a dairy farm and he knew something about farming. But I didn't so I went to TAFE (Technical and Further Education) and I did a twelve-month course on Women and Farm Management, learning what you do and how you do it and why you do it. Of course, with being so involved in that course, I didn't have the time to really meet the neighbours properly. Then one day I saw Ann, the lady next door, at her letter box — we all had mail boxes out on the road — and I stopped and invited her to morning tea and when she came along she asked if I belonged to CWA.

'No, I don't,' I said.

Ann was thinking of re-forming a Branch in Oura — there had been one from 1950 to 1955 — so she asked if I'd like to help. My memory of CWA, in Wollongong, was of older ladies having tea in the Rest Rooms and playing cards and things, so I said, 'No thanks, I'm not old enough yet.'

'Oh,' she said, 'it's not like that now.'

So I said, 'Yes, okay, I'll come along and we'll see how we go.'

Ann knew I'd been a maths teacher so she said that if she took on the job of President and someone else became the Secretary, perhaps I might like to be Treasurer. That's just what happened and so we re-formed the Oura Branch of CWA. We've now got about thirty-three members and even though my husband and I have since retired and moved into Wagga Wagga, I still belong to Oura.

I really enjoy CWA. As I said, I didn't join it till late. I have no daughters, no sisters, no mums or anything now so I guess you could say that all the CWA ladies are my adopted family, and I do enjoy the friendship. That's probably the biggest plus of CWA, the friendship, and you can get as involved as you like, depending on yourself. The organisation's umbrella covers whatever you want to do, be it cooking, cultural, handicraft, international, even bush walking if you want start that up in your Group or within your Branch; anything at all — perhaps even a book club. It's very wide and it covers anything that concerns and advances the interests of women and children.

These days the International Section of CWA is my passion. I suppose that came about from right back to school geography where I enjoyed learning about other countries and their cultures. I always found that interesting and CWA have an International Fund that's supported by all of the Branches throughout the state. Actually, many different organisations, from different countries, come under the banner of the Associated Country Women of the World (ACWW). In the South Pacific area they might be called Rural Women or Country Women of PNG (Papua New Guinea). Some of them are Catholic Women's Institutions. In Australia it's the Country Women's Association. In New Zealand they call themselves New Zealand Rural Women's Group. But it's women working together, worldwide, hence the title of Associated Country Women of the World.

New South Wales CWA is part of what's called the South Pacific Area and we have a triennial conference where we discuss issues and hear the stories from the ladies from the islands, be it Papua New Guinea, Samoa, Fiji, Tonga, Tuvalu. Then they prepare a 'Wish List'. Each association then decides if help — financially or otherwise — can be given to those in need.

In the past, CWA of NSW has provided tanks for water. We've provided tools for the women to work their gardens. We've provided funding for fencing to keep the animals out. More recently we have supported, and still are supporting, a school in PNG by sending them Education Packs, which include school books and rulers and pencils: all the things that children need for the classroom.

At the moment we're collecting Mother–Baby Packs ready to send to the ladies in PNG. That came about when one of our members went over there and worked as a volunteer in different hospitals. Upon her return she reported in our journal — the *Country Women* — that many of the poorer women of PNG didn't have many of the things we take for granted. She suggested that we prepare Mother–Baby Packs. So a list was made of what could go in them and it was circulated to all our CWA members. That's how that started. Now we're making up the Mother–Baby Packs, which consist of nappies, soap, baby power, towels, nighties, undies — anything that might be useful for the mothers and their babies. We've also been asked to include a one metre square sheet of clear clean plastic and a one-sided razor blade for birthing. That's because many of the ladies out in the villages can't get to a hospital so they're delivering their babies out in the bush and they're cutting their umbilical cord with glass, resulting in infections and complications.

So the Mother–Baby Packs we're now packing go to a Sydney depot and Rotary are helping us to get the container over to Papua New Guinea. They're then sent out into the villages, where they're needed. And that's why I think the international work that CWA does is just so important. Plus, of course, with the current world situation, if people are to get along there needs to be a lot more care and understanding and CWA does all that because, when all is said and done, we are all a part of the one world, aren't we?

Valerie Asche
Darwin, Northern Territory

I've been living in Darwin now for twenty-four years, though my husband, Keith Asche, he came here, from Melbourne, back in the 1920s, as a child, with his family. They then lived here until his father died in 1940 and they returned to Melbourne, and that's where he finished his schooling. Then during the war, Keith joined the air force and he came back up north and worked on a radar station out on Bathurst Island. After he was demobbed he studied law at the University of Melbourne, and that's where we met. He was doing law and I was doing science. We married in 1958 and Keith practiced as a barrister until he was appointed Queen's Council in 1972. Following that he became a Judge of the Family Court of Australia and was Acting Chief Justice until he returned to Darwin as a Supreme Court Judge. That was in 1986 and, of course, I accompanied him and I worked as a senior research fellow at the Menzies School of Health Research.

Keith remained a Supreme Court Judge here until 1993, which was when he was appointed the Administrator of the Northern Territory, and he held that position until early 1997. Also of importance is that, during that time, he received a Companion of the Order of Australia (AC) for his service to the law, education, and to the community, particularly with the people of the Northern Territory. We have one son and one daughter.

But it was in 1993, when my husband became the Administrator of the Northern Territory, that I was asked to be the Northern Territory's Patron of CWA. I wasn't a member until then but my mother had been for most of her married life. That was when we were living in the small town of Rupanyup, which is near Horsham, in the central west of Victoria. So I was pretty familiar with CWA. Then, when I finished as the Patron in 1997, I was a

CWA member for a few years before I was asked to be President of the Northern Territory, and I'm still Vice-President today.

As for special CWA memories, I guess my visiting the various Branches was special; though one particular time, very early on, I remember I went down to Tennant Creek and it was as hot as hot and I was staying in the hostel there and the building wasn't air-conditioned. Oh, dear it was hot. I think I might've been there to open an exhibition because they seemed to run a craft exhibition every year, and of a very high quality too, I might add. So that was one memorable event.

Unfortunately I didn't get over to Groote Eylandt, but I still hope to one day, and then there was Alice Springs, of course. I've been down there a few times with CWA and I've always enjoyed it. Also there was Nhulunbuy, over on the Gove Peninsula. I very much enjoyed Nhulunbuy. Back then they only had a small membership of perhaps less than ten. I particularly remember the time I went over there for a CWA meeting and I took my husband with me. Of course, they have a lot of crocodiles over that way but there was a specially designated area where it was safe to swim. So, with it being so hot, Keith went for a swim there and later, when he told someone about it, they said, 'Gee, you were lucky, there's been a few crocodiles seen in that area too.'

But the women at Nhulunbuy, they met at the little local hotel and some of them did extremely nice craft work. Of course, they often have a table at our conference each year. I don't know whether you know or not, but each year we have a specific theme and the various Branches produce a table at our conference with that theme in mind. We also have certain categories which are set down: so there might be a certain cake that they've got to bake or there might be a certain jam and they have to make that type of jam or there could be a certain type of sewing or embroidery which they have to present. Well even the very small Branches, like Nhulunbuy, they could produce a table with beautiful work.

I find that in those smaller towns, if someone enjoys doing craftwork they're naturally drawn to CWA, whereas in the bigger places like Darwin that's not necessarily the case. More often the than not, we have to seek them out. But it's those same ladies, from the smaller places, that keep coming to the conference each year. Tennant Creek, particularly, have a strong core group of women. In fact, three have just received Certificates of Long Service. So CWA does well in those smaller towns where the women have to be quite self-sufficient because, not being close to the wide variety of shops we have in places like Palmerston and Darwin, they have to learn to sew and they have to learn to knit and they have to learn to cook as a means of basic family survival. And really, other than a need for companionship, that's what CWA is all about.

Melinda Beckett
Boulder and Metropolitan, Western Australia

I used to belong to Boulder Branch of CWA but now I'm a member of Metropolitan, in Perth. I'm still only thirty-eight which is quite young for the CWA though, over the last twelve months, four new Branches have formed and we now we have a number of new members who are under the age of thirty.

Actually, I didn't have any CWA background at all. None of my family or friends were members. I was even brought up in the Hunter Valley, in New South Wales, where CWA is pretty big and, even still, I'd never heard of it. So I guess that I'm a bit out of the square, compared to many of the others who grew up with it.

Then how I came to live in Western Australia was that my other half was originally from here and he'd gone to New South Wales for work. But he always wanted to return home because all his family is here. That's how I landed in WA. I was only nineteen then. For the first six months we were living in Perth, then he got an offer to go out to Kalgoorlie for work. So we did that and, at that time, I used to ride my pushbike from Kalgoorlie out to a shop in Boulder to get bobbins for my sewing machine and I always said, 'I'll never live in Boulder.' Anyhow, after spending a fortune on rent in Kalgoorlie, we decided to buy a house and the first place we looked at was in Boulder and we bought it.

I still hadn't heard of CWA. Then it was sort of 'curiosity killed the cat' really because, when I was twenty-one I decided to get a CWA cook book. And I don't really known why but I got quite emotional when I read it. Then how I joined was that I was heavily pregnant and I was going to a craft group on Mondays and there was this girl there. She was a couple of years older than me. She was left-handed and, I don't know if you've ever watched a left-hander knit or not but, they're quite amazing. So she quite fascinated me and also, while everyone else would be doing the same craft work, she'd be doing something different. I remember one thing she used to do was that she'd come in with an orange and she'd knit like a little beanie type thing to fit this orange. Each week she'd do a bit more to it and put it over her orange and I'm thinking, Okay, so yes she is a little bit different. Then on the days she wasn't knitting the beanie for her orange she'd be knitting these things that were about twenty centimetres in width and a metre long. Anyhow, as it turned out, they were bandages for lepers, which was a project that CWA had done for many years.

So one day I plucked up the courage and I rang her and I said, 'I hope you don't mind but you fascinate me because it's amazing to watch how left-handers knit and,' I said, 'I'm also wondering what you're doing with the orange?'

'Oh,' she said, 'I need the orange because I'm making beanies for premmie babies and the rule is that the beanie has to fit over an orange. I do it for CWA. We meet on a Tuesday morning. You'd be more than welcome to come along.'

'Okay,' I said, but the next Tuesday I forgot all about it.

Then one Tuesday I remembered. The CWA met within walking distance from my house. I went along. Knocked on the door. The girl from the craft group wasn't there so I didn't know anyone from a bar of soap. But as soon as they saw me it was, 'Oh, hello, you must be Melinda, the pregnant one.'

And that's how I came to join CWA. It was with the Boulder Branch and that was in 1996. Anyway, most Branches in Western Australia meet once a month for their business meeting and they have another day for their social meetings. Boulder Branch was rare in that it met weekly. So I'd go along every week. As I said, I was heavily pregnant. Then one Tuesday I went into labour. In a way it was quite funny because I wasn't able to let any of the CWA members know where I was because I didn't even know any of their last names or where they lived or their phone numbers or anything. Then I was in hospital for a week and on the following

Tuesday I said to my other half, 'Before we go home can we go by the CWA so that I can show them the baby and let them know I'm okay.'

But by the time we arrived they'd already left. Then on the Friday we went on our first shopping adventure and I came across one of the Boulder CWA members and she said, 'Oh, I can't wait to tell the others that I saw the baby before they had.'

So that was the Friday. Then on the Tuesday I went to Branch and they'd all been busy knitting items for my baby. I was absolutely blown away, and one of the members said to me, 'Oh we were so worried when you didn't turn up for the meeting. We thought that, perhaps, something was terribly wrong.' And so they'd gone around to the house and knocked on all the doors and windows, wondering where I was.

From then on, because I didn't have an alternative, every time I went to a CWA function I always took my daughter. She became the baby of the Branch and we became quite popular because, still now, you go to CWA functions and you don't see a lot of children, which is a shame.

Then 1998 was pretty special. It was getting close to the State Conference, which is a big thing in CWA. Anyhow I was a little bit late to one of our Branch meetings and when I got there they said, 'Would you like to go to the state conference?'

I said, 'I can't. I've got a child and I know nothing, really, about the association and how it works.'

They said, 'Well, we need delegates to go.'

I said, 'What happened to the two that were going to go?'

'They're sick.'

'Well,' I said, 'what about the others?'

'Oh, they're not well and someone's doing something else, and so you're it.' They said, 'We'll give you a cheque and organise your train tickets. You're going on Sunday.'

The whole week I was as nervous as anything then, on the Sunday, me and my fifteen-month-old daughter, we got on the train and off we went to Perth. That year the conference was being held at Observation City, at Scarborough, along the beach there. So I arrived. I walked up the steps. They were setting up. Not one CWA member had a badge on so I didn't know anyone from a bar of soap, but it was, 'Oh hello, you must be Melinda and this must be your daughter.'

So it wasn't till some months later that our Branch Secretary admitted that she'd rung Head Office and a few other people and told them that I was coming along to the conference with a baby. And my daughter sat with me throughout the conference. I remember on the third night, we had a Divisional dinner and the State President was there and she said that she had no idea a child had even been attending the conference. Then, come the fourth day — the final day of Conference — the State President announced to everyone, 'I've got a special presentation to do today. It's going to be a first.' She said, 'Do you know there's been a baby in Conference?' and she got me up on stage with my daughter and she presented her with a koala. It was fantastic.

'Oh, she'll be back,' everyone said.

And they were right. I haven't missed a conference since. And it's only been because my daughter's now going to school that she hasn't gone along with me. Actually, I've just come back from a State Conference and still, even to this day, they're all saying, 'Where's your little girl?'

'Well,' I say, 'that little girl is now thirteen and she's as tall as me.'

So they still remember when she was a little baby and she came along and she slept through the conference and didn't say 'Boo'. And it's quite funny now because a lot of the members, they absolutely adore their grandchildren and I say to them, 'Are you going to such and such a CWA meeting or function?' and they say, 'No, I'm looking after my grandchildren.'

I say, 'Well why don't you bring them?'

'Oh, I can't bring them,' they say, and yet they talk about them like they're the bee's knees.

But 2010 is going to be a first because they're going to hold the State Conference during the school holidays. So we'll see what happens there. It'll be quite interesting to see how many members end up going because, these days, we do have crèches and things like that at our conference to cater for the children. Because, really, it is a bit disappointing that the older members don't bring their grandchildren or that the mothers don't bring their children along to CWA.

Jean Black
Casterton, Victoria

Yes, well I didn't come off the land. I grew up in the country town of Daylesford, just out of Ballarat, in central Victoria. Dad worked at various jobs before he became a wardsman at the Daylesford Hospital, then he did that for twenty-five or thirty years. I was the eldest of six and so, with there being so many of us, Mum was at home.

I did my schooling at the combined Daylesford Primary and Technical High School, then I went to Ballarat Teacher's College for three years before going out into the wide world. I specialised in infant training, and I loved it. At that stage the children have still got that marvellous wonder of life. They believe everything you tell them, and they also love hearing stories about what you did when you were little. That's 'you' as in me. So I taught in Ballarat for a couple of years, at Eureka Street Primary School, and then I went down to the western district. That was to a small two-teacher school just out of Casterton, at a little place called Dunrobin. At that time there were a lot of soldiers' settlement farms throughout that area. At Eureka Street I'd taught forty-eight four-and-a-half-year-olds, while at Dunrobin there were just forty-eight children in the whole school. So, with there being two teachers, I had a ball. And I guess, like a lot of young girls back in those days, the main idea was for me to save up for the big trip overseas. I still haven't been. I met my husband instead and, as they say, the rest is sort of history.

My husband was a dairy farmer. This was back in the 1960s and before I got married I was actually boarding at the mother-in-law-to-be's friend's place and she and her friend were my link into CWA. Neither of them had a car licence so, after I got married and had to resign from teaching, I'd drive them to the meetings.

Then I thought, Well if I'm driving them here I may as well join. It was known as the Dergholm Branch and my mother-in-law went on to become a life member there. Dergholm CWA has now closed, unfortunately, but when I joined there would've probably been fifteen or twenty members.

But then, after the fourth child arrived and the mother-in-law's friend got her car licence, I dropped out of CWA and went back teaching. At that stage I had the children to look after and also we were only a small farming concern and it was more economically viable for me to go back to work and my husband to go off-farm to work. So it was just circumstances really because, in the mid to late 70s and early 80s, things got very hard on the land and it was better for my husband to go out shearing or whatever. I mean, he'd get up and start the milking of a morning then, when he went off to work, I'd take over and finish the morning milking and feed up the cows before me and the kids went off to school. Then, because my husband wouldn't get home until after six at night, after school, the kids and I would do the evening milking. Oh, I couldn't do it now, but that was life back then. That's just what you did to keep afloat. At one stage, when my husband was very ill, the four kids and I would get up at five of a morning and milk a hundred and ten cows then we'd all go off to school and after our day's work we'd come back home and do the evening milking. And, mind you, you couldn't get financial assistance back then either. But I think it makes you a better person. It certainly made my children better people because they had to realise, from an early age, that the pocket wasn't endless, and those solid values have stayed with them, even to this day.

So I was out of CWA for a long time and just before I retired from teaching I was invited into an evening meeting at Casterton and I enjoyed it so much I said, 'Oh, I think I'll rejoin.' And I just wished I'd only done it a lot earlier. It's such a special organisation. I've only been back in it for the past ten years now but I've made friends everywhere and been to places that I'd never otherwise go to in a lifetime. It opens up so much, and you just don't see some of these places from the tourist point of view either. You see it how it is, and you'd be surprised just how many people don't realise all the good work that CWA does. That's because it's not in the nature of my generation, and perhaps the one behind me, to get up on our soap boxes and shout out, 'Look at us. We're doing this. We're doing that.' We just go about what we do and we do it quietly.

After rejoining I sort of got back in at state level, and that was because of a rash statement I made. Well, they have a State Public Speaking competition and one year one of the topics was 'Milking Time' and I happened to say, 'Oh gosh, I could talk about that for hours.' So I did and I've now been lucky enough to have won the State Public Speaking twice and I've been runner-up a couple of times. But that's what got me back in at state level and I became a Group President, then I was State Vice-President and now I'm Chairman of Social Issues.

Social Issues originally centred around CWA trying to make things better for rural women and children. But now we look at things like — and it may sound hilarious — we're currently looking into the condition of public toilets throughout Victoria. You'd be surprised at some of the comments we received when we carried out that particular survey. It's a real health issue. We're also looking at how we can improve the labelling of food products. Then there's the lack of signage at Southern Cross Railway Station in Melbourne, where there's no signage for the buses on the outside walls. Then, because there's been so many fatal accidents at level crossings, we're also looking at different forms of reflectors that can be put on trains. Luggage trolleys is another issue. You can't book your luggage through on the railways, nowadays. You've got to take your bags on the train yourself and could you imagine some of these ladies in their eighties, getting their luggage on and off trains. It's even worse if you're a young mother with a couple of littlies and you've got your luggage and you've got a pram and you've got to get everything off and on trains. So that's another issue we've been looking at.

And even though we're a non-political organisation we still have a strong voice with all political parties. They listen to us. Yes they do. So that's just some of the things that the Social Issues Committee does.

Anyway, it's a wonderful association. I just love it. As I said, I just wish I'd got back into it before I did because I would've been years younger and fitter. Though, in saying that, I do have one dubious honour within CWA and that's that I'm the only President at Dergholm CWA who's been pregnant twice while in office. I was pregnant during my first time as President of the Branch, then I was pregnant again at the end of my second term as President. Yes, I was pregnant both times. So there'd be some kind of claim to fame, I'd say.

Jessie Black
Barmoya, Queensland

I'm ninety-two years of age and I've been a member of Queensland CWA for over sixty years. I grew up on Sandringham Station, which is on the Greenlake Road, between Yeppoon and The Caves, just north of Rockhampton. It was a cattle property and I rode my horse from the farm to the primary school at Barmoya. After that I went to boarding school at Yeppoon. That was at Saint Faith's, a Church of England boarding school for girls. I was there for five years. To begin with there were about a hundred students but then the Depression came and in the end it got down to around thirty. People just couldn't afford it. But it was very good. I enjoyed it. We had our music lessons and we played tennis and basketball against other schools and every Saturday afternoon we used to go down the beach and have a little picnic, then we'd go to church every Sunday.

From boarding school I went back home. My mother wasn't well and so I looked after her. She wasn't a member of CWA because we were just forming the Barmoya Branch when she died. That was in 1948. We had about fifteen members to start with. They, too, mostly came off properties from around the district. I was one of the founding members. I was the first Treasurer and my two dear sisters, Rhoda and Mary, were foundation members as well. They're both younger than what I am: one is eighty-four and the next one is eighty-seven and I'm ninety-two. So you could say that CWA runs in the family because the three of us are foundation members and we're all still alive.

These days my memory's good but my back's no good and I'm not only back as Treasurer of the Barmoya Branch, which I have been lots of times, but I'm also, currently, the Vice-President of the Branch, yet again, and then I've been the President a lot of times as well. But we've had so many nice times. I remember when we used to give the school children a Christmas tree every year and we'd give them books and toys. That was all from our fundraising and a lot of that came out of the lovely Caulfield Cup afternoons we held. I guess why we had Caulfield Cup afternoons and not Melbourne Cup afternoons was because the Caulfield Cup is on a Saturday whereas the Melbourne Cup is on the Tuesday. But everyone really enjoyed them. People used to come out to Barmoya from all over the place. Sometimes we'd get over a hundred people and we'd have a sweep and we'd have raffles and lucky door prizes. Things like that. It was all fundraising, and we'd put on a lovely afternoon tea with cakes and sandwiches and there were slices, like a lemon slice or a vanilla slice. But then we got too old and we had to stop them.

Then something else we used to do for fundraising was our Barmoya CWA Ball. We held that every year out at The Caves and everyone enjoyed it. The Caves is about five miles from Barmoya and we'd start at about eight of an evening and we'd go right through to about one in the morning and we'd have a nice supper and we'd have raffles and lucky door prizes and, oh, all sorts of things and prizes. We'd have the Matron of the Ball. We'd have a three-piece orchestra: a piano, a violin and I suppose it was drums or maybe it was a guitar — something like that. The sort of dances we did were the old time dances. Everyone loved those; like the Mazurkas and the Alberts and the Oxford Waltz and all those lovely old ones. And that was also held once a year, generally in about September. I'm ninety-two years of age and I've been a member of Queensland CWA for over sixty years. So, with our CWA Ball in, say, the September and the Caulfield Cup afternoons in the October, they were two very busy months for us in Barmoya CWA. That was our busy time of the year. But then times change and we got too old to run the balls and so we had to stop them too.

Soups

Soup Accessories
CWA NSW

Croutons — Cut stale bread into small squares, about ⅓ inch. Fry in deep fat or sauté in just enough fat to prevent them burning.

Melba Toast — Cut bread in wafer thin slices and bake in slow oven till golden.

Mornay Toast — Cut bread in thin slices, sprinkle well with grated cheese. Dust with cayenne and paprika. Brown in slow oven.

Cheese Rolls — Butter wafer thin slices of bread and spread with grated cheese. Roll, fasten with toothpick and brown in oven.

Artichoke Soup
CWA NSW

3 lb artichoke
1 turnip
Half a head of celery
1 onion

2 quarts stock
2 quarts water
½ pint cream or milk
Pepper and salt to taste

Peel and cut the artichokes and other vegetables into slices, boil in the stock and water until tender and rub them through a fine sieve. Add the milk or cream, bring back to boil. Add pepper and salt and serve with fried croutons.

Chicken Soup
CWA NSW

1 fowl
1 onion
3 slices lean ham
2 quarts water
½ cup rice

Salt and pepper
Chopped parsley
1 cup milk
1 teaspoon flour
1 tablespoon chicken fat

Cut fowl into quarters and place in pan with onion, ham and water. Let simmer until very tender. Strain. The meat may be used in any way desired. Remove all fat. Add well-washed rice, chopped parsley, salt and pepper. Simmer until rice is tender, add milk and roux made from flour and chicken fat. Cook until mixture thickens — about 5 minutes.

Mulligatawny Soup

Mrs A.J. Barwick, CWA Tas

2 onions

1 apple

1 teaspoon curry
    powder

1 quart beef stock

1 small carrot

2 potatoes

1 teaspoon sugar

1 dessertspoon salt

2 tablespoons fat

2 tablespoons flour

1 tablespoon chutney

1 teaspoon lemon juice

Brown sliced onions and apple in hot dripping, stir in curry powder, stock, grated carrot, grated potato, sugar and salt. Simmer for ½ hour. Rub through sieve and thicken with blended fat and flour. Simmer for 5 minutes longer and add chutney and lemon juice. Serve with very thin toasted wafers.

Ox Tail Soup

CWA Tas

1 ox tail

1 slice ham

1 oz butter

2 carrots

2 turnips

3 onions

1 head celery

Pepper and salt

3 quarts water

2 tablespoons flour

Place all but flour in saucepan and simmer gently for 4 hours, skim well. When tail is tender take out. Skim and strain soup, thicken with flour, put back tail. Simmer 5 minutes and serve. Kangaroo tail soup may be made by the same recipe.

Pea Soup

CWA NSW

Ham bone
1 carrot
1 onion
2 potatoes

3 quarts boiling water
1 cup split peas
   (soaked overnight)
Salt and pepper and
   sprig mint

Place ham bone in large saucepan with carrot, onion, potatoes and boiling water. Add split peas and cook gently until tender. Strain through colander and season with salt, pepper and mint. Serve with croutons or mornay or Melba toast.

Sheep's Head Soup

Mrs H.R. Thomas, Northdown, CWA Tas

On sheep stations throughout the country where people kill their own mutton daily, this is the basic soup. Substitute dehydrated vegetables when fresh are unavailable.

1 sheep's head
1 tablespoon diced turnip
2 tablespoons diced carrot

3 tablespoons pearl
   barley
Salt and pepper to taste

Split and clean head, remove eyes, wash well and place in deep pan with all other ingredients. Cover with cold water. Bring slowly to the boil and simmer for 6 hours. Lift out head carefully and set aside. The soup is now ready for use. Garnish with chopped parsley or finely grated orange rind before serving.

Tomato Soup

E.A. French, Whitemore, CWA Tas

2 lb tomatoes
1 onion
½ teaspoon bicarbonate
   of soda

1 pint milk
Small piece butter
2 tablespoons flour

Cut tomato and onion. Add soda and cover with water. Boil till tender, strain and add milk and butter. Thicken with flour just before serving.

Kit Bright
Moss Vale, New South Wales

I'll tell you how I started in Country Women's Association; how would that be? Okay, my mother was big in the Kiama Branch and in my youth I was an extremely good knitter so I used to give my knitting to my mother and she would enter it in the annual *Land* newspaper competition. That's an annual competition that the *Land* newspaper runs which is open to all people throughout New South Wales, plus then there's a special section, which is only open to CWA members. So the, then, Handicraft Officer of Kiama CWA said to my mother, 'Would you please join Kit so we can put her knitting in the section that gets our group marks.'

So, as did my mother, I joined the Kiama Branch of Country Women's Association and it's just gone on from there. Then, years later, after I'd retired and my mother wasn't too well, I decided to move to Moss Vale Branch so that, when she died — which she did — the two events were not closely connected in my mind. I've now belonged to the Moss Vale Branch for about seven years. At the present I'm Branch Vice-President and I'm also what's called the 'Executive Representative' for the Wollondilly Group. To explain all that: well, as far as New South Wales goes, within CWA, the state's divided into thirty Groups and within those Groups there are over four hundred Branches. The Wollondilly Group takes in what we call the 'Highlands', which includes Mittagong, Bowral, Moss Vale, Exeter and Bundanoon. Then there's the coastal CWA Branches of Jamberoo, Kiama, Berry, Kangaroo Valley, Nowra, Jervis Bay and Jervis Bay Evening, Milton district and Mollymook. That's the fourteen branches in our Wollondilly Group.

As far as the highlights of my time in CWA go: one is that, at one stage, I was the Group President. I very much enjoyed that because it meant visiting all the various Branches for their international days or their birthdays or giving out long services badges. Nursing was my career so I'm quite happy to meet people and stand up and speak and do that sort of thing. So I did that and, of course, back then I had my mother who was behind me all the way and everything I did I had the thought of just how much Mum would also be enjoying all this. Maybe it's 'like mother, like daughter', though in my case my mother had the curliest hair on earth, which I don't. But when I see myself walking, I think, Gee, I'm walking just like my mother did.

So that was how I started, and my mother was a member of the Kiama CWA Branch for more than thirty years. And being involved was the biggest godsend for her, especially in her retirement. It was just something to go to, something to belong to and she made so many wonderful, wonderful friends. She enjoyed handicraft too, but cooking was her thing. She was a fantastic cook; one of the best cooks on earth, she was. She made the most wonderful sponges and scones. In fact, after she died, when I went through her things I must've found at least two or three first prizes for just about every single solitary thing that's mentioned in the *Land* Cookery schedule.

But I enjoy it. I think it's wonderful. As I say, 'Country Womens' Association is many things to many people.'

And so CWA offers you as much or as little as you want. For older people especially, there's the friendship, the companionship. Then in times of hardship — drought and such — it's important that there's women around to support women. And I really think that that's what CWA is all about. It certainly was with my mother. With my mother, people came first. I worked in the wilds of Canada once and I got a letter from her saying how one of my friends had just buried her little baby boy and she'd come down for a cuppa. He'd just lasted for three days, and my friend's immediate thought was, I'll go to Kit's mother for some company and help.

That was my mother. She was just that sort of person, and that's the CWA all over. We say, 'Come and have a cuppa. Come and have something to eat. Sit around the table. Have a chat.'

Of course, it goes far beyond that. I mean, food is a 'breaking of the bread' type of thing, isn't it? That's what it is. That's what my mother certainly believed. As our motto says: Honour to God. Loyalty to the Throne and Service to the Country, through Country Women, for Country Women, by Country Women. And it's definitely 'loyalty to the throne' — especially for my mother it was — as it is also for me.

Lillian Burgess
Palmerston, Northern Territory

I grew up north of Brisbane, at Strathpine. It's not far from Caboolture. I did my primary schooling at Strathpine State School but I didn't get to high school because I was the oldest girl in the family and there were seven of us kids. So I left school to help out the family. Yes, seven is quite a lot, isn't it, but we were actually made up from two families: Mum had been married before and she'd already had three of us kids then after she married my step-dad they had another four kids. That made seven of us kids in all.

So I left school before I was thirteen, then I went out to work at Golden Circle Cannery and my money came straight home to Mum and she'd give me back just enough to cover the cost of the train fare for work. That's all I got. Yes, they were tough days but they were still good days. I love my family. My mum's ninety-three. She's not too good, actually. She's in hospital at the moment and I'm just waiting for a call to see if I've got to go down there. Then my step-dad, he died ten years ago and he was a beautiful man. Absolutely beautiful, he was.

Yes, so I started work when I was thirteen and then I was married at nineteen and I'd had my first child before I was twenty. In all, I've got four boys so there's no CWA members there. But I'm very happy with what I've got. You don't have to be unhappy. My boys live all over Australia now: one lives in Perth, one lives in South Australia, one lives in Queensland and one's just moved back up here to be with me. I live out at Humpty Doo.

I didn't belong to CWA before I came up to the Northern Territory. Then as to how I got into CWA was, well, my husband died in March 2010. Exactly six months tomorrow actually. But after my husband died I just didn't want to sit around so I started looking for things to do, to get out. I've always been involved with horses, which is another passion of mine, and so I started doing things like helping friends out with their horses, and I also love to travel. Still, regardless of what I do, I just love helping people out. Just love it. But I think that, after my husband died, I really needed to go out and find myself and to see what I wanted to do next, and I've always loved the CWA. I've always collected their recipe books and that, so I thought, Well, if I can find a branch which is close to me I'll join. And I did. That's the Palmerston Branch and I love it. Absolutely love it.

We've only got, I think, about thirteen members at the moment. But I'm working on that because there's some younger ones out that way who are keen on joining. I've just got to make them realise how they can still be involved in CWA even if they can't make it to all the meetings or get-togethers; you know, that they'll still have that connection there. So that's what I'm working on at the moment, and they'll come along eventually. I've got one friend who'll probably join within the next twelve months and there's another one that will follow her. Another lady's retiring soon — she's keen — and so I'll get her in. So we'll keep on growing. I'm confident about that because CWA's such a great place to come to and it gives you a lot of friendships and contacts and support. That's what CWA is good for. And that's about it really, I guess, other than that I just love helping people, because you don't have to be unhappy, do you?

Roddy Calvert
Tennant Creek, Northern Territory

Well to start at the beginning, I grew up on a Jersey-stud dairy farm near Kangarilla, which is on the Fleurieu Peninsula of South Australia, south of Adelaide. I went to school at Kangarilla Primary. This was in the early 1960s. My parents then decided to live nearer the city, so we moved to Elizabeth and that's where I finished my schooling. My father was employed by a company that made demountable houses and he worked there for over twenty years before he and Mum got into property and decided to move out to the Barossa Valley.

By that time I'd finished my schooling and I'd met my husband and we decided to drive around Australia. We stopped and worked at a few places along the way and by the time we got to Darwin we needed to earn some more money and so we got work out on Douglas Daly Station. Douglas Daly's south of Darwin, on the way to Katherine. It was a cattle station, with some buffalo, but they also did experimental work for CSIRO. Basically it had to do with dew levels in relation to certain types of grasses, crop soils and pastures. So other than doing yard work I got involved in the experimental side of things and I also took readings for the Bureau of Meteorology.

So that's where we were living when Cyclone Tracy struck Darwin on Christmas Day, 1974. Though, actually, I was in Darwin when it hit. How that came about was that my daughter was due to be born on that particular Christmas Day so I'd gone to Darwin a couple of weeks beforehand and I was staying in a caravan. Of course, when Cyclone Tracy came through, I lost the lot. Yes, it was pretty scary. In fact I tried to get out of Darwin but all the roads were closed and the police advised me to go back and so I ended up at the DAC Club [Darwin Aviation

Club]. That's where they housed a lot of the people who'd been made homeless. It was also one of the points where you got your needles for typhoid and that. Of course, because we were already staying there we were among the first ones to get our jabs. But I can remember that whole day, there were just lines and lines of people coming in to get their injections.

Actually, just yesterday at the church that us CWA ladies went to, I related some of my experiences of the cyclone and of how we were only allowed a little mini-bucket of water — about a gallon or so — to wash ourselves and also when we flushed the toilets. But I can't get over the amazing support of the people in Darwin at that time. They kept bringing us cold drinks and there was always food being brought around. Always. Then on the third day we had to get up early and ready ourselves for evacuation to Adelaide. We were picked up by a bus and they'd take us somewhere then we'd just stay there for a while, waiting. Then they'd take us somewhere else and we'd wait again. I remember it was quite hot and we were stuck at the airport, sitting in the bus, and they brought us milkshakes to try and keep us cool. Then, when we were eventually allowed off the bus, we sat around the airport and we didn't leave for Adelaide till about eight o'clock that night. And I just couldn't believe my luck because, seeing how I was pregnant, I got to sit in the flight deck of the Hercules aeroplane while all the other poor people — the women and children — were squashed up together in those hanger-seat type things, at the back of the plane. Anyhow, we got down to Adelaide at about midnight and I had my baby girl on the 10th of January. She was actually a couple of weeks late. Yes, so that was certainly an experience and definitely one I wouldn't like to have to live through again. But as I said, the support of the people of Darwin was just amazing.

And now, as to CWA: that came about because after I'd had my daughter, whenever I went back to Darwin I'd go to the old CWA restrooms in Knuckey Street to change her nappies and all that. That's how I got involved with CWA and then, because I was still out on Douglas Daly, I became a mail bag member. That's when you don't live in a town where there's a CWA and so you can't be on any of the committees or get to their social events but you still want to be involved. So you become a mail bag member and CWA sends you out all the information, like newsletters and that, and if you come to Darwin you can get a member's discount when you stay in the hostel. So that was how I, initially, got involved with CWA.

Then after ten years out on Douglas Daly we came down to Tennant Creek to live and that was mainly for the children's education. I'm now involved in tourism. That all come about because, back in the late 80s, I decided to go for a tour guide job at an old ore crushing plant that was going to become a tourist precinct. From there I slowly became more involved until now I'm actually the manager of Battery Hill Mining Centre and the Tennant Creek Visitors Information Centre.

So I've been in Tennant Creek for about thirty years now and in our CWA we currently have about twenty members. But once again, due to the amount of station properties around the area, we have about eight mail bag members. Then as for special moments, perhaps one of the most memorable would've been when I went to the Associated Country Women of the World conference in Pretoria, South Africa. That was back in 1998 and I'd always been intrigued by South Africa and by the women's involvement there. Luckily, at that time, I could afford to go and so I went as the delegate from the Tennant Creek Branch of CWA. Of course, no one knew where Tennant Creek was but they were well aware that I was Australian and Australians, as a whole, are received quite well, worldwide. So I had a fantastic time there and it was a fascinating country. In fact, not unlike Australia in many ways. But I had to pinch myself at times because there I was as a representative of Tennant Creek CWA Northern Territory, attending a worldwide conference of country women, all the way over in South Africa.

Eva Campbell
Camden, New South Wales

My name is Eva Campbell — spelt the same as the soup but without the money. I was born in Crookwell, New South Wales, which is significant because the first official branch of CWA was established at Crookwell back in the early 1920s and my pathway into the Association would, I'd say, be different to most. To be honest, I had no intention of belonging to CWA, or any other women's organisation for that matter, because I didn't think they were truly reflective of society. Having grown up after 'the Sisterhood' had, supposedly, won the feminist revolution, I couldn't see any point in belonging to any segregated group.

Even so, though I wasn't a member, I'd had a long involvement with CWA as a judge and adjudicator for their various activities, like the public speaking and international project competitions that they ran for their own members and for school students. There were no entry fees. It was just an opportunity to give those in the community a life experience as part of the CWA's support of ongoing education. This is an ideal that went right back to the formation of the CWA. Nevertheless, whenever I visited various CWA Branches, it would always be, 'Come and join us.' But in those days, I had a 'real job'. Overcommitted really, being a wife, a mother and Head Teacher. Then I became a city councillor and following that, the Mayor of Camden. So to their comment about me joining CWA I used to jokingly reply, 'Seeing I have such a connection to the CWA already, by being born in the town where CWA officially started, I'll join when I have some spare time!'

Then, when Camden CWA opened its new Branch rooms, I was invited to attend. Which I did. That was back in about 2001 and at the very first meeting they didn't have an International Officer so I said, 'Well, what does the International Officer do?' and I ended up as the International Officer. After that the jobs came in rapid succession. To start with, no one could remember when we'd last held a Land Cookery competition in Camden so I tried to get that up and running again. I did some publicity and promotions. Had a bit of success. My daughter even wanted to join CWA as a junior member. Then my aunt joined our Branch — aged one hundred and one. My mum also joined. Mum would have never dreamt of belonging to a women's group either, until I got involved — and she's eighty-eight. Actually, since I've become the Branch President our numbers have more than doubled, which is very satisfying. And by the way, the new members are not all from my family.

Given my previous involvement with CWA I thought I knew what it was all about. But I didn't. At my first State Conference, in Mudgee, I found the debate and the guest speakers fascinating, as was the CWA system. My experience of attending local government conferences was of them being a two-ring political circus whereas, at Mudgee, goodness gracious me, they even marked the roll before each session. And when one woman came late for a session the Group President sort of ripped into her. 'Remind me never to be late,' I said. I mean, there was a part of me that thought this attitude was quite severe but you'd know if all the voting delegates were present or not, wouldn't you? Anyway, there's nothing wrong with a bit of precision and preciseness either, I guess. It certainly gets the job done.

I've also discovered that CWA encompasses 'everything'. You name it, the CWA will be doing it, literally. And I very much like the flexibility of being able to pursue your own interests within the Association and though I've never acquired any talents with handicrafts, I'm now the Executive Rep. to the State Land Cookery Committee. After I first suggested we bring the Land Cookery competition back to Camden, I volunteered to be a steward at the local agricultural Show. I've been doing that now for about five years and it's been a sharp learning curve. Amongst other duties, as a steward you assist the judge and write down her comments and I really enjoy that because you pick up so many tips from the 'expert' cooks.

So one of these days I'd like to go for my Judge's Cookery Badge. To get that you have to do both a written examination and a practical test. Basically, you need to know your sweets, your rum balls, macaroons, coconut ice and anything else that might come up. Plus there's every sort of cake and biscuit and, mind you, if the schedule says 'three distinct biscuits', it actually means three completely different biscuit recipes, not just making up a basic mix then putting chocolate in one and sultanas in another. It's a very thorough and complex process so I don't expect to pass the first time around, or the second, or even, perhaps, the third. But I'll get there.

Now you may wonder why someone who's led such a busy life, working in various institutions, is now doing voluntary work and homely things like cooking. Well I believe we've reached a point in society where we tend to assess a person on how much money they can earn. It's like, the more you're paid, the more possessions you can accumulate, which somehow equates to you being a more satisfied, significant and important person. So if you're cooking for a family, doing volunteer work, or undertaking personal study then, in the eyes of many, your personal worth is lessened. Whereas, in actual fact, many of the most satisfying and worthwhile activities you can undertake do not have a dollar value placed on them and the people who are doing these activities actually make massive contributions to society. Our values are all wrong because, it's my experience that, the more money people make, the bigger their houses are likely to be, so the larger the mortgages they take out, which leads to greater stress, larger numbers of family breakdowns and increased domestic violence.

As a society, we're losing our connections to reality. Thinking back over my 'former life', which I jokingly call 'my teaching career', at one school I replaced a tall, bearded bloke who taught Living Skills. I was the youngest head teacher in the state at that time and I had to take over his class and teach all these big, tough Year 10 boys — sixteen going on thirty-five, all footy players. Of course, the headmaster was concerned that here was this extremely young female — probably incompetent — replacing this macho male who knew everything. But I soon found out that these kids thought that pizza either came frozen in a box from the supermarket or was delivered, also in a box, from a fast food outlet. They didn't realise that you could make one. Now, if you don't know that you can actually make a pizza, where's the connection back to the farmer who grows the wheat and to the horticulturalist who grows the capsicums and the butcher who made the salami? Beyond 'takeaway' was just La La Land to these kids.

Just a couple of generations ago, having a fair knowledge of farming and how to cook would've been taken for granted. Now we've got a generation of young people who don't have a clue what life is really all about and, worse still, they're now becoming parents. So basically, in that school, I abandoned this macho bloke's program for Living Skills and I ended up doing things like getting the nursing mothers in to demonstrate bathing and feeding a baby. And, well, didn't that cause a stir in the community. I was summoned to the headmaster's office. 'What's this I'm hearing? A baby being fed in front of a class!'

Yes, so that's about it from the girl who was born in Crookwell and had no intention of ever joining CWA. However, she has become a member and it's something she's very passionate about. Maybe my involvement is a direct reflection of my personal values, which are also the values that are so strongly upheld by the CWA: where a broad knowledge of life skills is important and your worth is not measured by how much money you can earn but by how much difference you can make.

Bette Chapman
Palmerston, Northern Territory

My name is Bette Chapman. I'm eighty years of age. Originally I was from Adelaide and then, about twenty-four years ago, my husband Harold, and I, we came up to Darwin to help my son. He's in civil engineering. He had his own earth-moving business and he used to make roads and airports and things like that out at places like Oenpelli, where a lot of the Aboriginals are, and also Snake Bay and a few other places like that. Harold was a private pilot and so he used to fly my son around to the different places where he had his men working.

In the first place, we only planned to be here for six months and, as I said, that was twenty-four years ago. But that particular son, he's not here now. He's working in Indonesia, and I lost Harold two-and-a-half years ago. But I love it up here. I do go back down south a fair bit. Actually, I have to go to Adelaide later this month. But I'm not looking forward to it. Even though you get the high humidity up here I'd still prefer to live in Darwin. You can't have it both ways, can you?

We were among the few that first lived out at Palmerston. That's when Palmerston was just sort of getting built. In those days there was nothing much there except for the water tower and half of the shopping centre. Anyhow, I'd run a book exchange before I came to the Northern Territory so I knew the business, and when I first came up here I was so bored with being stuck at home that I decided to start up a book exchange in the new Statepack building. I ran that for ten years and I'd just started to make a bit of profit out of it, then Harold got sick. So I sold it and the lady who bought it from me, well, she made all the money from it, didn't she.

But I love meeting people and, about seventeen years ago, somebody talked me into going to the Berrimah Branch of CWA.

So I went to that and I enjoyed it. Then after two years, Elva Whitbread and I, we thought, Why don't we start up a Branch in Palmerston. So that's what we did; the two of us started the Palmerston Branch of CWA, and it's still going. We have about fifteen members in all, though only about eight members actually get to our meetings. But I think we do pretty well for a small group. Twice a year we have trading tables in our big main shopping centre, and every year we try and give Camp Quality a thousand dollars. Camp Quality is a charity that was formed to brighten up the lives of children and their families that are affected by cancer. Then we have a meeting day once a month plus once a month we also have a craft day. We've been very fortunate: the Palmerston Community Health Centre allows us the use of a room and they allocate cupboards for us and they don't charge us for anything. So that's really good. And if for some reason or other we can't get in there, Terry Mills, our local member of parliament, he lets us use his boardroom.

But I am a very lucky person: I have four children, ten grandchildren and seventeen great-grandchildren that I love and enjoy a wonderful relationship with, and I think CWA is a wonderful organisation because you get to meet lots of different people and you do lots of different things, and you also help so many people. And these days Palmerston's such a growing area. When I first came out here, as I said, there was basically nothing and since then the place has grown so much around me that I'm like one of the old bits of the town now. But I enjoy it out there, especially with the CWA. Oh, yes, Elva's still with us but she's very sick at the moment. That's why she's not here today, which is a shame because she'd just love a chat.

Helen Christie
Rochester, Victoria

I grew up in northern Victoria near a town called Nanneella, which is seven miles outside of Rochester. My family had a small dairy farm in the area. Back then Nanneella had a primary school and so I rode my pushbike to school or, if it was very wet, we were taken by car, which was a great luxury in those days. At that stage there were eighteen children at the school and so we described it as being a 'big' school because there were other times when our numbers got as low as ten or eleven. Then for my high schooling we were bussed into Rochester. After that I went down to Melbourne to do nursing. But I didn't finish that because I came back to get married.

My husband was a dairy farmer too, so I've virtually been dairy farming all my life. Milk runs in the blood. Well, farming certainly runs in the blood because at one stage we did leave our dairy farm and we had five years on a beef property at Tallarook. After that we went dairy farming again. That was in south Gippsland and then, as we were getting nearer to retirement and because two of our children were still in the Rochester area, we decided to go back home. One was, and still is, married to a wheat and sheep farmer. The other one was on dairy farming, though they've since left the industry because it wasn't that profitable and also we've lost a lot of dairy farmers in the area because the irrigation water isn't there any more. But dairying will improve. It'll come back again. I'm sure of that.

CWA was always very much part of our community. Very much. So I was well aware of it when I was younger. Then one day in November 1967, in our local paper, there was a notice that an Evening Branch was going to start up in Rochester. Evening Branches suited the young mothers and the women that were working. So another girlfriend and I went along and I've been a member of CWA ever since. I had two more children after I joined and all us younger mothers formed a great friendship, one that's still going today. For us it was a night out and so we left the children at home with our husbands. In that Evening Branch we had up to thirty members and even now we've got about twenty-six members. So we're still flourishing. We're actually called the Campaspe Branch, after the Campaspe River that goes through the town of Rochester.

But I've very much enjoyed being involved in CWA. I've held nearly all the offices at Branch and Group level. Then four years ago I got elected as State Vice-President and now here I am: I've nearly finished my first year as State President of Victoria. We generally have two-year terms but you're elected for one year at a time and so I'll do another year. Even though every state is different, and they have their own constitutions, we're all part of the national body of the Country Womens' Association of Australia — all bar South Australia and Western Australia that is. But we're hoping they may come back on board soon.

As for any special single or shining moment, to be honest, there's been so many that it's hard to pinpoint just the one. Well I couldn't because, for me, the best part of CWA is just being involved. Then there's also the knowledge you gain as you go along, as well as the personal development. And, of course, there's the wonderful friendships you make. They're very important; very much so because, even though I still live in the same area that I grew up in, I can go all over the state and meet people I know. All over. Everywhere.

Meat

Beef Olives
CWA NSW

1 lb thick steak
¼ lb veal forcemeat (an eschalot is nice in forcemeat)
1 oz flour
1 oz dripping
½ pint stock or gravy
A puree of spinach or mashed potatoes for serving

Cut steak into pieces 3 to 4 inches square and a ½ inch thick. Place a little roll of forcemeat in each. Roll up, tie with fine string. Roll in flour. Make dripping hot and fry them till brown. Add water or stock to pan and simmer slowly for about 2 hours. Lift out and serve on a puree of spinach or mashed potatoes. Strain the gravy and pour little around dish. If liked, some olives may be finely minced and mixed with the forcemeat and 1 dozen whole olives may be stewed with the meat and served with the gravy.

Beef Stroganoff
CWA NSW

1½ lb topside or round steak
Lemon juice
Flour
1 cup finely chopped onion
1 cup chopped mushrooms
Butter
1 cup sour cream
Boiled rice for serving

Cut the steak in shreds and sprinkle with lemon juice and allow to stand for ½ hour. Lightly flour the steak. Cook the onions and mushrooms separately in a little butter. Cook meat in a little butter at sizzling heat for about 5 minutes, stirring all the time. Add the onions and mushrooms and cook for a further 3 minutes. Pour on the sour cream and serve with a border of fluffy white rice.

Corned Silverside of Beef
CWA Tas

Place corned silverside in pot of cold water, enough to cover. Boil and skim. Simmer gently for ¾ hour or until almost cooked then add carrots, parsnips and turnips, 3 or 4 peppercorns and simmer for ¼ hour.

Serve with dumplings (see below) round the meat. Serve with Parsley Sauce or Mustard Sauce. (See p139.)

Dumplings for Silverside and Stews etc
CWA NSW

1 lb flour
1 heaped teaspoon baking powder
½ teaspoon salt
Milk and water to mix

Put the flour, baking powder and salt through a sieve then form a stiff dough with milk and water. Roll out lightly, form into dumplings and either put them in the stew for one hour or the better way is to steam the dumplings and then serve them with the stew. If steaming, to keep them dry and light, put a piece of greased paper at the bottom of the steamer before putting the dumplings in.

Add 2 oz of finely grated suet to the above if suet dumplings are required.

Cornish Pasties
CWA NSW

1 lb skirt steak
1 teaspoon salt
½ teaspoon pepper
1 onion
1 large potato
1 white turnip
1 egg beaten with
    1 tablespoon milk

SHORT CRUST PASTRY
¾ lb flour
¾ teaspoon baking powder
½ teaspoon salt
½ lb clarified fat or dripping
¾ cup of water

Prepare the mixture of meat and vegetables first. Chop the meat finely, put into a basin and sprinkle with salt and pepper. Cut vegetables into small dice and mix with meat.

Prepare short crust: sift the flour, baking powder and salt. Rub in fat until mixture looks like breadcrumbs, add water, gradually making into stiff paste. Turn on to floured board and knead gently. Divide the dough into six equal parts. Roll out about ¼ inch thick, keeping it circular. Place about one-sixth of the meat and vegetable mixture on half of each round, moisten the dough edges with water, fold over the other half and press the edges together. Crimp the cut edges to form a frill. Prick with a fork and brush over with beaten egg and milk. Put into hot (200°C) oven and cook for 10 minutes. Then lower the heat (160°C) and continue cooking very gently for 40 minutes.

Goulash (Austrian style)
CWA Tas

1 lb lean beef or veal
Salt and pepper
3 oz butter
½ small onion, finely chopped
1 red pepper
1 dessertspoon flour

½ wineglass red wine
1 gill brown stock
½ teaspoon caraway
    seed
4 oz bacon
2 potatoes, cut into dice

Remove all fat and skin from the meat, cut and dice and season lightly with pepper and salt. Heat half the butter in a frying pan. Fry onion and red pepper slightly then add meat and cook slowly for 10 to 15 minutes on low, sprinkle on the flour. Add the wine, stock and caraway seeds and continue to cook slowly. Heat remaining butter, fry bacon then add prepared potatoes and fry until golden brown, drain well, add to contents of frying pan. Cook slowly, occasionally stirring gently.

Irish Stew
CWA Tas

1½ lb neck chops
    (mutton or lamb)
Flour
Salt and pepper

Water
2 onions
3 potatoes

Cut meat into small pieces. Roll into flour, pepper and salt. Put into saucepan with water. Cut onions into rings and add and allow to simmer for about 1 hour. Peel and chop potatoes and put on top and simmer slowly until cooked. Remove fat from gravy if necessary.

Lamb's Fry and Bacon

Mrs Mollross, Moonah Branch, CWA Tas

1 lamb's fry

Salt

Flour

½ lb bacon

1 onion

Prepare lamb's fry by cutting into pieces, soak in water with salt, drain water off and dry, flour and fry brown. Place in casserole with bacon on top and sliced onion. Pour all the fat out of the pan and use to make gravy. Pour over lamb's fry and bake in oven. Very nice.

Meat Loaf

CWA Tas

1 lb beef

3 oz bacon

1 teaspoon onion

Stock

1 egg

Nutmeg

Salt and pepper

3 oz breadcrumbs

Mince beef, bacon and onion and add stock and beaten egg. Mix in a bowl with seasonings and breadcrumbs. Press into Pyrex dish and cover with buttered paper. Bake 1½ hours in moderate (180°C) oven. Take out and glaze with gelatine stock warmed.

Ox Tongue

CWA NSW

Soak the tongue in cold water for a few hours. Wash it well in fresh water, trim the root, put into tepid water, bring very slowly to the boil, removing any scum as it rises. Simmer gently until the tongue is tender — about 3 or 4 hours, according to the size. Skim when necessary. Add a bunch of herbs while cooking. When cooked, skin the tongue while hot, trim the root, remove any small bones. If to be eaten hot, brush it over with glaze. Serve on a hot dish. Garnish with small heaps of cooked vegetables or with slices of lemon and sprigs of parsley.

If to be served cold and pressed, roll the tongue round, place in a meat press and leave all night. Turn out and serve. Garnish with parsley or lettuce and tomato.

Roast Pork

CWA NSW

The leg or loin is generally chosen for roasting and the skin must be well scored. A leg is scored round and round in narrow rows from the knuckle and a loin the way of the chop bones.

The crackling is one of the titbits of roast pork but often we find, when it comes to the table, it is hard, tough and uneatable. This is easily prevented by brushing it over well with salad oil before putting it into the oven. It will then be deliciously crisp, but not tough.

The joint must be put into a hot (220°C) oven, which should be kept at a fairly fierce heat for 10 minutes, then slackened to moderate (180°C) until the meat is thoroughly cooked through, basting it occasionally to keep it moist. Allow 25 minutes for each pound of pork and 20 minutes over.

Pork must be served very hot. Do not start dishing up until the dish, plate and gravy tureen are all hot. Put the joint on the dish and keep it hot while you make the gravy.

Slowly pour off the fat from the dripping pan, leaving just the brown sediment at the bottom. Add half a teaspoon of salt and half a pint of boiling water or broth made from the knuckle bone. Stand the pan over gentle heat and stir for a minute whilst it boils, scraping every particle of meat essence from the bottom of the tin. Strain into hot tureen. Serve pork with apple sauce.

Steak and Kidney Casserole

Mrs Mollross, Moonah Branch, CWA Tas.

1½ lb stewing steak	1 onion
2 tablespoons flour	1 dessertspoon vinegar
2 tablespoons sugar	2 dessertspoons
1 dessertspoon salt	tomato sauce
4 kidneys	

Cut the steak into fair size squares. Mix half the flour, all the sugar and half the salt and rub into steak with spoon. Cut kidneys in half and place all in casserole dish with sliced onion. Mix the remaining flour with vinegar, tomato sauce and half the salt. Add enough water to make a good cup and a half of liquid. Pour over contents and bake for 3 hours. Very tasty.

Steak Diane

CWA NSW

Allow ½ lb topside or round steak
    (all fat and gristle removed) per person
A clove of garlic
Flour
1 tablespoon of butter
1 teaspoon Worcestershire sauce per four servings
1 dessertspoon lemon juice
Salt and pepper

With a meat mallet pound the steaks carefully until they are ⅓ inch thick. Rub with garlic and lightly flour them. Cook in a thick-bottomed frypan in butter, quickly browning on each side. Add the Worcestershire sauce and lemon juice and cook slowly on each side for 2 minutes. Serve immediately with the juice from the pan as sauce. Salt and pepper to taste. If desired a little brandy or wine may be added to the sauce.

Tripe and Onions

CWA NSW

5 or 6 whole onions
2 lb tripe
Salt and pepper
2 oz butter
2 oz flour
1 pint of milk

Peel the onions. Wash the tripe. Blanch it as follows: cover with cold water and bring to the boil. Drain away the water. Repeat this blanching process. Return the tripe to the saucepan. Cover with 3 or 4 pints cold water. Add onions and season with salt and pepper. Cover the pan. Bring to the boil and simmer till the tripe is tender, about 3 hours. Strain and reserve 1 cup of liquor. Chop the tripe into pieces about 1½ inches square. Chop the onion roughly. Melt the butter in a saucepan. Add the flour and blend well. Remover from fire. Gradually stir in the milk and liquor. Return to the fire and stir till it boils. Add the tripe and onions and simmer for 15 minutes.

Veal and Ham Pie or Pork Pie

CWA Tas

FOR PASTRY
1 lb flour
6 oz lard
Salt
Cold water

FOR PORK PIE
1¼ lb lean pork
Salt and pepper
Sage
Stock

FOR VEAL AND HAM PIE
1 lb veal
¼ lb ham
Parsley
Thyme
2 teaspoons grated
    lemon rind
1 hard boiled egg

Put flour and lard in a basin in warm place. Boil salt rapidly in water for about 5 minutes, let stand for a few minutes then add to flour and lard, kneading all the time. Knead well and allow to stand in a warm place for ½ hour. Roll out and place round a flat or loose bottomed cake tin.

For the pork pie, fill pastry case with pork. Season well with salt, pepper and a little sage. Add a little stock to moisten, put on pastry lid and decorate then stand in a cool place to set. Bake in a moderate (180°C) oven for 2 hours. (You may need to add a little stock when pie comes out of oven).

For veal and ham pie: cut the veal and ham into squares. Cook in 1 pint of water for 1 hour with parsley, thyme, lemon rind. Drain and pack the meat into pastry case. Put hard boiled eggs in centre. Put on pastry lid and decorate. Stand in cool place to set. Bake as for pork pie.

Elizabeth Clark
Cressy, Tasmania

I'm a Tasmanian, definitely. I grew up in the northern midlands, at Cressy, which is a forty-minute drive south of Launceston. Actually, I still live there and have done so for sixty-two years, and counting. Cressy has a population of about a thousand people. It's a farming community. I don't live in the township itself. I live a kilometre out on the very same property that my mother and father bought nearly seventy years ago. It's unusual I know but, because there were no sons in the family, when my parents deceased, the property was left to my sister and I. So I'm a farmer. Actually, I've retired. Well I'm trying to retire, but we farmers don't ever really retire, do we?

Originally it was a mixed farm with sheep and cropping but I've sold all the sheep. We ran Merino wethers but it was a struggle economically and there was so much paperwork involved. A terrible lot. Paperwork for this. Paperwork for that. It became such a nightmare that the actual farming side of things got lost along the way. So I now live in the house and look after the garden and we've leased the land to friends who do the cropping part of it and they just give us a cheque at the end. For me, that's the easy way of farming.

As for my education, I went to the local primary and high school in Cressy. Then after I left school I went to Launceston Technical College and did a secretarial course. During that time, I sat for an exam as a telephonist with what was then known as the Postmaster General's Department. I was lucky enough to pass that and so I started work at the Cressy Post Office as a telephonist. I did that for, oh goodness gracious, for about fifteen years I think and, when the post office went automatic, I got a job as a receptionist in a solicitor's office in Launceston. I worked there for about five years, then I went overseas for three months to see the world. After my travels I came home and I started managing the farm. My father had passed away by then but my mother was still alive and when she died in 1982, that's when my sister and I formed our partnership.

But I grew up with CWA. Cressy Branch celebrated its seventieth birthday in August 2009. My grandmother was a foundation member, and a very staunch one at that. She loved her CWA and she loved her handicraft. She had three children, all sons, then there were nine grandchildren and I guarantee you, for each of our birthdays and Christmases we'd get something she'd made at CWA. And I just loved the gifts Nanna used to give us. She'd knit things like jumpers and cardigans, then she'd do little bookmarks and shoes made out of paper, and I've still got a handkerchief box she made, which I treasure. It's a cardboard handkerchief box and you put material over the top of it. It's actually got roses on it. It's sewn down the sides and the top's sewn on as well.

Because of my grandmother's influence I joined Cressy CWA in 1982. My sister didn't join for a long time but she's now a member. Mind you, she's not as staunch of a CWA lady as I've been over the years — I wanted to go from one level to another within the organisation. That was my driving passion — but she's still only young and she works as well. So from Branch level I became Group President. From there I've progressed and once you get to the top level it becomes very interesting indeed. I was State International Officer for four years and we used to pack up parcels to send away to the island girls. I loved doing that and I've also been very lucky that I love the conferences. Triennially, we have a National Conference. There's the South Pacific Area Conference, a World Conference and with my travels to the various conferences I've met a lot of people and I very much cherish the friendships I've made from those. They'll remain for the rest of my life.

But my greatest ambition was to become State President and I've achieved that. My term finished in about 2008 and during that time I worked in all sorts of areas. I was on the Drought Taskforce Committee. That was a Tasmanian State Government initiative where, along with representatives from other organisations, we got together around a table and we were asked for our input as to how we could help those in the drought areas. Of course, CWA Tasmania was given money from the state government which we then distributed to the affected families. I was also part of the Woolworths days where they donated a day's profit to help drought relief.

Then, because I've had breast cancer and have had a double mastectomy, I really think that the highlight of my era was my working with the National Breast and Ovarian Cancer Council. I was very, very happy and grateful to have had that opportunity because, after I had the breast cancer, I had lymphoedema. So I actually went to Sydney as a representative of not only Tasmania but also of the National Body of CWA and I had input into the writing of the Lymphoedema Booklet. Basically, it's an instruction book, with photos, advising people with lymphoedema as to what can happen and what treatments are available, plus your do's and don'ts. And believe me, there's a lot of do's and don'ts. Mind you, you don't have to have had breast cancer to get lymphoedema. It affects men as well, especially after they've had leg operations or groin operations. Anyhow, that book has now been published Australia wide and it's also going to be done in different languages as well. So, yes, I was and still am very proud of doing that and, well, really, that's about my life's story in CWA.

Faye Clark
Molong, New South Wales

During my working years I was a Relieving Manager with the Commonwealth Bank, and so I was going all around the countryside, which I loved. But one of the problems was that you could be in some of these towns for anything up to six months and, when you're female and you don't know anyone your own age, and you're living in a hotel room, like I was at one place, that faced north in the summer and there was no air conditioning, it can be quite soul destroying. Then, when the bank manager at Molong went on long-service leave, I did an extended relief up there. Then I was at a CWA function one time and the State President was there and we got talking and I had the brainwave that if I joined CWA then, when I went to these towns, I could go to their meetings and make myself known.

That was the idea of it and I joined in February 1987 and that made it much easier when I went out to some of these places. Then, when I retired in 1990, I was living in a unit at Cronulla. It was a three-storey block and I was on the top floor and my doctor said, 'Because of your knees, you'll have to get out of there.'

I couldn't afford a decent house in the Sydney area and I was thinking about going down the coast. My family came from Huskisson, just south of Nowra, where there was a reasonably large retired population. But I soon realised that it's very difficult for a single female to be accepted amongst retired people because the wives think you're out to pinch their husbands. Mind you, just between you and me, most of the blokes I wouldn't touch with a forty-foot barge pole. But that's beside the point. But I'd loved it at Molong. I'd already made friends there and I enjoyed the bowling club so that's where I decided to retire and, basically, it flowed on from there.

At that stage the Molong CWA had its own building but it wasn't in the best of conditions. Because it was close to a creek, the foundation stones were giving way and it would've cost us over $30,000 to be fixed. Whilst we could've got a ten-year, interest-free loan from CWA State Head Office it still meant that we'd have to find nearly $3000 dollars a year to pay for the rates, the insurance and the electricity. We were struggling for members anyway and so my thinking was that we should sell the old building and relocate somewhere else.

But with our small membership, it was a battle. And as far as dwindling memberships go, it isn't only us. Apex has folded at Molong. The Rotary Club is just struggling along. Red Cross has recently picked up but, prior to that, it was struggling. Hospital Auxiliary is struggling and, of those organisations that are still viable, most of their members are at least in their sixties. It's just that it's very difficult to get the under-fifties to join any organisation, throughout Australia, where they've got to attend a meeting once a month. Yes, they'll come along and help for the day or maybe a weekend, like at our Molong Festival, but they're not prepared to commit themselves to one day a month.

My thoughts on the matter are that my generation and the generation before me, we all went through the Depression and the Second World War. The younger people haven't had that experience so they haven't grown up with the natural idea of helping one another. It's an intriguing facet of life and it's going to be very interesting to see if this crisis, with the global economy and recession, will change that. We have it in us in Australia. That's evident by the huge success of the Bush Fire Appeal. But when you ask them to join a group the answer is, 'What's in it for me?' instead of, 'What can I do to help?' And that's the satisfaction of being in an organisation like CWA. It's not a monetary thing. In fact it costs. It's simply the reward of helping others.

Anyway, all that aside, it proved a hard enough task to get through the sale of the old CWA building. We needed a seventy-five per cent majority vote and we had an elderly group of members who were very attached to the place. It was that notion of it being 'our building'. So we had a first meeting and it didn't go through. We had a second meeting. Still no good. Then I brought the State President into the third meeting and there was still no resolution. Then one of our ladies' sons was a carpenter-builder and he told his mother, 'You're mad.' He said, 'There's no way you can ever pay for fixing that building up.'

In the end we had four Special General Meetings before we finally got the sale up. Then we agreed to give the council some of the proceeds to assist them to build a new Community Centre, which they're currently in the throes of doing. In return, we're to have free use of a meeting hall there. We won't have a room of our own, completely, but we're going to have a locked cupboard and we'll have our honour boards up on the wall, which will be marvellous, and we won't have to pay rates or for electricity and insurance, which is even better. That's what was killing us because most of our standard jobs, like catering, had been taken up by the United Protestants' Association. Plus, years ago, the old CWA building was an economical place to hold your birthday parties and Christmas parties, your wedding receptions and so forth. These days, of course, people want to go where they can have alcohol, so they go to the clubs, and that too had reduced our income. Also, back when I was first relieving at Molong, the Baby Health Centre was in our old building. But then, when they decided to rebuild the Mitchell Highway, that ran right past our door, and there was no way the women could get their prams across the road so they moved the Baby Health down to the Community Health Centre. Of course, when the road was finally finished we didn't get them back, did we? And that too made a huge dent in our income.

Still, I was very surprised at our meeting last Friday, in our temporary digs in the United Protestants' Association Hall, when we got two new members. That's five new members this year, which is good, because most of our ladies are in their eighties and they're just finding it a little too difficult. They've done tremendous work over the years and they can still be a support but as far as being active, that's something different.

So, yes, it is difficult — very difficult — but it won't be long before we'll be in our new home. Actually, the Community Centre was going to be finished by June but, when they first started to dig down, they found asbestos in the soil. Following that they were delayed by drainage problems or something. They've got the foundations in now so I'm thinking it might be nearer to Christmas. It's coming to fruition and as it turned out it was just lucky that we did sell the old CWA building because we had huge floods in Molong, eighteen months after, and, if we would've stayed on and hadn't had the foundations fixed, we would've been washed down the creek.

Carol Clay
Packenham, Victoria

I come from an orcharding family that's lived at East Doncaster for over a hundred and sixty years. When I was growing up, the area was known as the food bowl of Melbourne. I'm the eldest of four girls — no boys — and I went to the local primary school. In those days East Doncaster was one of only three primary schools in Victoria that had a swimming pool and my grandfather helped build that pool with a horse and scoop. Then seeing that there wasn't a local high school nearby, I went to MLC [Methodists Ladies College] in Hawthorn, as a shy little country girl. I didn't board. I went as a day girl, which was really a major trek in those days.

One of my sisters would've just loved to have taken over the orchard but, unfortunately, girls weren't allowed to do those things back then. It wasn't the done thing. So it was sort of the end of the dynasty really, which was a disappointment for our father. Also, of course, progress had started to take its toll and when the natural gas pipeline was laid through our property the crop was ruined because of all the dust they made. Then, with the rising land prices and the new housing estates, the rates started to go up. Yes, so that was the end of that and I'm talking as if it was eighty years ago, but it's not. Times change and, when they do, they change quickly, and so the little country dirt road that went by our place is now a major four-laned thoroughfare and where our orchard and house was there's now a hockey club. There's traffic lights where our gateway used to be and my parents moved into the new housing estate that had been part of my husband's family orchard. So, yes, it's been a huge change.

Then I married the so-called boy next door — who was also an orchardist — had two children and then moved down to the

Mornington Peninsula. That's where a lot of the orchardists had moved, to get away from the urban sprawl and also the rates weren't so high. Of course, little did we know at that time how the peninsula would become a much sought-after place to live and plant vineyards. But my eldest son wasn't interested in orcharding because it became economically unviable and so he went off to university to study electronic engineering. Then, later on, I married an ex-orchardist and I had another baby and we lived on the peninsula for twenty years and when all the children had left home we moved to the dairy farming community of South Gippsland, just outside Leongatha. And now I'm on my own and I live fifty-seven kilometres out of Melbourne, at Pakenham, and that's as close to the city as I ever want to be.

But none of my family was involved in CWA and I've only been a member since 2001. I'm a so-called 'new girl'. I only came to it after we'd moved to South Gippsland and my elderly next door neighbour invited me along. But like many do, I thought you had to be good at craft to join CWA, and I wasn't a crafty person. Anyway, being new to the area, I went to that first meeting full of trepidation. It was a great connection to the local people and so I joined CWA and I also joined Red Cross and the tennis club. But it was actually the CWA magazine that really got me in because it was full of all the good stuff they were doing; stuff that non-members rarely know about. As you may have guessed, CWA is not very good at marketing itself. Anyhow, I was an ordinary member for a bit over a year then, at the Group's annual meeting, they needed a new Group President and, even though I hadn't done anything at Group level, I was duly elected. To be honest, I was quite daunted by it all. I thought, Oh no, I'll never be able to do this. But then I thought, Well if all those other old ducks can do it, why can't I? So I took on the job.

The rest, as they say, is history because after two years as Groupie I was elected a state Vice-President for a year and following that, Club Chairman. Club Chairman looks after the twenty-six room B&B (bed and breakfast) here in Toorak. The house itself was built in 1875 for the Chief Secretary of the Victorian Parliament and CWA bought it in 1948 for 28,000 pounds. Our administration offices weren't here then. The building was used purely as a residential club, providing accommodation and full board. But by 2005 we were losing money hand over fist. That's when I came into it with the brief of, 'There's no money. Make some.' So to put it kindly, all the staff were sacked and we turned it into a B&B and, even though there were those who weren't originally keen on the idea, it hasn't looked back and for the time I was Club Chairman we went from a loss to a profit. Mind you, it was very hard work but it was right up my alley because I love cooking and I love to meet people, and it worked.

After that stint I was elected Performing Arts Chairman, which I also loved. Performing Arts includes public speaking where we have competitions at Branch level, then on to Group and finally the State Public Speaking final is held in conjunction with our state conference. We also have a Song and Costume Festival which consists of beautifully costumed musical comedy items. That's also held in conjunction with our state conference. Then in September or October we have our Choral and Drama Festival and we go to a different country town each year for that. We have a State Choir as well, and some Branches have their own choirs. Believe it or not, some CWA Branches only exist for the music and drama. But eight or nine years ago I never thought I'd be able to stand up in front of a thousand people and compere a program. But I've done it now and I loved it, and that's the confidence you gain with being in CWA where you're mixing with so many strong and capable women.

So I did that and now I'm into my second year as Deputy State President. It's exhausting, I tell you. Once you get in a senior position you're rarely home. I'm always heading off left, right and centre and, mind you, it's all voluntary, so it's a huge commitment. If you let it, it can take over your life, and that can put a strain on relationships. It's pretty damn difficult actually. As I said, I'm on my own now and, although CWA wasn't the reason we broke up, you absolutely need that solid support. We find it can be a big problem sometimes when the husbands aren't supportive. Really, it's hard to believe that, in this day and age, some men aren't keen on their wives being involved in CWA just because they might be away from home a few times a year. I don't know, maybe they feel threatened by a wife who's out there doing things instead of being at home in the more traditional way. Yet that's odd because, when most wives leave home for a couple of days, they've usually got all the food labelled in the fridge with 'Eat this for lunch. Eat this for dinner' and even then some of the men still don't like it. Then, of course, there's the others who probably look forward to a little peace and quiet.

Still, we love it, even though, like in every large organisation, there's always the, you know, the back room stuff and the politics that goes on. So really, that's been my nine years in CWA. But I think it's a great testament to any organisation to see just how many of its members stay members for so long. It's a lifetime commitment really and, in our case, a lot of our older members, they're still willing to work hard. Take the Royal Melbourne Show for instance, that's the most amazing team effort of volunteers you're ever likely to see. You're on your feet from six in the morning till nine at night and, really, it's the older ones who never seem to complain. If there's a job to be done they just damn well do it. It's the mind-set that comes from a country-type background where you have to be self-sufficient and you have to show perseverance and forbearance. So you just grit your teeth and you do it. You just do it, and I think that's a great trait of not only the CWA character but of the Australian female character as well.

Mavis Cooper, OBE
Jamestown, South Australia

I was a city person. I grew up in Victoria and went into a nursing career. By that stage my parents had moved to South Australia. Then I came home on holidays, fell in love, and decided not to go back to Victoria, nursing. And I can say that it was a great shock to fall in love with a farmer and go through that transition from being a city girl to becoming a country girl, along with all the things it implied.

So all of a sudden my life changed, but very much for the better. I moved to Jamestown, in the mid-north of the state, and then in 1957 I joined the Country Women's Association. In those days there were about thirty members in our Jamestown Branch. At that stage I was a young mother, and the association offered all sorts of activities that I was interested in, primarily singing. I loved singing, and back then there was no other outlet for singing in Jamestown except for the CWA Choir, and that had been going for quite some time. And it was a good choir. We had a choir mistress who was conservitorily trained. She had majored in pipe organ and voice so she really was a person well worth working with. We used to go and sing down in Adelaide in the big choral festivals, with massed choirs from all the other various CWA Branches. When that happened we'd come down to Adelaide and have training sessions through CWA, with Professor Bishop from the conservatorium, at Adelaide University. It was quite a big part of the association in those days and so there were a good number of CWA choirs.

After I joined CWA I started becoming more and more involved. I became Branch Committee Member, Branch President. Then I went on to Group President, Divisional President, State President and National President, plus I've been a State Officer in every aspect except Treasurer. That's one thing I don't think they're ever going to ask me to do. It's not my forte.

I received the OBE after I finished my national work. That was in appreciation for what I did for health and education in the various states. Back then, Queensland had the highest incidence of skin cancer in Australia and Australia has the highest incidence of skin cancer in the world. So that really tells you how bad it was, particularly in outback Queensland, around Julia Creek and those areas. And I helped manage to get decent health services for those people. Through CWA I had access to the federal government and so I was able to lobby. We held the first ever Rural Health Conference in my time as National President. I was one of the key-note speakers. Ralph Hunt was then the Minister for Health and I put a lot of pressure on him during that conference, and the media loved it. In fact, I don't think I saw too much of the conference because the media wanted to know more about what I was saying about rural health.

Another thing I was heavily involved in was that there was no psychiatric care in Alice Springs at all. None at all. So when people needed help they were put in the Alice Springs jail until they could be transferred down to Adelaide. Now that, to me, was an appalling situation and, of course, as soon as I pointed the situation out the media took up the issue and we did end up getting a psychiatric unit in Alice Springs Hospital.

Something else that was achieved during my time as National President was that a lot of children in isolated areas were lacking education. Believe it or not, but there were children who were getting no education at all on some of those remote station properties and, quite often, the parents didn't have the wherewithall to teach the kids. We got a fair bit of help there with organising their correspondence lessons to be flown out to those isolated children, and on a regular basis. To help get things going, money to pay for those contract aircraft was made available through some of the State Country Women's Associations.

Those were just a couple of the things I received my OBE for at national level. Then at state level: in South Australia we've always raised enormous amounts of money for all sorts of other good projects; wonderful things. If you have a look at our State Treasurer's report there's one paragraph in particular that absolutely says it all about the huge amount of money we've raised for Emergency Aid, and that's just over the last twelve months. That money is used to help people who are really suffering; people who even struggle to put food on the table.

As for avenues of raising the money: one is the Dorothy Dolling Memorial Trust Fund. She was one of our South Australian founding members and when she died, her family established the trust fund. It's used to help children from country areas with their education. This last year, alone, we gave out twenty-eight awards, and that's just one area our members put money into. There's also the Emergency Aid Fund, which I've previously mentioned helps those in need. Then this year, our State Objective is a programme called Take-a-Break. That's made available for people who have suffered badly though the drought and we help give them some time off to have a holiday. We've already raised quite a bit of money to go into that. State Holiday Cottages have offered their support for free and our association helps pay for the people to get there. We also pay for their accommodation, where it's not been offered gratis. Our Branches also give money to hospitals to help pay for much needed equipment. They support their local CFS [Country Fire Service] as well as all sorts of other things in their local communities, and that's quite apart from what they're doing at a state level, here in Adelaide.

So there's just a few of the many projects that are undertaken through our fundraising activities. Only our subscription money goes to the State association and that's only to make us a legal member of an incorporated body. But the rest of the money that's raised by each Branch, they do with it what they will. It works better that way. People just love to feel that they're actually directly involved and responsible for helping those less fortunate. They're much closer to it.

So in all, the association is definitely one of the best things that's ever happened in my life. In actual fact, I was made a Member of Honour of the South Australian State Country Women's Association. That's the highest honour they can give you. It's given for outstanding and diverse service to the association and it's the thing I'm most proud of. To me, it means a great deal more than the OBE. As far as I'm concerned, Julia Materne summed it up perfectly in this year's report when she said that the sharing and caring and looking out for other people glows as brightly within the association as it's ever done. And that is my reason for still being an enthusiastic member after fifty-two years.

Rosalie Crocker
Bordertown, South Australia

During my life I haven't moved very far from home, actually. Most of my time's been spent around Bordertown, South Australia, which is on the Adelaide–Melbourne highway, over near the Victorian border. I was an only child who grew up on a mixed farm between Bordertown and Wolseley. We had sheep and cattle and cereal crops and I'd come home after school and milk the cows and help out on the farm, wherever I could. It was part of your living in those day. We only had six hundred and forty acres, as it was in those days, and that was enough to cope with. Not like nowadays where you'd need at least four times that size.

The little school I first went to was at a small place called Pine Hill. It was a one-teacher school. When I first started, there were just six girls and one boy and that boy eventually became my debutante partner. I'm not sure who the other five girls had for their debutante partners, but I took first choice. Then I remember that some of us had to walk through a creek to get to school and when it rained our boots would get all wet and so, while we did our lessons, we'd put our shoes around a little pot belly stove to dry out. But like a lot of those small schools, Pine Hill school closed. We were only seven mile from Bordertown so I went to school there. At that stage, you couldn't do your matriculation at Bordertown, you could only do your Intermediate, so I only went there for two years then I went to Alexandra College, at Hamilton, in Victoria.

My mother was a CWA member. She had joined CWA when I was about fourteen. In those days, because we lived out on the farm, we only went into Bordertown once a week and we always did that trip on the Tuesday to coincide with their CWA meeting. I'd always tag along with Mum, then, when I reached the age of sixteen, I also joined. You don't get too many sixteen-year-olds joining nowadays. But that's how I kind of started and I've been a member ever since.

Then after I married I moved to a little place between Bordertown and Francis, called Pooginagoric. Pooginagoric was just a little settlement with a church. That's all. Years before there'd been a school there but, by that stage, it'd also closed. I was still living close to Bordertown so I kept going to the CWA in there. Then, when the children came along, as children do, you couldn't have the little ones running around during the CWA meetings so we started an Evening Branch. Actually, the Bordertown Evening Branch was the first Evening Branch formed in South Australia. The idea of having an Evening Branch was that you could leave the children at home, with your husband, and that gave the young mums the chance to have a night out together and learn something as well. I was their foundation Vice-President and then President. In fact, during my time I've held just about every position except Treasurer. Yes, I can help somebody with money but balancing ledgers and things like that doesn't really interest me.

When the children got older we came into Bordertown to live. By that stage all the 'young mums' were getting older and so the Evening Branch closed early in the 1990s. That's when we joined the two Branches together — the Evening Branch and the day Branch — and I became Branch President, then Secretary and then, at one meeting, I was asked to be Group President. I had a florist shop at that stage and I thought, Well, it'll be a bit hard to work full time and be Group President as well, so I said, 'Oh no, I couldn't possibly do that.'

The State President was at the meeting that day and she said, 'Well I'm not going to go home until we get a Group President.'

So that's how I became Group President and from there I went on to be the Divisional President, then I was asked to be State Handicraft Officer, which I enjoyed very much. Following that, I became State General Officer and, on 1st July 2008, I was voted in as State President of the South Australian Country Women's Association. State President's a three-year term though you get re-elected each year just in case something happens and you feel like you can't cope or things aren't working out.

But no, I've enjoyed it. It's been a very busy life. CWA not only does a lot for the various communities and the people who are in need, we also do a lot of political-type lobbying. So much so that the government now see us as a force to be reckoned with. And I do love meeting people and I love being with people and I think that the friendships and networking are a big part of our association. And that was one of the main reasons why Mrs Warne first started our association, here in South Australia, in 1929 — for the companionship and friendship. At that stage she was living at Koomaloo Station, out from Burra, in the mid-north, and, as you might be able to imagine, living out on a big station property with nobody close by, it would've been quite a lonely existence for a woman in those days. So she realised then the great need for country women to be able to get together. It started from there and, of course, back then, with the problems of not being able to travel any great distance, CWA Branches sprung up all around the place.

Then as transport improved, unfortunately, many of those smaller Branches closed. But we've still got a hundred and forty Branches around the state, with a current state membership of around two thousand five hundred and, as Betty said just yesterday, we have a few new members this week. So it all evens out. Actually, this year, 2009, has been our eightieth birthday and I've gone around South Australia with the CWA banner and, at today's meeting, we're reading the first minutes of our first ever conference meeting.

And that's about it, really, other than I never thought I'd ever become State President when I first started with CWA fifty years ago as a sixteen-year-old, and I hope to continue for a long time to come. Yes, it's had its challenges but I think you've got to face those challenges in life to get somewhere. You've got to have an aim. So even if, as I said at the beginning, I haven't physically moved very far in my life, you could say that I've certainly come a long way.

Alice Davies
Bencubbin, Western Australia

I'm an elderly member of the CWA. I was born in 1926 so I'm touching eighty-three. I grew up in Western Australia, on the farm at Welbungin. It's between Mukinbudin and Bencubbin. It's a funny name, Welbungin. The town's not there any more. Only the name's there and the wheat bin and the hall and the tennis courts, which are still well used. Our farm was a wheat and sheep property. My mum went to Welbungin CWA back in about 1927 or '28, I think it was. But things got bad, with the bad seasons, the Depression and so on, and Welbungin CWA eventually closed down and they all came into Bencubbin. Bencubbin started up in 1932 and my mum was one of the early members there.

As kids, me and my younger sister, Laura, we used to go to Bencubbin CWA with Mum. We'd play while they had their meeting. Then I joined Bencubbin CWA in 1946, when I was about twenty. I was married in 1955 and after I had my first daughter I also took her to the meetings. Then, when she was about nine months old — you know, she was just at that age where they don't shut up and they've got to bang things on chairs and make a din — well, two or three of the ladies yelled at me, 'Keep that child quiet.' They were absolutely disgusted. So that was it. I went. I pulled out, and I pulled out for several years, which was unfortunate because I would've now been a long-time member otherwise. But I made that break.

Mum, Rose Wren, was a university-trained voice and music teacher. She was very good too, and I've always liked music, myself. It's one of the joys of life, so when Mum wanted to get a CWA choir started up in Bencubbin, to take to the 1962 CWA State Conference, I wanted to go too. So that's when I rejoined and I've been in CWA ever since. We did very well too, at the

Conference. After that, Mum had the choir going for quite a few years and we'd go around to the different towns, like Kwelkan, Kununoppin, Nungarin, and do musical nights, which was quite good. Welbungin CWA was well and truly dead by then.

As for memories — oh, there was one funny time. Back when I was a child we weren't flash enough to have anything like a car. We only had a horse and cart. The old truck that we did have, the big end had gone through the engine. But Dad, Joseph Wren, was a very sick man. He'd been in the 10th Light Horse Regiment and when his horse had been shot from under him, as it went down, it kicked him in the head and he used to get these crippling pains and headaches all the time after that. Anyway, he needed to get into Bencubbin hospital quite a lot and when that happened I had to ride a horse over to a neighbour and ask him to drive Dad the eighteen mile into town. So it wasn't easy. Anyway, the policeman from Bencubbin, Constable Gray, he got onto the RSL to do something about it and someone out on one of the farms had an old Buick car just sitting in their chicken yard being used as a chook's roost. This was in 1941, perhaps, and the RSL got it into town and it was fixed and cleaned up and made it into a utility and they gave it to us.

After that, whenever there was a CWA meeting, Dad would drive us all into Bencubbin. We two girls always had to sit in the back of the ute. What happened was that they put a board across the back of the ute and they'd put a wheat bag over it for us to sit on. Either that or we'd just put a wheat bag over an old tyre. Of course, in those days, you daren't go into town unless you were done up to the nines, with matching shoes, gloves, hat and handbag, and you daren't go without stockings. Never. Not like they do nowadays. It's so much easier these days.

There was no bitumen roads back then and it was all heavy clay country so, when it rained, we'd slip and slide all over the place. We girls thought it was great fun. Then, one particular day — in 1942 I think it was — it'd been raining quite heavily and Mum wanted to go the CWA meeting. Seeing the main road was so bad, Dad decided he'd take us to Bencubbin the back way. Of course, we got stuck in this very greasy ground and Dad just couldn't get a grip with the tyres. We got stuck good and proper, didn't we? Dad was the only one of us that could drive so it was left up to Mum and us two girls to push the car out of the bog. And we sure got spattered. We got in such a mess, I don't mind admitting. Oh, we got covered all over in mud. Anyhow, we finished up having to wash our legs, hands and faces from the water lying around the road. So you can imagine what we looked like by the time we got to town.

That's one of my memories of going to a CWA meeting. Then later on, in 1944, Dad bought an old second-hand Dodge car and sometimes the battery would go flat. So, when Mum wanted to go to the CWA and Dad couldn't get the car to start, one of us girls would have to race the twenty-five chain, up to the stable in our good clothes and grab a horse. We didn't have any saddles because they were all team horses, so then you'd ride it back to the house bareback and hook it onto this damned old vehicle and give it a tow to try and get it going.

Another memory I have is when we used to have the CWA Balls. In Bencubbin they were held once a year in May. Dad wouldn't let me go until I was eighteen. Then, when I did turn eighteen, Dad always drove us in and, of course, with Mum being a CWA lady, she'd be working in the kitchen or organise things while Dad used to sit on the door and take the door takings. That's how we'd get to the dances. We weren't allowed to go by ourselves and I used to think it was terrible; I was eighteen and you'd see all these other youngsters going to the dance by themselves. But Dad would never allow it. Yes, I was 'chaperoned', and very much so. But we used to have such lovely balls at Bencubbin. And they were balls in those days. They weren't dances, they were balls; very formal and proper and so it was very hard for some of the ladies, especially when the seasons were bad and no one had much money to spend on expensive things like ball gowns. But we made do. We made our own.

Oh, they were wonderful times. In those days we did a lot of cooking and when you had your CWA meetings everybody brought in beautiful sponge cakes. Of course everyone used to compare each other's cooking to see who had the best cake or scones. It was very competitive at times. Not like today's attitude. Things are more casual now. It's different. Not better or worse, just different. But we had such a lot of fun back then, even when times were hard everyone could be cheered up by having a good sing-along in the choir.

Poultry

Chicken Casserole
CWA Tas

1 chicken
3 or 4 tomatoes
3 tablespoons melted
   butter
Sprinkling flour
¼ cup tomato puree
½ cup white wine

½ cup stock
10 small onions
10 mushroom
Salt and pepper
Small piece garlic
Chopped parsley

Cut the chicken into neat joints. Skin tomatoes. Heat butter. Cook chicken until golden brown. Sprinkle with flour and when flour is brown add tomatoes, puree, wine and stock. Brown the whole onions and mushrooms in butter and add seasoning and garlic and simmer for 1½ hours in casserole, 2½ hours if boiling fowl. Put chicken on a hot dish, garnish with mushrooms and onions. Pour sauce over all. Sprinkle with chopped parsley and serve with fried bread croutons.

Chicken a la King
CWA NSW

2 tablespoons
   shortening
1 cup sliced
   mushrooms
1 green pepper,
   chopped finely
2 tablespoons flour

1 cup chicken stock
2 cups diced cooked
   chicken
1 cup sour cream
2 egg yolks
1 tablespoon sherry

Melt shortening and sauté mushrooms and pepper. Lift out, add flour and then chicken stock and cook till thickened. Add chicken and, when hot, the cream and beaten egg yolks, mushroom and pepper. Add sherry and serve immediately.

Chicken Fricassee

CWA NSW

1 chicken

1 onion

1 carrot

Peppercorns

Salt

Lemon

Milk

Flour

Parsley

Joint the chicken, put into a saucepan with sufficient water to cover with onion, carrot, peppercorns, salt, a piece of lemon rind and boil. Then simmer until tender. Lift out. Strain liquid and add 1 cup milk to 1¼ cups of stock. Blend 2 tablespoons flour with cold milk to make into a paste, then add to stock and milk. Stir until it boils and simmer for 5 minutes. Return the meat to saucepan, add chopped parsley and 1 tablespoon lemon juice.

Chicken Roast

CWA NSW

1 good-sized chicken

½ lb breadcrumbs

¼ lb chopped suet

1 grated lemon rind

Chopped parsley

Salt and pepper

1 egg

A little milk (if necessary)

The size of the chicken depends on the number of guests. From a good-sized bird at least six helpings may be carved with the seasoning to help out. Make the seasoning with the breadcrumbs, suet, lemon rind, parsley, salt and pepper, eggs and a little milk if necessary. Mix all together and stuff the bird at the neck end. To roast, put chicken in a roasting dish, cover breast with good dripping or lard and place a sheet of greased paper over it. Put into a moderately hot (200°C) oven for 20 minutes after which turn the bird over on its breast and leave to cook for the remainder of the time — about one hour altogether. Re-cover with paper before returning to the oven.

Duck Roast with Orange Sauce

CWA NSW

1 duck 3–5 lb
Salt and pepper
Flour
Orange rind and slices

SAGE AND ONION STUFFING

½ lb breadcrumbs
¼ lb chopped suet
1 grated orange rind
Chopped sage
Salt and pepper
1 egg
A little milk (if necessary)

Make the stuffing with the breadcrumbs, suet, orange rind, sage, salt and pepper, eggs and a little milk if necessary and mix together.

To choose a duck for tenderness the windpipe will give easily when pressed. Singe the duck, wipe the inside with a slightly damp cloth, sprinkle well inside with salt and pepper, dredge with flour. Put the grated rind of ½ orange into the baking dish with fat. Stuff duck with sage and onion stuffing. Cover the breast of the duck with thin slices of orange, cover with a well-greased sheet of brown paper and place in a hot (220°C) oven for 15 minutes, reduce the temperature and cook at an even (180°C) temperature, basting every 10 minutes for half an hour. Remove the paper from the bird and baste well; allow to brown. Allow 20 minutes to the pound.

Orange Sauce for Duck

3 tablespoons butter
4 tablespoons plain flour
1½ cups water
Salt and pepper
⅔ cup orange juice
Grated rind of half an orange
1 tablespoon sherry

Add flour to hot butter and allow to brown well. Add water gradually, stirring until smooth. Season to taste. Just before serving add orange juice and rind and the sherry.

Turkey Rissoles

CWA NSW

1 breakfast-cupful cold turkey
2 level tablespoonfuls minced mushrooms
Salt
Few grains cayenne pepper
½ gill thick white sauce
Flaky pastry
1 egg
Tablespoonful milk
Breadcrumbs

Mince the turkey very finely. Mix it with the mushroom, seasoning and sauce. Cook it for one minute and leave the paste to cool. Roll out the pastry very thinly and cut into twelve 4-inch rounds. Divide the paste into twelve portions and place one on each round of pastry, a little to one side of the centre. Flatten each slightly. Wet the rim of the pastry with the eggwhite and fold it over to form half a moon. Mix the remainder of the eggwhite and yolk together and beat in 1 tablespoonful of milk. Brush the rissoles with the mixture very carefully and cover with breadcrumbs. Cook the rissoles in hot fat until they are golden brown. Drain on paper and serve at once.

Mary Edwards
Arno Bay, South Australia

I actually grew up in the Adelaide Hills then, when I was about eighteen, I went over to live at Arno Bay, on the Eyre Peninsula of South Australia, to work for my sister. She'd previously gone over there to work and she'd married and she missed home and she'd had her first child. So I went there, more or less, to help out and to keep her company for two pounds a week and my keep. Her husband was a farmer: wheat, barley and sheep. Anyway, my sister was already a member of Arno Bay CWA so I joined as well. Then after a couple of years I also got married. My husband had a property at Cleve so I went there to live. There was a CWA Branch in Cleve but, with my sister being at Arno Bay, I just continued going there. It was only about twenty-five kilometres away anyway, and I'm still there. I'm still an active member.

But one of the first things I got involved in at Arno Bay was that we used to have a big community Christmas Day down on the foreshore and, as I was new to the district and not too many of the kids knew who I was, I acted a Father Christmas. I was 'Mother Christmas' really but I dressed up as Father Christmas, beard and all. After that, schools asked me to be their Father Christmas. Then I acted as Father Christmas for the street procession through Cleve and I was Father Christmas at the Arno Bay CWA Christmas Tea. Of course, these days, everybody knows who I am but I think they just enjoy it. It was just something a bit different, you could say. It even got to the stage where I was Father Christmas for the Lions Club. Still am. They book me up halfway through the year.

I've also worked my way through CWA. I had six children and I'd take them along to the meetings. Those days they were okay with children, though I had one son who was a bit of a nuisance.

When it got to the time that I could leave the children at home with my husband, I became Arno Bay's Branch President. I also joined our CWA choir. It was just a small choir of around twelve members and we'd sing at church functions and that. The choir isn't going now, unfortunately; not in Arno Bay CWA it isn't. Then I become Group President. Our Group had eleven Branches. Also, in those days, we had the Division and that took in all of Eyre Peninsula. The CWA structure went: Branch, Group, Division and State. They've now cut out the Divisions so it's just Branch, Group then State these days.

From there I became a State Officer with the arts and crafts, which I really enjoyed. I'm not too sure where my love of the arts and performing comes from, because my parents didn't have much opportunity to do those things. Though, when we heard Dad sing, which wasn't that often, he was a good singer, as was one of my brothers. But I seem to be the only one in my immediate family that does all this entertaining, and I really do love it. I've sung at cabarets and I've done skits and, do you know the Strawberry Fetes we had years ago? Well, they used to hold what they called a Strawberry Fete to raise money for the church and they'd sell strawberries and they'd sell items at trading tables and I used to sing or act or do something at all the Strawberry Fetes around the district, and I still do.

There's also something else that I've become very interested in: years ago one of the CWA ladies from Queensland organised a trip through the Pacific Islands, to help out the locals by teaching them sewing and things like that. I went along on that, which I thoroughly enjoyed. Following that, a woman, Valerie Fisher — I think, at that stage, she was World President of the Associated Country Women of the World (ACWW) — well, one day she spoke at our conference and she said that she was taking a group of people to the islands and so I put my name down to go on that and, luckily, I got called up. The trip was run through the ACWW and we were called a Resource Team and we'd go to countries like Kirabati, or Kirabas as it's better known, and Samoa and

Nui and about four women students from each village would come along and we'd teach them basic sewing skills and that, and then they'd take that knowledge back to their villages. So we taught them how to make children's clothes, shirts and shorts. In Kirabas we also taught them how to make bras because they couldn't buy them there. Another thing we taught them was how to make ladies' pants out of that stretch-net material.

I was very lucky because then I went to Papua New Guinea. Some of the places had sewing machines. Most of them were those old types where you had to turn the handle on the machine by hand. One poor girl, she didn't have a spindle on the top, to put the cotton in, so she dropped the cotton over the side of the table to take the tension off. In the end we made a spindle for her out of a long knitting needle. So you have to be inventive in situations like that. She was one of the students. They came from all the islands. In lots of places we had between sixty to eighty students. It was a wonderful experience and when they'd finish a garment we'd all sing, 'If you're happy and you know it, clap your hands', which caused a lot of excitement and it brought attention to each girl, which was important.

We'd be away for about four weeks at a time. So I've been through many of those Pacific Island countries and we also went to Ernabella Aboriginal Community, as they call it these days. That's in the far north and we worked up there for a couple of weeks, doing the same type of thing, teaching sewing and handicrafts and all that sort of jazz. That was very different, I must say, but it was still a good experience. They even took us rabbiting and they cooked a goanna for us. So we ate a goanna.

Then, with the International Committee, I was Chairman of that for several years and so I've been to a lot of World Conferences and South Pacific Conferences. Actually, I must say that I've discovered all my talents through our association, and it's given me more confidence. Not that I'm a great speaker but I do speak at a few different places and I enjoy that. So there's a lot going for CWA though, sometimes, these days I think they're getting a bit too bogged down by all the administration they have to do. But that's life, isn't it? It changes and you've got to change with it.

So I've been lucky in my life. My husband was very good and supportive though, oddly enough, all my children grew up with the CWA and not even one of my daughters has become a CWA member. They're all so busy working. I didn't work when the kids were at home and so I was always at CWA or I was always doing something for CWA. These days I just feel a little sad that I'm getting older and age tends to slow you up a lot. But if the dates don't coincide with our CWA Christmas Tea, I'll still be Father Christmas for the Lions Club again this year.

Nikki Egginton
Quairading, Western Australia

To some extent I'm a city slicker who went to the bush as part of a career move. Bush was out at Narrogin, and that's where I met my husband and that was it. He was from Quairading and so I moved up there. Quairading's in the wheat belt, two hours east of Perth. I was a podiatrist so I'm a long way from doing that now.

While I was at Narrogin I was a member of an organisation called Rural Youth, which was previously known as Junior Farmers, and during that time I met many wonderful ladies from CWA. We even had Barbara Dinnie, an ex-CWA State President, come along. Rural Youth was for both males and females and we had what was called Adult Advisors, who were esteemed people from the community and they sort of mentored Rural Youth. For example, say, if we had a heated debate at the Annual General Meeting on some constitutional matter or other, these Adult Advisors would come along and talk us through the correct procedure of the meeting. They'd also advise us on things like financial matters or helping judge our various competitions.

We also ran an International Exchange Program and we'd often have a CWA representative come along and they might ask the applicants general knowledge questions or judge the public speaking side of things. So because of my Rural Youth background I'd always had an interest in CWA and I had some knowledge of what they did. And it was through Rural Youth that I won an International Exchange to Canada. While I was there I came across an organisation known as the Associated Country Women of the World (ACWW), which is something else the CWA is involved in, and through the ACWW I gathered information as to what we women were doing to improve the lives of other women throughout the world.

Then, as I said, I met my husband and so, from Narrogin, I moved up to Quairading and we started having a family, and that's where I saw more of the relevance of CWA. At that time I still wasn't a member but a few of us mums were looking for somewhere to have a childcare facility. Then in Quairading there were quite a few elderly ladies involved in CWA and they took the challenge on and put forward the suggestion, 'Why don't you lease our building and use it for childcare?'

At that stage I was actually on the cusp of joining CWA but I didn't want to be seen to be putting pressure on them in any way. Well basically, I was just a bit worried that some of the older ladies might think, Oh these young ladies are coming in and taking over our building for childcare and that's it for us. As if we were coming in and taking over the whole show. So I just sat off for a little while and, when that had sorted itself out, then I joined.

So after seven years of trying, we finally got a place for our childcare, and even though I wasn't actually a CWA member just then, for me, getting that up and going would still be one of my highlights. It was fantastic. I mean, it wasn't as simple as all that but it was because these CWA ladies were willing to give us a go that the childcare is now up and running and it's going wonderfully. Actually, it's so successful that it looks like increasing from its current two days per week.

As I said, until then, a lot of the CWA members were quite old and in many ways they were still very traditional. Basically, Quairading was a dying Branch and I think they saw that they had to do something to increase their membership. But what I admired about them was that they took the challenge on and they embraced change and, I think, by doing that, it just opened up the organisation of CWA to many of the younger ladies who may not have previously thought about it.

Actually, the Quairading Branch has now been going for eighty-four years. That's in 2009, so it's quite an old Branch. At the moment I'm President and probably fifty per cent of our members are younger than forty and, of those, a fair majority would be in their early thirties. So it's done a real turn around. And because we've got quite a few younger mums as members, we now have a lot of kids come to our CWA meetings and things and some of the most gorgeous moments are when you'll see a ninety-year-old playing with a two-year-old. It's such a huge generational gap and it's really lovely because I don't think you'd get to see something like that happening in too many other organisations.

Maude Ellis
Darwin, Northern Territory

I was born in 1929 in a little town called Dajarra, in western Queensland. But I didn't grow up there. I grew up in Camooweal, which is right over near the Northern Territory border. Camooweal was a big droving place in those days. I started school there in about 1935 and, when I left in Grade 7, we moved to Mount Isa. That was during the war years. I was twelve going on thirteen by that stage and I got a job at the Mount Isa hospital doing housekeeping and that in the Nurse's Quarters. Then I had my first child to the man who was going to become my first husband and in 1948 and when our second child was coming we got married. We had two more children after that and we moved back to Camooweal.

My first husband, he'd go out of town a lot, droving and working on stations and that, and so we separated after a while and I went cooking out on a station property at Anthony's Lagoon. I took two of the children with me, the baby and another one, and Mum looked after the other two. And it was while I was out at Anthony's Lagoon that I met my second husband, Bill Ellis. Bill and I, we'd known each other from a long time before. Bill was a drover and this time he was coming through with some cattle. There was quite a story about that because some of the cattle were cross-branded, which means that someone had branded the cattle over someone else's brand. Yes, so they were stolen cattle. It wasn't Bill's fault because he didn't own the cattle. He was just the drover. Anyhow, at different points along the trip the drovers had to get the cattle dipped and at those dipping points there was usually a police station. That's how they found out about the cattle being cross-branded. It was in the paper and everything. But these cattle, they come from off Coolabah Station and Bill was held up for a while because he couldn't move them till it was all sorted out.

But the thing was, by then, there wasn't anyone to look after Coolabah Station and the travelling manager from Townsville, he come along and he asked Bill if he'd go out and look after Coolabah till they got a new manager in. So that's how I came to live in the Northern Territory. My four children and I, we went out to Coolabah with Bill. It was in January 1954 and we travelled up to Katherine by car. I can remember it clearly because it was raining and there were mosquitoes and lavender bugs and lots of things I'd never seen before. Then from Katherine we flew out to Coolabah. I was twenty-five and that was my first time in an aeroplane and I was so scared because we were flying in the rainy weather and through all the big rain clouds and that.

Actually, they made the film *Jeddah* out that way. I think they must've done that in 1952 or '53, just before we got there, because they used Coolabah homestead in the film. Though we didn't live in the homestead. We lived in another cottage because they were keeping the homestead for the new manager. So Bill was looking after the station, then the new manager came out with his wife and family. I was going to have my fifth child by then and so we moved into Katherine. Bill got a job on the railways there and my last child was born in the December of 1954.

As to how I came to join CWA was that, well, we lived in Katherine for twelve years before we came up to Darwin. Then I worked for the Health Department for a while and also for Community Welfare and, one time, a friend of mine asked me to go to a CWA dinner at Mrs bin Sallik's. Mrs bin Sallik is Mary-Ann bin Sallik's mother. Mary-Ann's a big professor in Darwin now and she's well known all throughout the Territory because of all the good work she's done for the Aboriginal people. Anyhow, my friend asked me to go to this CWA dinner. It was actually a Christmas lunch and so I went along. That was in December 1979 and I joined the Darwin Branch of CWA in January 1980, so I've been a member now for thirty-one years.

What makes CWA important to me is the friendships you make and I also enjoy the fundraising. Some of the charities we help are the ACWW [Associated Country Women of the World]. With that, the money goes to help less fortunate women all over the world, particularly in the Pacific Islands. Then any time there's floods or bushfires, we help out there. Also there's the Woolies Days where Woolworths donate all their profits from that one day and the money goes to help the farmers who are in need. On those days we all go along to Woolies and set up our stalls and sell lamingtons or whatever and the money goes to the farmers throughout Australia. We also raise money to help some of the young people go to the agricultural college down at Katherine. That's like a training centre about fifteen miles out of Katherine, on the Darwin side. It's joined up now with the university.

As for special moments, for me, I've got to see a lot of the Northern Territory through going to the different CWA meetings. I've been to Gove, which is now called Nhulunbuy. I've been to Jabiru — that's when they had a CWA Branch out there — and to a meeting at Katherine, when they used to have a Branch. I've also been to Tennant Creek and Alice Springs for different Annual General Meetings. Oh, lots of places. But I'd have to say that the most special moment is the one we're having now, with the Northern Territory CWA celebrating our fifty years. It's a very, very special time for all of us.

Coral Elsden
Keppoch, South Australia

I was born in Victoria, actually, but due to my father's employment we moved to the south-east of South Australia. I was educated in Millicent and Mount Gambier, then, when I was about seventeen, I was called into the Education Department in Adelaide to do a one-year teaching course. That was during the war years and I can still remember Darwin being bombed, which was a bit scary.

After my year's course I was sent up to Washpool, near Spalding, for a short while and following that I was sent down the south-east to Keppoch. Back then, Keppoch was just a small farming community. I was eighteen and I was known as Head of the School and I taught all the grades from 1 to 7. There were about twenty students and we had a pump and a garden and we had a low-drop toilet, which was new to me. I boarded with a family who lived about four mile from the school. There were three children in the family and, at first, we rode pushbikes to school but we were always getting punctures, so then we started to ride horses. I'd never been on a horse in my life and so I was given an old rundown racehorse. The children used to ride ponies and I'd be dead scared that these jolly ponies would take off and my fellow would want to go with them and I'd have a buster, which I did on one occasion. But that was country life in those days.

Seeing that the school was the only public building in the town, that's where the Keppoch CWA met on a Saturday afternoon. They'd started their Branch in the October or November of 1942 and I joined in the February of 1943. That was my introduction to CWA and the first thing they got me to do was to write a report for the newspaper. Being the war years, in Handicraft, our main project was to make hand-stitched leather gloves for the war effort. As for fundraising activities, one of the big ones was when we sponsored the woolshed dances. They were wonderful occasions really because all the families went and so you'd not only see the children again but you also met the parents. Of course, you had to set an example and in those days the teacher was a special person in the community. You were looked upon and looked after and so, if anybody was driving into Naracoorte, which they might have done just once a month, you'd be invited along as well.

From Keppoch I went to another little place, Lachaber, before moving down to Penola. I got married down there and when I got married, I married a farmer. I didn't marry a grazier. I married a farmer, and we were proud of it. We had an old army truck that I used to drive and, when we were making cane baskets in Handicraft, all the cane was loaded on the back of the truck and the shortest way to get to the meeting was over a creek and when it rained that creek got so high that it was just jolly lucky that I was driving a big truck. And we made our own fun. Of course, it was a different lifestyle then. Now it's different, but we still go to CWA for that companionship and for what we can learn. You learn something new every time you go to a meeting. I'm eighty-five now and I'm still learning.

As for any highlights of my time in CWA: the first one that comes to mind was when I won the State Pork Casserole Competition. That was many years ago now, of course, but I remember the prize was a week at the beach, in one of the CWA's Country Cottages. The only trouble was that my husband wasn't keen on the beach so we never took it up. But, oh, there's been so many highlights. There's four Branches in our Bowman Group. I've been President of our Group then I went on to be a Divisional President. The Division took in an area from Talem Bend right down to Allendale and with all the travelling I did as Divisional President I think I wore out about two sets of car tyres.

But the real joy of it all is simply just meeting and talking to people. To me, that's what it's all about. Then, when I was on the International Committee, I'd come to Adelaide once a month. That was very interesting and I'm still our Group International Officer. It's a little-known fact that CWA has been helping people overseas, who are in need, for seventy-odd years now and you look around these days and it seems that certain groups — and I won't mention who — have just discovered that there are poor people in this world. So I've learned a lot about how the other half live and, in that work, I instigated taking our committee out to the country for meetings and they're still continuing on with that, which is great to see.

But you met so many people, in so many different situations. I remember one member, up in the Mallee, who impressed me with the way she could speak and do things, so I told her that they'd proposed her to be their Floriculture Officer. 'I can't do it,' she said.

So I went to her afterwards and I said, 'I know you want to do the job, you're capable, and so why are you saying that you can't take it on?'

'Well,' she said, 'I'd love to do it but I can't drive so I can only get out from the farm once a week, and that's to do the shopping and go to our CWA meeting.'

You wouldn't believe it, would you? But a lot of those women never ever learned to drive and so, there they were, they were more or less stuck out on properties. Oh, talk about driving — I remember when one of our members drove me into Naracoorte. It might've even been her first time out in their new car and it took what seemed like an hour to drive the twenty miles and when I said, 'Gee, that took a while,' she said, 'Well Coral,' she said, 'I still didn't know how to get out of second gear.'

But, of course, I suppose, I always drove. I mean, my husband was farming and if you couldn't drive, well, you just sat at home. So there was me, I drove this great big truck and when I had the children I'd load them up and I'd have a pram on the back of the thing and off we'd all go, off to CWA, where I'd take their shoes off and put a rug down and let them play. And those kids grew up like that. With that companionship. It was really great.

Anyhow, I lived out on the farm for sixty-two years. That includes the ten years I was on my own, after my husband died. I've now moved into Naracoorte. Town life is a different life but there's still four of us who drive out to Keppoch for the CWA meetings. We've got a membership of about twelve and I've got my Fifty-Years Membership Badge. I'm a Life Member.

Valerie Fisher AO, OBE
Barnawartha, Victoria

I grew up in Melbourne actually, then I married a farmer and I went to live at Barnawartha, where I still am. Barnawartha's in Victoria. It's right on the Murray River, about twenty kilometres from Wodonga. These days there's only about sixty houses there and two churches, a store, a post office and a soldiers' memorial hall. That's about it, really.

Then after I'd only been living there for a short while, a neighbour knocked on the door. 'We're thinking about forming a branch of CWA in Barnawartha,' she said. 'I know you go to church but CWA embraces everybody and you'll get to know a wider field of people. We're having a meeting on Thursday night to see if we can get it up and running. Come along.'

Well being a city girl, to be perfectly honest, I'd never even heard of the CWA so when my husband came in at lunch time I said, 'Do you know anything about CWA?'

He didn't know much about CWA either but he said there was one in the next town and he thought they supported things like local charities and all that. We agreed that I should go along to this meeting so I went along and that's when the Barnawartha Branch of CWA was formed and I became a foundation member. About forty or fifty women joined — not on the first night, mind you, but eventually. They were all ages. There were newlyweds, like myself. There were grandmothers. There were also some single women because, in those days, more of the younger people stayed on the family property and worked as farm hands, which, of course, is very different to today where many of the women have to get employment off-farm to enable the farm to survive.

So that's what happened and, having worked as a secretary in Melbourne, I quick-smart found myself as Secretary of our

Branch, then President and then Group President. Following that I became State President of Victoria and then National President of Australia. After that I was elected into the international field. Do you know about the Associated Country Women of the World (ACWW)? Well CWA is under the umbrella of the worldwide organisation known as ACWW. It has nine-million members spread over seventy countries and we're divided in to nine areas and the Presidents from each area form the board of ACWW. Initially I was elected South Pacific Area President. Up until then I hadn't been out of Australia. Never. I knew nothing about the South Pacific and my husband said to me, 'You'd better get to know it,' so I travelled around all the islands to places like Tonga, Fiji. Oh, and I shall never forget the first visit I made to Cook Islands. I was booked to fly out in the middle of the night and they said, 'We'll come and see you off.'

I said, 'No, please don't. I'm not leaving until the middle of the night.'

But they still came. In the middle of the night they were there in their dozens to see me off and after I arrived home I said to my husband, 'I love the people of the South Pacific and there's so much needing to be done to help them.' That's because they were telling me about how much they wanted to improve things like their health and they wanted a decent education for their children. For instance, education wasn't free in Tonga and, with the average family having around eight children, education was extremely expensive. So the week before a tourist boat arrived, the women would stay up every night, making baskets and mats and things to sell to the tourists so that they could afford an education for their children. And it used to break my heart when I'd walk among the likes of the Americans and the Australians and you'd hear them trying to barter these poor women down, down, down. Oh, it used to break my heart.

So I began to develop projects to help these women. For instance, in Tonga, they have a very high rainfall — up to two hundred inches annually — and their kitchens were separate from their houses. Basically, they were just a little thatched hut with an open fire and, of course, with the rain, they often couldn't get their fires to light of a morning and so their children went without breakfast. So we took on the huge project of helping them build cement kitchen huts, where they could cook in all sorts of weather.

I also organised resource training teams to go over to the island countries, taking experts in whatever field of support the women wanted. I got in touch not only with CWA, but also with other groups and societies throughout Australia and asked them for a list of their members who might be experienced in various fields. In the case of health issues it might mean nurses or people who had been nurses or even doctors for that matter. It was everything, whether it was learning needle and thread work or learning about diet and food or income-generating projects. Then, when some of the women wanted to take on a more meaningful leadership role in village life, we organised leadership training courses for them. In Fiji, three women have since become government senators and they said it was largely due to the training and the confidence they'd received from us that had enabled them to do that.

So yes, I found that a very rewarding experience. Then I was asked whether I'd like to be Chairman of World Development Projects within the ACWW and after they'd rung, my husband said, 'What was that all about?'

'Oh,' I said, 'they've just called from the ACWW head office in London to ask whether I'd like to be Chairman of World Development Projects and I told them that I couldn't possibly do it because I didn't know the world well enough.'

Anyhow, they explained that the principle would be the same as what I was doing in the Pacific and my husband was supportive so I took the position on and for the next six years I travelled the world, setting up projects. From there I went on to become Deputy World President, then World President of ACWW. One of my most pleasing achievements during that time was with the annual telethon they held in Norway. They contacted me and asked if I, on behalf of ACWW, would like to put forward a proposal for the Norwegian Government to have a look at with regard to our possible use of the telethon monies that year. So I drafted a programme for us to run workshops in different places around the world. These were to focus on the specific needs of the women in each region and then, two years later, we'd go back and assess the development. And we were accepted. They held the telethon and we got 600,000 pounds. I thought that was just absolutely wonderful. Yes, it was a lot of money but it proved to be money well spent.

So there's just a couple of the things that ACWW and CWA have done to help those less fortunate. Then I finished as President of ACWW in the mid 90s. It was a tremendous experience. I loved it and it's something I was, and still am, very passionate about. As I said, it's the practical work that I push for and even though I'm out of it now I still keep in touch with the many, many friends and godchildren I've gathered throughout the world. For instance, when the Solomon Islands had that nasty tsunami a few years ago, I rang one of my ACWW friends, Eva. Eva does wonderful work with Women in Development. I knew that her family came from Western Province where the tsunami struck and I said, 'Are you okay, Eva? How's things with your family?'

'They're all right,' she said. 'Their houses were back from the water so while they got a bit of damage, they didn't lose everything.'

Eva can never ring me because they don't have the funds so, three weeks later I was feeling anxious and I rang her again and she said, 'It's a very different story now.' She said, 'There was an underground rumble, back from the water, and one day the ground just opened up and swallowed all the houses and the people lost everything.'

Apparently one of the big concerns there was that the hospital in that area once had a mental counselling department but they'd let it go because they could no longer afford to run it. Now of course, since that tsunami, with so many people having lost everything, many of those people were living on the streets, which was a very traumatic experience for them. So they contacted Eva, and asked if there was any way she could get help to set a counselling service up again. So we were able to be of some assistance there as well.

There's always so much to do. I mean, yes, governments go in after an event like that and they help with housing and that but, when it comes to the practicalities of setting up your house again — after you've lost everything —that's a very different story. We've just passed it here in CWA Victoria to send a certain amount of money to Samoa to help buy pots and pans because that's what the women said they most needed.

Of course, we have no right to tell them how they should run their own lives because, in many ways, they live a far more moral life than what we do. But it's those more practical development projects where we can make a difference — even if it's providing a cow for somebody. Oh yes, we often provide animals in little villages anywhere around the world. It's a project to help start them off. Then, as those animals reproduce, they build up a herd and it expands like that from village to village. It's just those simple little things, but it's those simple little things that grow into giving people a better life.

So that's a bit about my time in CWA and ACWW and I've been very, very lucky with having such a supportive husband and family. In fact, when I was so involved with ACWW, I'd be away for months on end and, mind you, I went right out into some of those places and I slept on stone floors, the lot, and I just loved it because you got to know the real people. But anyway, people used to say to me, 'Valerie, don't you think all this travel and so forth will be putting a strain on your relationship with your husband?'

And I'd come straight back at them and say, 'Don't you think it might be an even greater strain if I was at home with him all the time?'

But he remained very interested in what I was doing and he'd hold the fort while I was away. He'd go through all the correspondence and prioritise it for me and then, if I was only home for a few days, he'd say, 'You've got to do this first. You should do that second and that can wait till you come back again.'

So yes, that made it easier. A lot easier, actually. But unfortunately I lost him four years ago, which is sad. My family do the farm work now. They live either side of me. But I still live on the farm, oh yes, and I'm still active within CWA and I hope to be for a good while longer.

Dulcie French
West Ulverstone, Tasmania

I was born here in Tasmania and I grew up in the small country town of Birralee. I suppose there'd only be about two hundred people living there now. It fluctuates. They come and they go. Birralee's just north of Westbury and Westbury's along the Bass Highway, between Launceston and Deloraine, heading towards the north-west coast. My dad was a carpenter. He did a lot of building renovations. During the war years someone always wanted something or other renovated. Then after the war he built a lot of cool stores for apples, down the west Tamar, at Glengarry, which is just up from where we were at Birralee.

Back then, Birralee School went from Kindergarten to Grade 9. There were only about twenty-five of us kids and, with so few of us, if you wanted to form two teams to have a game of cricket, everyone had to play, even the girls. Then, when we'd play netball, the boys would join in with us. The same thing happened if you wanted to play football, though I didn't get into that very much. I always tried to find something else to do when the football was on. It was only a one-teacher school so the teachers had to be multi-skilled and also the bigger kids helped teach the littler ones. Then quite often the teacher had a wife who came in and showed us how to do some sewing and sometimes the teacher's wife would also show us how to do a bit of cooking.

I remember one teacher we had, when I was in Grade 8. He was married. They were a fairly elderly couple so he would've been just about to retire. Anyhow, they arrived. It was only a very small school residence and he had all this antique furniture so he complained to the education department that the house wasn't big enough for him. And because of that they closed Birralee School down and we had to go down to Exeter on a bus. That was about a twelve or fifteen mile trip, there and back, each day, which meant we had to leave home a lot earlier every morning to get to school.

But the funny thing with that old teacher was that the education department then sent him and his wife to Frankford, which was the next little town up the road and, believe it or not, he did the same thing there: he complained about the size of the school residence. Then they went and they closed Frankford School down and the kids from there were also sent to Exeter. So we all ended up at Exeter. But I don't know what happened to him after that. Maybe he retired, like I said. Anyhow, Exeter only went through to Grade 9 and if you wanted to go any further you had to go to Launceston. But we only ever went to Grade 9. That was enough.

There wasn't a CWA in Birralee and so it wasn't until after I'd been married for a while that my mother-in-law took me and a friend from down the road to Hagley CWA. By then I'd had a little toddler and so did my friend from down the road and, apparently, the children made a little bit too much noise for the CWA ladies so we were politely asked not to come any more. That was a bad part of CWA in the early years. Some Branches didn't like children disturbing their meetings and that probably put a lot of the younger women off.

Anyway, it was about another four years before I decided to go back to CWA. This time it was at Selbourne and they said it didn't matter how much noise the children made, so I joined and I went on to became Branch President. Then I went to Group President of Central Group. Then, with our numbers falling, Central Group merged with West Tamar and we became Centrewest Group and, as more of the smaller Branches closed down, the Groups merged and Centrewest Group went with the Greater Launceston area and made it Greater Northern Group. Then the Esk Valley and Greater Northern combined and now it's just the Northern Region Group.

As for special moments in my time with CWA: well, I'd say the World Conference that was held in about 2004 in the big hotel near the Hobart waterfront stands out for me. That was for the Associated Country Women of the World (ACWW) and women from just about everywhere in the world came to that. It was a very big thing. Adriana Taylor, who's currently the mayor of Glenorchy, she was one of the vice-presidents of CWA at that time and she helped organise it along with Jill Hayes.

Back then we had a special CWA choir. Unfortunately, the choir's just about all gone now because everyone's too old. But I think, back then, there were nearly two hundred CWA members in that choir, from all over Tasmania, and, as a welcome to the women of the world, we sang 'Waltzing Matilda' and several of our members got dressed up and acted it out. Then Scottsdale CWA had a bell ringer's group. They used to ring the hand bells to different tunes and one of the ladies' husbands used to come along to help carry the bells because they were quite heavy. Anyway, they played on that night and, oh, in the background you could hear the humming of all the ladies while the bells were playing. It was beautiful. It really was a fantastic time, those two or three days. But the thing about us hosting that World Conference was that, when we first applied to do it, the organisers said, 'Oh, I don't think CWA Tasmania can manage such a large event like that,' and we said, 'Oh yes, we can ...' and we did it and we did a magnificent job of it too. So there.

Fish

Hints on Fish
CWA Tas

When purchasing fish, the following points should be borne in mind.

1. The fish should be quite fresh and should not smell at all unpleasant.
2. The skin should not be wrinkled; the scales should be plentiful and easily removed.
3. The eyes and colours should be bright. Gills should also be bright red in colour.
4. The flesh, in the case of cod, hake etc, should be firm and the body stiff.
5. Medium-sized fish have a better flavour than small and are less coarse than large fish.

The general directions for preparing fish are as follows:

1. Clean, if necessary. Cut off the tail and fins (cutting from the tail towards the head) and scale. Remove the eyes if the fish is to be cooked with the head on.
2. Wash well in cold water, using salt to remove any blood etc, and dry in a clean cloth.

Baked Stuffed Fish
CWA NSW

Select fish of medium size, wash, wipe, dry and salt.

> 1 teacup stale breadcrumbs (not dried breadcrumbs but couple-of-days old crumbs from a loaf)
> 1 tablespoon melted butter
> ½ teaspoon salt
> ¼ teaspoon pepper

Mix all ingredients. A little, very finely powdered sage or chopped parsley and a couple of eggs could be added if liked.

Stuff whole fish (head on, eyes removed) with mixture. Wrap with fine string to keep the seasoning inside. Place the fish in a well-buttered pan with greased paper under it, dredge flour, salt and pepper on the fish and add 1 cup of boiling water. Bake in hot (200°C) oven about 15 minutes to each pound of fish, basting with the gravy that forms in the pan. Be sure to bake fish until a nice brown. When done slide carefully into a dish, garnish with lemon and parsley. Some people add tomato sauce to the dressing, others like fish covered with layers of tomatoes. Some stew tomatoes separately and serve as a sauce to the fish.

Barracouta or Smoked Cod, in Milk
Mrs C. A. Chambers, Kettering, CWA Tas

Barracouta or smoked cod
Milk — enough for shallow pan
1 oz butter
1 oz plain flour
Sliced lemon and parsley for garnish

Wash or wipe fish and have milk boiling in shallow pan. Simmer fish in milk for about 10 minutes. In another pan melt butter and stir in plain flour till blended. Strain off milk and gradually add to flour and butter blend, stirring sauce until nice and thick. Garnish with lemon slices and parsley. There is enough salt in fish without adding.

Curried Prawns
CWA NSW

1 chopped onion
2 oz butter
A good dessertspoon curry
    powder
½ chopped apple
1 oz rice flour
½ teaspoon sugar
Salt

3 gills white stock
½ teaspoon curry paste
1 dessertspoon chutney
1 tablespoon desiccated
    coconut
1 lb prawns
2 tablespoons cream
Squeeze of lemon juice

Fry onions in butter 15 minutes without colouring them then add curry powder and fry few minutes. Add apple, flour, sugar and salt. Put in stock and all other ingredients except prawns, cream and lemon juice, and cook for about ½ hour. Add prawns. Be sure to wash and cleanse prawns after they are shelled and dry on a cloth before adding to curry mixture. Cook 10 minutes. Before serving, add cream and lemon juice, just at the last, and give them just one boil. Serve in a border of well-boiled rice and decorate with a few whole cooked prawns.

Fish in Batter

C. Blackwell, Campbell Town, CWA Tas

4 oz flour

Salt and cayenne to
    taste

Pinch baking powder

1 egg yolk

1½ gills milk

3 fish

Lemon juice

Lemon slices

Parsley

Sift flour, salt, cayenne and baking powder into a basin. Make a well in the centre of flour. Pour egg yolk into well. Mix till it begins to thicken. Add milk gradually. Beat well till batter is smooth. Allow to stand for ½ hour. Cut fish into pieces. Sprinkle with lemon juice and pepper. Dip in batter. Fry in boiling fat till brown. Garnish with lemon slices and parsley.

Fish Paste

Dulcie James, Clarendon Home, Kingston Beach, CWA Tas

1 small tin of salmon or sardines

2 eggs

½ teaspoon cayenne

1 large tablespoon butter

1 tablespoon vinegar

Chop up the fish finely, put into a basin, add the eggs and beat well, then add the cayenne. Heat the butter and the vinegar in a saucepan and when boiling, add the fish and egg mix. Cook till the eggs are thoroughly done. This paste will keep for several days if kept in a cool place.

Kedgeree

Mrs A. Acton, Taroona, CWA Tas

4 oz rice
2–3 oz margarine or dripping
8 oz cooked dried haddock or other fish such as barracouta or
    flathead, well drained and cut into small pieces
Pepper and salt
Pinch of nutmeg
1 hard-boiled egg
Chopped parsley
Cayenne pepper

Boil rice until tender. Drain well. Melt fat in pan, when hot add rice and fish, mix thoroughly. Season with salt, pepper and nutmeg. When hot through, pile up on a hot dish and sprinkle with chopped hard-boiled egg and parsley. Dust with cayenne pepper. Use plenty of fat otherwise dish may be dry and disappointing.

Salmon Loaf

CWA NSW

Place tin of salmon into a bowl, remove bones and break into flakes with a fork. Add 4 tablespoons melted butter, 1 cup breadcrumbs, ½ teaspoon salt and 4 well-beaten eggs. Put into a well-greased pudding dish and steam for 1 hour. It is delicious served hot with diced potatoes and cream gravy or sliced cold with a garnishing of lettuce or parsley and lemon.

Nancy Fuchs
Darwin, Northern Territory

Having grown up in the small country town of Kulin, in Western Australia, I must say, I have managed to travel quite a lot. You'll find Kulin west of Perth. It's in the wheat belt area, along the railway line between Narrogin and Merredin. Actually, it's only recently celebrated its centenary year, and how I came to live there is quite a story in itself. I was born during the Depression times of 1929. Both my parents were school teachers and they were left some money, so they decided to buy an old soldier settlement block of around two thousand acres and go farming.

The land was mostly undeveloped so I think they had a pretty rough time of it for a while. But we still all survived, and the land had a little house that Dad expanded on, as the family grew. My father liked to buy a block and do it up, to make it viable, then sell it and go off and buy another block. My mother always said how she'd lived in eleven different houses on five different properties. Anyhow, I was brought up there on that original sheep and wheat property. Of course, in the beginning it was pretty basic living and everything was done by hand; like the wheat was bagged and taken by horse and dray to the railway siding whereas later on all that was done with tractors and trucks.

The farm was quite isolated in those days and for our education, my older brother and I did our schooling by correspondence. That came out by mail. We didn't even have radio in those early days so, oh, it was a big event just getting the mail. Then when we were older, my brother and I were sent to boarding school in Perth. I went to the Methodist Ladies College and my brother went to Wesley Boys School. For me, boarding school was a bit daunting, frankly, especially with not ever having had other children to play with, other than my brother, that is. In a way I always felt like an observer. This was also war time when young men and women were a rarity, so many of the teachers were elderly — past retirement age. But they were wonderful people so, overall, I quite enjoyed it, not like some. Still, I longed for the farm life and so, when I finished my schooling, I went back on the farm and worked for my parents and I also did some correspondence courses in typing and art.

Then when I was twenty I got a job at a photography place in Perth. It was a business where people used to bring in their old photos and we re-enhanced them — enlarged them and coloured them in. Some were so ragged that you had to virtually retrace the people and everything. Because I enjoyed art so much, it was good fun, even though they did promise to give me a pay rise after six weeks and that never happened. So when I saw a job advertised at the *Daily News* in Perth and everyone said, 'You're mad if you don't go for it', I did and I got the job. Then when I gave in my notice at the photography place I was shouted out of the room, which wasn't very nice.

With the *Daily News*, I worked in what was called the 'Morgue'. It was actually the archives area where all the photos were catalogued and the biographies were kept. So, say, if someone important died in America or England then we'd go through and find their photograph and they'd use it in the newspaper article. Or, say, they needed a photograph of the horse that had just won the Melbourne Cup. Those sorts of things. It was very interesting, actually.

My father didn't go to the war. Other than being in a 'required occupation' — farming — he was just past the age limit. But then, after the war, he wanted to go overseas to visit his family in England so I went back on the farm to help my brother and Mum. Mum didn't go overseas with my father because by then she'd had three more children. There was a big gap between my brother and I and the rest of the children. About ten years, actually. I call my brother and I the 'Depression kids' and the younger ones are known as the 'credit-card kids'. Anyway, Dad was away for six months or more and that's when I got very involved in the Junior Farmers organisation. That really suited me and it was through Junior Farmers that I won a trip to New Zealand for three months in 1945, and I had a wonderful time over there. So good in fact that I'd been engaged just before I went and when I returned that sort of fizzed.

After Dad came back from his trip he purchased more land in Albany, with a cottage — all to be done up and made viable, of course — and I stayed in Kulin to helped my brother.

Then one day a girlfriend mentioned that she was going over to England. 'Well, I'll go too,' I said, and we spent a year overseas. That was in 1955. I visited and stayed with many of our relations and we travelled all over England, Scotland and Wales. I still had to make money of course and as well as doing other jobs I also worked for the Young Farmers' London Office. But one trip I very much remember was when five of us spent six weeks on the continent, going all over Europe, in an old Austin car I'd bought in England. That was fantastic, though I remember arriving in Vienna just as the Russians were leaving, and that was quite scary because they had absolutely stripped the eastern sector, and nothing was repaired. Oh, they took everything they could lay their hands on. Anyhow, we finished out the year and we left at Christmas and came back to Australia on a P&O liner, along with many of the ten-pound Poms who, I must say, were mostly very brave people setting out for a new life.

When I got back to Australia, luckily I was offered a secretarial job with the Junior Farmers in Perth, and that went right through until I left to marry Peter. And that's another long story too. Well, one time, my English cousin, Susan, and I went on a boat trip up the west coast to Darwin and Peter just happened to get on at Onslow. He's a Swiss instrument maker by trade and he was touring the country. The two of us got on well and then, when I left him in Darwin and returned to Perth, we corresponded. But fortunately or unfortunately, depending on how you look at it, Peter had a horrific accident while he was in Darwin and he was told that he couldn't leave until the court case had been completed. So he had to wait. And he waited and waited and, in the meantime, for something to occupy his time he bought a block of land and built a house on it. Anyhow the court case finally worked out well and over that time our relationship had grown strong enough for us to decide to marry. That will be fifty years in October 2010 and we have three married daughters and six wonderful grandchildren and during that time we've been on many trips to Europe and round Australia. Oh, and I must also mention Cyclone Tracy in 1974. That was an unforgettable experience, one I hope never happens again.

As for my involvement with CWA: my mother was a staunch member and had been a State President of CWA Western Australia. So she always took a great and continued interest in my life. But it wasn't until I was up here in Darwin, back in the early 1960s, that I joined CWA and, with the experience I had of secretarial work with the Junior Farmers, it was easy for me to fit in. But I think what really changed my attitude and made me want to commit so much more of my time and energy to CWA was when the World President of the Associated Country Women of the World, Aroti Dutt, came to Darwin in the mid 60s. Aroti Dutt was a very high-class Indian lady, but she was just so interesting and uplifting — 'inspiring', I suppose the word might be — and that gave me my real kick off to do things and become more involved in CWA. I've now been a member for forty-five years or so and over that time I've held most positions. I've been Territorial President twice and travelled to all our Branches and been to all the various Territorial and National Conferences. I've even found the time to make it to two World Conferences, one in Hamburg and one in New Zealand.

So it's been a great experience and through my work in CWA I've found myself being involved in wider social issues. When I finished as Territorial President the first time, Roger Steel, who was in the NT Government, he nominated me to go on a parliamentary enquiry into the cost of freight throughout the

Northern Territory. At that time there were many complaints about the high costs of transport. So I was part of a panel of three and, basically, the brief was to prove that we, in the Territory, were being charged equitable rates for freight. That inquiry went on over a period of about eighteen months and I got to visit just about every state in Australia, interviewing people. Of course, I wasn't away all that time. We came and we went and, thankfully, I was able to leave the children at home with Peter. And I must say, it is important to have that family support. Very important indeed.

With the parliamentary enquiry we also went all over the Territory, out to Aboriginal Communities and to many other places I'd normally never have visited. And that was a very exciting time for me, and it was a very interesting experience because I was able to meet with women from all these different places and find out just what their particular problems were. Oh, and I'll never forget: we were out in the Wave Hill area one time and this woman said to me, 'I really think, for the exorbitant amount they charge for freight, they could at least provide us with decent lettuce.'

And I thought, Out here? And you're complaining about the lettuce. You're lucky to even get lettuce.

But, the funny thing was, wherever we went I seemed to keep running into people I knew and, at one stage, one of the other panel members remarked, 'How is it that whenever we go somewhere, you always seem to know someone?'

I said, 'It's because I belong to CWA.'

Judy Fulton
Broadford-Mount Piper, Victoria

I grew up in Bright, a well-known tourist town in the north-east of Victoria. That's where I went to school and I worked there until I met my husband, who was a forester. Then I left Bright as a married woman and we shifted around in his job. First we went to Forest, down in the Otways, near Colac, then to Swifts Creek. Following that we went to Kallista, which is in the Dandenong Ranges then, finally, they shifted us here to Broadford, where we've now retired.

As for CWA, when I first came to Broadford a friend asked if I'd like to go along to a meeting. I knew CWA existed because there'd been a Branch in Bright but at that stage, being young and single, I was more interested in other activities. So anyway, I joined the Broadford-Mount Piper Branch and I'm very happy to say that that was twenty-eight years ago. We've got a great Branch of up to twenty members. They're a great lot of girls. Over the years we've lost a few but we've also started to get some new ones. At the moment our youngest member is thirty-nine. She's got two kiddies at school and two at home and she's really, really loving it. Then we have another new member; she's only been with us for five months but she really fits in.

Perhaps you haven't heard but, CWA was very involved during the Victorian bushfires. We helped with the welfare fund, which included giving out money vouchers to those who'd been affected. As President of the Hume-Goulburn Group, cookery books and pamper packs were sent to me from State Headquarters and, in turn, I went around and gave them out to those who'd lost their homes. As well as the larger government relief fund and the donations CWA Victoria had collected, money also came in from various CWAs throughout New South Wales and Queensland.

Some of those CWAs wanted their donations to go toward special things like kitchen utensils et cetera, because, while we'd given out the cook books, many people had lost their basics, like their pots and pans. Some people didn't even have spoons or anything to beat eggs with. Then other CWAs wanted their money to go to the actual towns that had been affected, or even to different organisations within those towns. Like in one place, the Girl Guides lost everything so we helped them out. Then there were groups like one Junior cricket club who'd also lost everything. We helped them as well. So that was our involvement during that terrible time.

Then also, within CWA, at Branch level we do organise our own programmes for the year. You can have whatever guest speakers you want and you can run your own special days et cetera, but just as long as you kept within CWA Victoria's guidelines as to where the money goes. That's because, in CWA, you not only support your local community but you also support your state association for their fundraising activities. An example of that would be our State Thanksgiving Fund. That's where we raise money for a specially designated cause. This year it's the bionic ear people, and so you might have tins at your meetings and all the small change goes into them or you might hold a special event to raise money.

Then at the end of the year all the money that's been raised throughout the state gets collected in at CWA Head Office and it goes to the Thanksgiving Fund which, as I said, this year is to go into research by the Bionic Ear Institute. Then next year we may raise money for something else, like we've raised money for cancer research then another year it went into special cots for the Children's Hospital. But no one knows how much we've raised until the final cheque is handed over at our annual conference. Though, mind you, it's usually in the thousands of dollars, so it's worthwhile.

But no, it's a great organisation. It's become such a part of my life that I say, 'Yes, sometimes it gets hectic but if it's for a worthwhile cause then it's worthwhile doing.' That's what I say. And because of the bushfires and the connections I had, I, more or less, had to stay on as Group President. I'll now finish my term in May, and I'll miss it. Of course I'll still be involved at Branch level and you're always encouraged to go on to other state committees. Patchwork and quilting are one of my hobbies. I love doing handicrafts so I'm already on the State Creative Arts Committee. I could go further there and, maybe, become Chairman. A couple of women are pushing me in that direction but I'm not that interested. Though my husband's supportive. He's in Lions and so he knows all about working for your community. But I don't know. I'm just happy to go along and come to Melbourne for the committee meeting every three months or so.

That's all for the present, anyhow, because our members are very active at Branch level. There's not only our craft days but we join in at swap-meets and sell cakes and cooking books to help raise money for our various projects. We also have our Christmas-in-July meeting. That's something special. Then on Australia Day we have a get-together where our husbands come along and it's great for the men to see each other again. Actually, last year we held it at one of our members' newly built house in town because she'd lost her previous one in the bushfires. She's settled down really well now and a lot of that's to do with the support she gets from her friends in CWA because, one thing I tell our members is that, if you belong to CWA and you lose your house or you lose your husband, you've always got someone to come to. We'll help you. And actually, we do cater for quite a few funerals where members have lost their husbands or close relations. And that's our service, to help them, and really, to be honest, we're all going to go one day, aren't we? So you may as well do it with CWA there.

Lorraine Greenfield
Branch of the Air, South Australia

When my husband and I semi-retired, to let our son and daughter-in-law take over the pastoral property, we then bought a farming place out of Port Pirie and I decided that I was now close enough to Adelaide to become more fully involved with CWA. To that end, I'm currently Chairman of the Show Cafe Committee, where we run the CWA cafe at the Adelaide Show, and I'm also on various other committees.

I'm a country girl and until we moved to Port Pirie I'd been too isolated to do much more. I was actually born at Innamincka, in the north-east of South Australia, and I grew up on a couple of pastoral properties on the Strzelecki Track. When I was born my parents were managing Cordillo Downs, then we moved to Murnpeowie Station, at the bottom of the Strzelecki. Basically, that's where I grew up, along with my seven brothers. I had no sisters. I was the only girl in the family. My father tried to keep me as a 'girl' but it was a bit difficult, given that situation.

As far as my schooling went, other than a very short stint in Adelaide, it was mainly done by correspondence. Our lessons came by post from the Correspondence School in Adelaide. School of the Air only started in 1956, from Broken Hill, so virtually all my schooling was done via correspondence. Then after I was married I moved to the north-west of South Australia, out from Kingoonya. That was also on a pastoral property called Billa Kalina Station, which is a hundred and seventy-five kilometres north of Woomera, in that direct line between Woomera and Coober Pedy. Then when my children started school, I decided I needed something else. Really, I guess that I was looking for the companionship and friendship of other women so, in 1978, I joined the CWA's Branch of the Air and it's certainly filled a big gap in my life. Originally we were known as the Port Augusta Branch of the Air but now we're simply the Branch of the Air.

With all of us members being from isolated areas we originally had our meetings over the flying doctor radio through School of the Air in Port Augusta. It's a little similar to the more general Galah-chat sessions they used to have but ours were more structured. We held an hour-long meeting, once a month, and our president would call us all in at three o'clock in the afternoon. Actually, considering the poor reception we sometimes got in the outback, it was amazing how those meetings managed to continue at times. But they did and it's a very successful little Branch. It's still going today and, even though I now live out of Port Pirie, I'm still a member of the CWA Branch of the Air.

We cover the entire state. Currently there's eleven of us members and we come from places like Port Augusta, Carrieton, Eden Valley and through the mid-north and the upper-north area of South Australia. With the advances in technology we now hold our meetings over the telephone. As for the fundraising, yes, we still manage to do it. There's various ways and means. At times we may set up a stall at the local pageant at Port Augusta. Things like that. Some of the members come into town for those; not all of them, obviously, but many of the women members are ex-School of the Air parents so we tend to get together occasionally.

But even though our membership isn't large, we're still very active. Actually, we've just started a new project within CWA where we're taking arts and crafts into the outback, for the isolated women who live there. Because we've all lived in similar situations, we fully realised how the girls in those more remote areas were in need of something else besides the everyday cooking and cleaning and trying to teach kids through School of the Air. They all have so many commitments. Even when they go out as a family it's, more often than not, to attend meetings. So that's why we decided to try and provide a more social time for these ladies. It's currently just getting off the ground but we've already had two of these weekends — one at Marree and we've had one over in the

Glendambo area — and in a month's time we're taking a trailer of crafts out to Yunta. We try and give the outback women an enjoyable, relaxed time by taking out handicrafts of all different types. Then, because they hardly ever get the chance to pamper themselves, we also give them the opportunity to experience things like aromatherapy and massage.

It's definitely a positive project. As I said, we're still just getting it off the ground but it's been very popular so far. Women have started to look forward to it now that the word's got out. So we've applied for funding through CWA South Australia and we're hoping that comes through because it's what those isolated women are in need of and, really, that's basically what CWA is all about.

Margaret Hampel
Loxton, South Australia

I came off a very small dairy farm in the Adelaide Hills. I was the eldest of five children and I went to a one-teacher school at a place called Cromer, which not many people would know of. Cromer's between Mount Pleasant and Williamstown. It's right on the watershed, with one side running into the Torrens River and the other side running into the Para River. The town's still there but it's changed a lot. Actually, the school building also doubled as the district's hall and that's still there, as is a tennis club.

After Cromer, I finished my schooling at Birdwood and went to Teacher's College. I was then posted to Waikerie, up in the Riverland. We're talking about 1961–62. That was back in the 'good old days' when you had fifty children in your class. It was a primary school. That first year I ended up teaching all the children who had learning difficulties and the itinerants that just came and went. It was a good steep learning curve because, in those days, there were also quite a few Italians in the area that didn't speak any English at all.

Then I met my husband. He was a grain farmer from Meribah, which is out near the Victorian border. Actually, one of our farm fences is the state border fence, so you could say I'm on the border of being a Victorian. When I went to live there I taught at the little one-teacher school at Meribah and when that closed and the children all went to Brown's Well District Area School, that's where I began my twenty-nine-year stint as what was loosely called a teacher–librarian. Since then, the Brown's Well school has also closed down and the children are now bussed into Loxton. But that's what happens in these rural areas. When I first went there, every little place had a tennis team and a football team and now they're struggling. It's changed dramatically. I'd say that I'd be about the second oldest woman in the district these days because a lot of the farmers now live in the township of Loxton and come out to work on their farms. The population mix has also changed because these days there seems to be more of the alternative types living in the old farm houses.

The same changes are happening within CWA as well because, when I first arrived, there was a Branch at Meribah, which I belonged to, and another one at Malpas and, when Malpas closed, instead of having Meribah Branch one end of the district and Malpas Branch at the other end, they formed one in the middle and called it the Brown's Well Branch. That happened in 1979, then in July 2009 we amalgamated with Loxton as the Loxton District Branch. They've got about twenty-eight members now, which is good as it brings more activity and stimulus into the Branch. So that's how things have changed and, actually, I was one of those who pushed for women to be able to join the association without being attached to a Branch because a lot of women these days are working full-time or are on a farm full-time or caring for their grandchildren. You name it, but they just don't have the hours in the day to devote to the activities of a CWA Branch, yet they're often willing to join. Then, like me, when they retire they're able to become more active.

As for me, I think CWA is a fantastic organisation; one that's terribly important for isolated women. Even with living in quite a rural community there's the need for mental stimulation from outside of that small community and CWA offers that. There's also the lasting friendships, from right across the state, because you get to meet so many women. I've been State Treasurer, State Property Officer, General Dogsbody — you name it — the list goes on but the thing is, you get out and you meet so many people.

Also, in the early 1990s, I was invited onto the Social Issues Fact-Finding Team and that's been one of my most rewarding experiences. We did a rural poverty survey and the result was totally damning because, back then, a farmer couldn't get any social security benefits at all. Nothing. So if you were in the middle of a drought, things were very tough in farming communities and our report found that there were many, many rural people living in poverty. So we had a big launch of our report and from that they set up a parliamentary enquiry into rural poverty, which resulted in drought assistance. That included a lot more federal–state co-operation in as much as there were changes to things like the school system, where the school card was introduced. That's where families who need help are given a card so their children can receive benefits, like they don't have to pay for their books or their school fees. Also more recognition was given to community needs, as in community grants to maintain community activities.

That's what the Social Issues Fact-Finding Team does, and still does to this day. At the moment I'm chairman for a committee that's delving into just how many university places are set aside for full-paying rural students who want to do medicine. To date, the South Australia government has tried to ignore us and they go on about scholarships and all the rest of it. But we're not on about that. We want to know just how many places are set aside for our rural students; and we do know that there are rural students who have been refused entry yet they would've made very good doctors. One young person that I know of has decided to give up on being a doctor and has gone into dentistry. Another has found a place interstate. And we need doctors, especially out in the rural areas where many of these students come from. It's a waste, an absolute waste. So that's the sort of thing we do, and we'll get answers, I can assure you of that because, we're not only very busy ladies in CWA but, we're also very determined ones.

Lynette Harris
Carlisle River, Victoria

My husband, Ken, and I live down in the Otway Ranges, at a place called Barongarook. It's about ten minutes out of Colac. I belong to the Carlisle River Branch of CWA and we're now sixty-four years old. At the moment we have ten members, which mightn't sound a lot, but its okay for a little country town. I think that in some ways, these days, with the ease of travel it's destroyed some of these smaller settlements. I know with Carlisle, when Ken and I were first married, Carlisle had a football team, then, when people started moving out and the farmers started buying their next-door neighbours out, our footy club amalgamated with the Otway Rovers. Then later on they amalgamated with Gellibrand. So those three footy clubs are now just the one club, and this is what happens in these small communities. The people are just not there anymore and the children go away to be educated, they find work, and they stay away with their work.

The same has happened to us. Ken's family were pioneers of Carlisle River. They'd lived there for a hundred and eighteen years. It was mostly dairying and we also had the dairy farm down there. We were milking four hundred and fifty cows and, even though we did employ people, it was still a lot of work for just the two of us. It got to the stage where we felt that we had to get out and start afresh and refresh the spirit before we were too old. So we decided to sell and because Ken couldn't live in the city, we downsized to two small beef properties at Barongarook. It's more like a hobby farm really but we'd been on that dairy farm at Carlisle for thirty-seven years and with the family history and all of that, yes, it was a little bit sad to sell up.

But in our case we had four sons and none of them were interested in taking over the farm. They'd grown up on the farm and they didn't want to go dairying, where you have to get up at the crack of dawn, seven days a week, and you don't finish until sunset, or after. So when we discussed it with them they said, 'Go ahead and sell the farm. We don't want it.'

They'd already made lives for themselves. One's an electrician, one's a builder, one's a concreter and one's a teacher, and they're very happy in what they do. And anyhow, the eldest son's allergic to cows. When he goes near a cow he comes out in a rash all over his body and his eyes swell up. He was probably about fourteen when it first happened. We did take him to a specialist for treatment but when that failed, the specialist said to him, 'I hope you're not going to be a farmer?'

He said, 'No,' and he's now the builder and he lives in Colac. So he was definitely not going back on the farm. That was one down. Then the others are very involved with their football and these days, if they were out on a dairy farm, football would be completely out of the question. My husband, Ken, he used to play football but he sometimes couldn't get to training and then, when they played, he had to do the milking in the morning before he went to footy then, after the game, he'd have to come back home and milk the cows again at night. That was the way it was back then. You could get away with doing that, but not any more.

As for myself, I grew up in a little town called Timboon, which is south of Simpson, in the heart of the Heytesbury Settlement. You've probably heard of Port Campbell. Well Timboon's fifteen kilometres from Port Campbell. My parents also owned a dairy farm at Timboon so I sort of had an idea as to what I was getting myself in for although, mind you, I hadn't done a lot of milking. But that soon changed when I got married. And I also didn't really know that much about CWA until I came to Carlisle River. I was still only quite young — not quite twenty — and of course I hardly knew anyone at Carlisle. Then I was invited along to a CWA function and the Group President, Mrs Montgomery, asked me if I would like to join CWA. So I did and, look, CWA has been just great.

Unlike some of the other CWA Branches, when I had my babies I took them along to our meetings and there wasn't a problem at all. The ladies were wonderful, they really were. They made me feel so welcome and I learned to cook lots of things and it's just snowballed from there. I've become more and more involved with CWA and now I am a State Office Bearer. I'm in my second year as Chairman of Associated Country Women of the World/International/Community Support for CWA of Victoria and I've really enjoyed coming to Melbourne for meetings. I love it actually. I come here once a week with International to help organise and pack clothes and other goods to send to the South Pacific Islands and local areas and hospitals.

Another place we support is Chernobyl. Remember Chernobyl, in Russia, where they had that nuclear accident about nineteen years ago? In Melbourne we help Mr Nikolai Grigorovitch who is the president of a charity known as the Victims of Chernobyl National Relief Fund. He works out of a warehouse, here in Melbourne, and twice a year he sends shipping containers of clothing and other goods over to Chernobyl. It's a big concern because there's an ongoing problem with radiation poisoning and that's been passed down through generations and so a lot of the children are suffering badly from ill health. And also they don't have the nice sunshine and fresh fruit and vegies that we have here in Australia. So along with other organisations we send jumpers and socks, beanies, mittens and knitted rugs over to Chernobyl in an attempt to make these people's lives just that little bit more comfortable. Then a few years ago, the Echuca Branch of CWA helped to support some of the Chernobyl children to come over to Australia for a holiday. So that's just some of the things we do through our international work.

Now would you like to hear a humorous little story about the Carlisle River CWA ladies? This is going back a few years now to before I was married, and I've been married for forty-one years. It was back in my mother-in-law's time and she helped to write this story for the *Back to Carlisle* book when she was a CWA member there. It was when cars were becoming more plentiful in the district and the dirt road between Carlisle and Colac was very rough and windy. Anyhow, the CWA members decided to push for an all weather road. So they kept inviting the people from the Country Roads Board down for a chat and to make them aware of the poor condition of the road. And every time they came down, the CWA ladies would supply them with cups of tea and beautiful home-cooked cream cakes, puffs and sponges. Then after many, many lunches and a lot of lobbying, an all weather road was eventually built between Carlisle and Colac and at the opening, one of the Members of the Country Roads Board described it as being 'The Ladies Cream Puff Road'. That's true. He called it 'The Ladies Cream Puff Road'. It's all in the book that Ken's mother helped to write. So that might just give you an idea as to what lengths CWA will go to, to change things, even in the smaller communities.

But Ken and I, we did miss Carlisle when we first left, although we're happy where we are now. We're very settled. Ken's got his bowls and I have CWA, and I still go back to Carlisle for that. Actually there's five of us from Colac who travel back to Carlisle to attend the monthly CWA meetings. And with just the ten members, if we didn't go we wouldn't have a Branch there. It's not that far really, just half an hour's drive and travel's nothing to us because we're used to travelling long distances and, of course, the road's pretty good these days, too.

Shauna Hartig
Alice Springs, Northern Territory

Originally I come from Bowen in north Queensland. That's where I was born and raised and I was married there when I was seventeen. We then went to Dunk Island and I worked in the gift shop there for just over a year before we shifted across to Townsville where my husband got a job in the bank. Well, he's actually my ex-husband now. After that, we went to Mareeba, then to Mount Isa and that's where we parted ways. No, we didn't have any children. Anyhow, Mount Isa was where I met my current husband, Steve. He was a mechanic by trade and his mother lived over in the Northern Territory at Daly Waters so that's where we decided to move to, and we've been living in the Territory ever since, and the Territory has been very good to us.

When we first came to Daly Waters, Steve drove one of those super-liners that transported cattle. The company he worked for was owned by the Beebe family and they also owned several cattle stations throughout the territory. So we were out bush a lot and that's when Steve taught me how to drive those huge cattle trucks, which is a little bit different for a woman I suppose. Actually, Coral Beebe is one of our CWA members and we used to go to Katherine a lot, to go shopping, and we'd always go to the CWA and have a lunch of beautiful fresh sandwiches and scones and a nice fresh cup of tea. I remember that clearly and so its sad how the Katherine Branch no longer exists. But I guess times change. Still, you never know, do you? You live in hope.

Anyhow, after Daly Waters we worked out on a road construction camp and I was the cook. When we finished up there we went caretaking at the Moly Hill mine. Moly Hill's about four hundred kilometres out on the Plenty Highway. What they do with a lot of these old mines is that, when they stop mining, they leave all the infrastructure and that on site and take on a caretaker to maintain everything, just in case they want to start up again. So that's what we were out there doing. Actually, it was a bit of an eye-opener, with just the two of us, being out in the middle of nowhere. But we got to know each other very well and we thought nothing of driving a couple of hundred kilometres for a barbecue, just to catch up with the neighbours. And we're still friends with many of the people we met during our time at Moly Hill.

We spent eighteen months at Moly Hill then they decided to close the mine and auction everything off. So we moved to Tennant Creek and Steve got a job managing a company that bituminised roads. But no sooner had we got all that up and running than they turned around and said, 'Sorry, we can't afford to pay you anymore,' and that's when we went out to Warrego mine. Steve worked as an ore truck driver and I had a few different jobs. I worked in the purchasing office as a clerk. I worked in the main office. I worked at the Warrego Club as a bar person. For a while I had a job in the shop and I also did some book-keeping for a hardware store in at Tennant Creek. It was all pretty free and easy but we had no children at that stage so we didn't have those sort of ties that parents have.

Anyway we stayed at Warrego for about a year then another caretaking job came up, out at Plenty River mine. Plenty River was a bit further out on the Plenty Highway, and so then we were out there for nearly three years. That was quite isolated as well. I mean, a small mail plane brought out bread and stuff but we still had to come into Alice about once a month to do our bigger grocery shopping and that. It would've been about a four-and-a-half-hour drive each way — nine hours in all — so we'd come in and do our odds and ends then stay overnight and go back out the next day.

But Harts Range was reasonably close and so we'd to go there a bit and we became very good friends with the policeman and his wife, there. Actually, we first met them when we were out at Warrego. At that time he was a policeman in Tennant Creek then after we went to Plenty River they moved to Harts Range. They're in Perth now. But it's funny how in those isolated areas you create such strong bonds of friendship. I mean, you might not see someone for years and when you do, it's like, 'My God, it's great to see you again,' and you just pick up from where you last saw them. But it was a wonderful lifestyle out at Plenty River and we'd go to the Harts Range races and we'd go to the ball and I love to sing. I'm a country singer and years later I actually got to play at the Harts Range races and we performed at the Harts Range Fiftieth Anniversary. But then they did the same thing as they did at Moly Hill; they decided to close the mine down, so we shifted into Alice Springs and we've been there ever since. That'll be twenty-two years ago, at the end of 2010.

I'd known about CWA. When I was a child we had CWA in Bowen and we'd been to Charters Towers and there was a CWA there and, of course, you see the CWA halls when ever you trip around. But CWA in Alice Springs had previously folded. Then in the late 1990s or early 2000s, a lady by the name of Marie Lally, who was then the National President of CWA, she came up to Alice Springs and wanted to get it going again. And so, along with Steve's aunty, Elsie Anderson, and others, the CWA in Alice Springs was reformed. Of course, Elsie soon roped me into becoming a member. She's seventy-seven this year and she's still a member. She comes along to our meetings. So yes, that's how I got into CWA and that was about ten years ago. The Alice Springs Branch has about twenty members these days. Not everyone comes to our monthly meetings of course because some are quite old. Then there's our postal members. They're more like associate members who live out on cattle stations and that and can't get to meetings but they still want to feel a part of CWA and hear what's going on, so they get the newsletter and any other forms of support we can give them.

As for fundraising, we've had food stalls at the Masters Games opening and closing ceremonies. At the Camel Cup we usually have a food stall. We've also been doing the barbecues at the local drag racing and we do a bit of catering for the senior citizens. Every two years they hold a national conference in Alice Springs and all us CWA ladies pitch in, making cakes and sandwiches. Oh, we also have an Easter raffle where we do up a big basket of Easter eggs and other goodies and we sell tickets in at the Alice Plaza. That raises quite a bit of money. But we're always trying to think up new ideas because a lot of the ladies are getting on a bit and they can't spend a long time on their feet, selling things. To that end we've just come up with the idea of a plant sale where the older ladies can potter around through the months, potting plants, getting them ready for us younger ones to sell. And they're happy doing that kind of thing, most of them.

For special memories? Well, I remember, not long after I joined CWA, we had a huge reunion dinner and CWA members came from all over, especially for the occasion, and I sang. Marie Lally organised it and we held it at the Blue Grass Restaurant in Alice Springs. What was so special about it being held there was that the building where the restaurant is had once been the old CWA hall. And so that was a lovely night.

But for me, the positives of the organisation are that I love the interaction with people and I love getting out and meeting different people. I also love the conferences, and probably the biggest buzz for me in CWA was coming to the National Conference, in Darwin, a few years back. My birthday was on that same weekend and on the second day I walked into the conference and everyone stood up and sang 'Happy Birthday', and they had flowers on my table and everything, and I just thought it was such a lovely thing to do. So that was a very memorable birthday. And that's what's so special about CWA — everyone cares for everyone else and so, yes, it would be nice if Katherine CWA got up and going again.

Sauces

Apple Sauce
(Ideal for roast pork)
CWA Tas

4 apples
Juice of half a lemon
2 tablespoons water

½ oz butter
Pinch salt
1 oz sugar

Peel and slice the apples. Put in a pan with lemon juice, water and butter. Cook till soft. Add a pitch of salt and sweeten with sugar. Beat smooth or rub through a sieve.

Béchamel Sauce
CWA NSW

2½ oz butter
1½ oz plain flour
1 pint of chicken or veal stock in which
    a few mushrooms have been simmering
Salt and pepper

Melt butter and stir in flour. Cook for 2 minutes without browning. Add strained stock. Stir until thick. Add seasoning. Put through a fine sieve then reheat and serve.

Hollandaise Sauce
CWA NSW

1 oz butter
¾ oz flour
½ pint water

Yolks of 4 eggs
Salt and cayenne
1 dessertspoon of lemon juice

Melt butter, add the flour, and fry gently without browning for a few minutes. Add the water and stir till boiling. Boil for 5 minutes, remove from the fire and stir in the egg yolks one by one. Place the saucepan in a pan of boiling water and stir till the sauce thickens. It must on no account be allowed to boil or it will curdle. Season with salt and cayenne. Just before serving add the lemon juice.

Mint Sauce

(All year round)
CWA Tas

Gather the mint in October or November. Chop very finely and for each cup of chopped mint allow one cup of vinegar and one cup of sugar. Boil vinegar and sugar and allow to cool. Add mint and keep in screw top jars. When needed for use on table, thin down with cold vinegar.

Important — do not return to jar any sauce that is left over.

Tomato Sauce
CWA NSW

Put into a saucepan 2 or 3 cut up tomatoes, 1 teaspoon chopped onion, ½ cup water, some thyme or mint, pepper and salt. Cook until tender and put through a sieve. Melt 1 oz butter, mix with it 1 oz flour, add the puree and stir well over the fire until it boils.

White Sauce with Variations
CWA Tas

FOUNDATION RECIPE

¾ oz butter

¾ oz flour

½ pint liquid seasoning, this liquid may be milk, water, milk and
water, or the liquid in which foods have been cooked

Melt the butter in saucepan. Remove from fire and stir in flour. Return saucepan to the heat and cook gently about a minute. Remove from heat and stir in the liquid. Bring the sauce to the boil and cook for 2 minutes, stirring briskly. The brisk stirring gives the sauce a glossy appearance. Season as required.

Cheese — ⅓ oz grated cheese and half a teaspoon of made
    mustard

Egg — 1 hard-boiled finely chopped egg

Mustard — 1 teaspoon made mustard and 1 teaspoon vinegar

Onion — 1 large onion cooked and finely chopped

Parsley — 1 tablespoon freshly chopped parsley

Anchovy — ⅓ teaspoon of anchovy essence

Any of the above should be added just before serving. Allow the sauce to
come to the boil again.

Worcestershire Sauce
CWA NSW

6 cups dark vinegar
1 cup treacle
1 oz garlic
1 cup dark plum jam
½ oz cloves

½ oz allspice
9 small chillies
½ teaspoon cayenne
    pepper
1 teaspoon salt

Put all the ingredients together in saucepan and boil for 1 hour. Strain and
bottle. This keeps well.

Jo Hawkins
Perth Belles, Western Australia

I was born in Mullewa, in the south-west of Western Australia. I'm twenty-eight years old now. Actually, many years ago, my nanna was President of the Mullewa Branch of CWA so, during my childhood, back in the 1980s, CWA was a big part of our community. I can probably only talk for Western Australia but I think that, from my mum's generation on, the CWA started to lose its relevance and women, like my mum, felt that it just wasn't for them. Now it's kind of skipped a generation, from when my nanna was heavily involved, to where I can see so much of value in CWA, especially for younger women like myself.

Then, while I was in England, working in the music industry, I saw all the innovative things that the Women's Institute was doing over there. The Women's Institute is kind of like an English version of our CWA. You might remember that it was the basis of the film *Calendar Girls*. But the Women's Institute was doing a very good job of keeping itself relevant and getting younger women in and, other than their charity work, they were getting involved in a lot of projects, some of which were quite political. So yeah, it was fantastic.

So after five years overseas I moved back to Australia and one day I saw a newspaper article which basically said that over the last forty years the CWA membership in Western Australia had fallen from something like 11,000 down to approximately twenty-three hundred. It was really dwindling and I thought, Gee, that seems crazy because there's a lot of sustainability issues at the moment and women of around my age — the mid-twenties to the mid-thirties — we're really passionate about reusing things and not wasting resources and, you know, not wasting money. At that time I was living in Geraldton with my grandparents so I basically rang Pam Batten, who was the State President of CWA and we had a chat. From that conversation I wrote, I guess it could be called a manifesto, for the want of a better word, about how I thought that this eighty-five-year-old organisation of the CWA could connect with a brand-new generation of women, particularly in metropolitan areas. And Pam really bought into that.

Then when I became a history student in Perth, I attended a meeting of the King's Park Branch of CWA and not long after that we had the first meeting of our group, the Perth Belles. We're one of the newest Branches in Western Australia. We launched only four or five months ago and, other than by word of mouth, a lot of awareness about our group got out pretty much totally online. We've now got about twenty officially paid-up members. But we're just really passionate about CWA. Everyone's welcome and though we don't have any kind of age limit, mostly we're between twenty-five and thirty-five. There's mums. Some members are foster-mums. There's a broad group of full-on professions. We've got quite a few scientists for some reason I'm not sure about and one of the girls runs her own law firm. And that's one of our main challenges because many of us have such busy lives and stressful jobs we don't have lot of time so, what we do is, we go online to connect. We have web sites and blogs. We also have a Facebook group, where other friends of friends see this Facebook group and, all of a sudden, we now have a hundred and fifty online Facebook members, which is quite cool.

By doing all that we now have a large network of friends and contacts and we always get a lot more people coming along to our meetings than we have paid-up members. We expect that that's because a lot of those girls aren't from the country and so they're interested in finding out who and what the CWA is all about. Also, I think they want to know what we, the Perth Belles, are on about and whether or not they'll be comfortable in joining us. And so I kind of say, 'It's basically up to all of us to work out where we want to go and what we want to do.'

So, being so new on the CWA scene, I think we've really just been trying to get to know each other properly and get to know what everyone does and work out in what direction we'll head. Then over the next six months we want to start getting into a little bit more community work.

I know that, recently, here in Western Australia, because the numbers have been decreasing and the age of members has been increasing, CWA's been making some really big changes. I mean, we've found that they're just so open to different things. We've had ideas about having tea and cake stalls at music festivals, where we could also run craft workshops and sell craft items. Different things to what was considered to be traditional. We even held burlesque lessons at CWA House, here in Perth. That was fantastic. We were all prancing around with feather boas and that, doing burlesque, and the State President just couldn't believe her eyes.

But the main area we're interested in is fundraising, really. We'd kind of do that ad hoc, anyway, I guess. But we'll try to make it as much fun as possible. Our first big project is going to be a Sunday lawn bowls afternoon with DJs [Disc Jockeys] and a meat raffle with beers; so we'll have music and maybe a band. It'll be more like a huge party kind of thing, really. I'd also like to think that we'd be big on sharing knowledge. I'll tell you one of the most hilarious things. A while back we had a jam making session at CWA House. I didn't really know how many people would come. I mean, we advertised on our web site and there was Facebook but, even though people might RSVP, you still don't really know how many will turn up, do you? And it was almost like a movie. It was absolutely hilarious.

I'd previously had a phone conversation about it with two of the older CWA members, Gwen and Beryl, and they'd agreed to come along as our 'gurus' for the day and demonstrate this jam making session. I had no idea what age they were and Gwen turned out to be about seventy-seven and Beryl was something like eighty-two. They had, like, over a hundred and fifty years of cumulative jam-making experience between them. And they were just fantastic because, all of a sudden, on this Sunday afternoon, about fifty women turned up. It was crazy. We'd bought everything, like the fruit and that and all our members had brought different things like pots and pans. But people just kept coming through the door. Most of them were all new. They'd heard about us and they just wanted to meet us. Some of them even came by themselves, which I think is great, because I'd love us to become a group where you could just call in and make networks. So all these young women turned up and my jaw just dropped. I thought, Oh my God, I don't know what to do here, because most of us didn't have the first clue about how to go about jam making. But Gwen and Beryl, they were fantastic. They were just so good at handling us all. They were completely relaxed about the whole thing. As cool as cucumbers, they were.

Jill Hayes
Huonville, Tasmania

Even though I was born in Hobart, I'm not a city girl. It's just that Hobart's where my parents decided they'd have me, instead of one of the country hospitals. I actually grew up on an apple orchard, south-west of Hobart, at Grove, and I really haven't moved too far from there in my seventy or so years. My family has a long history in Tasmania. My great-grandfather came out as a convict in about 1830. He was at Port Arthur. That's where he met his wife. She was a convict too. I mean, my father didn't find all this out until he was dying and I said to him, 'It's just as well because Mum's parents wouldn't have let you marry her if they knew about all this.'

After my great-grandfather had served his term he was given a land grant at Grove. That was in the 1850s. The property already had a house on it by then but that was wiped out with floods so he built a homestead in 1855. Then as time went by and bits and pieces were sold off or divided between sons, my grandfather eventually built the house near the main road at Grove, in about 1910. When I got married, I lived in the house that my father built in 1930 and I'm still there. But seeing that there were no sons in our family and both my husband and my brother-in-law had found good work elsewhere, the orchard was cleared in 1983. I've now only got an acre of land and the house, and I'm certainly hanging on to that because I don't want to move into the town. Not yet anyway, though I guess the time will come.

For my primary education I went the six miles down the road to the Area School at Huonville. Then if you wanted to go further in your education you had to sit for an exam. So I sat the exam and passed and I went to Hobart High. Hobart High was a co-educational school back then and I boarded within walking distance at the all-girl's Woodlands Hostel in Newton. I didn't like that one little bit. Anyway, I survived and the building, which was Hobart High, is now a funeral home and, oh, they've done marvellous things with it. But the old school-days memories are still there because you go to a funeral and you look around and you think, Oh yes, I remember what used to go on in this room or that.

Then in my last year of high school, my mother died unexpectedly. I'd already put my name down to go nursing by that stage but, because I had a younger sister to look after and all that, I went home to helped out my father and run the house. But my mother, she used to tell us such wonderful stories about her childhood and I often think, If I could only go back and ask her about different things. Like some of us were only talking the other day and a friend asked, 'Who was in such and such building in Huonville?' and I said, 'Well there was the barber shop and the barber's name was ...' And do you know what? For the life of me I just could not remember the barber's name. Then another lady happened to come in and I said, 'Who used to be the barber at Huonville?' and she said, 'That was Nip Salter.' And of course, Nip Salter was also the coach of the Huonville Football Club. But I thought, If only I'd written down the things my mother had told me about.

Anyway, at the time my mother died, she was President of the Huonville Branch of CWA and I can tell you, she used to work extremely hard in the community. I often think that that was probably part of her problem because, even though we didn't know it at the time, she had high blood pressure. Then I got involved in CWA just after I was married. I would've only been twenty-four or something and by the end of the second meeting I'd been elected as the treasurer, and I've just about been everything else since then. The only position I wouldn't take on is Branch Secretary.

Then in about 1970 there was this dear lady — her family name was Roberts — and she said, 'I can see you as Group President.'

So I became a Group President. I've also been involved in handicraft and eventually I became State Vice-President. After that I had a little gap then I was asked, unexpectedly, whether I'd stand for State President of Tasmania. 'Oh all right,' I said and actually I was a bit surprised that I got in.

That was back in about 2001 when we were leading up to hosting the Associated Country Women of the World Conference (ACWW). Really, I think a lot of people doubted that a little place like Hobart, Tasmania, could take on something as big as that. But we had a wonderful coordinator and also Adriana Taylor, the current Mayor of Glenorchy, she was keen that we have this conference. So we did and even though I wasn't State President at the time of the conference, I was still Chairman of the Committee and I must say we did a terrific job. It was a real eye-opener and I think the ACWW people were really surprised because, apparently, where they'd held the world conference the time before, it'd been a bit of a fizzer. But, oh, we had a wonderful band of women who worked extremely hard and very well together.

Then for me, personally, CWA has given me more confidence. I remember when my son was involved in scouts. They needed a new chairman and that position had always been held by a man. Anyway I was elected and after the first meeting the District Commissioner looked at me and said, 'Gee, you can really run a meeting, can't you?'

And, oh, that really stirred me. I thought, You male chauvinist pig. So I said to him, 'Well I've been running meetings for a number of years now, through CWA and other organisations so I should know what I'm doing.'

By that stage I'd already been chairman of the Parents and Friends at the local primary school. I was the current Treasurer of the mother's club and at the high school and, with CWA, I'd also been involved with the Hobart Show and the Huon Show. We're all involved with the shows. Just recently I said to someone, 'Some of these shows would fall in a heap without CWA,' because one of the things that really stands out is that us women can, and do, get the job done. Too right we do. Just like last night: the Elder Care Homes at Franklin had their ecumenical service and the minister didn't turn up and the pianist hadn't turned up because the minister didn't turn up and so we all looked at each other and thought, Well, the residents are all there, waiting for the service to begin. What are we going to do? Then they looked at me and they said, 'Well you can do it.'

'Okay,' I said, and I led them in a little bit of a service and everything went well. And it's been through my involvement in CWA that's given me the confidence to do these things. Whereas before, I was a very quiet, shy person and so I'd just sit back and hope that someone else would rise to the occasion. But not any more.

So if only we, in CWA, could get the message out to other women that, 'Yes, you can do it and together we can do these amazing things and also be able to help so many people.'

Sometimes I think we might be doing a lot better if we waved the flag a bit more than what we do. But then you sort of think, Well, perhaps, that might be a bit brash of us. So we don't. With CWA, we're more your quiet but determined achievers.

Eulie Henderson
Port Germein and Adelaide, South Australia

In my day we were appointed as a junior teacher, straight from high school, with absolutely no teaching experience at all. So I did my Fourth-year exams in November and in the February I started teaching at Houghton, in the Adelaide Hills region of South Australia. I'd lived in Adelaide all my life, I was seventeen, and I arrived at Houghton on the bus and somebody met me and took me up to the school. It was a two-roomed situation — just me and the Headmaster, as they were called in those days — and he said, 'This is your room, Miss Dunn. That's my room. You've got Grades One, Two and Three. I've got the rest.' And that was it. He didn't even have the time to sit down and explain things to a greenhorn like me. He just gave me a copy of the previous teacher's class notes and I had to learn from those. It was a real case of learning on the job. Yet it was a wonderful experience and I'd guarantee that every child I taught learned to read and write and add up.

I then went to Adelaide Teacher's College where, in trepidation, we tossed around possible appointments to places like Nunjikompita and Pinkawillinnie — names that you could hardly pronounce let alone know where they were. And if you were sent there, that's where you went, no questions asked. Luckily I was sent to Port Germein, a costal town in the St Vincent Gulf. I was nineteen and I met my husband during my second year. He was a farmer who lived just north, at Baroota. It's a place that everybody drives through and never bothers to stop. It's between Port Pirie and Port Augusta, south of Mambray Creek. We were on a mixed farm of wheat, sheep and cereal crops. Originally we also grew dry-land table peas, in the winter months, when there was rain. That was a wonderful money-spinner, but once frozen and tinned peas came to the fore there was no further call for our peas and we went back to mixed farming. Then toward the end of our farming career we put up a piggery. It was huge place with a type of under-floor heating. It was very intensive. Like caged chooks, actually. But that's what we did and it worked very well for us.

I got into CWA because, simply, it was the thing that the women in that area did. That was in the mid 50s. Until the first child came along CWA didn't hold much appeal for me as I considered it to be an 'old lady's thing'. But once my daughter got to be a take-able age, while you weren't compelled to join, it was more or less expected that you would. It was an interesting situation, actually, because the meetings were held on a Saturday afternoon, which is a bit unusual. That came about because, back then, apart from playing tennis during the tennis months there was nothing in Port Germein to hold your interest. Other than a 4-Square store there were no shops so, once you'd bought the bread for the next week and had been to the post office, there was little else to do. So the men went to the hotel for their Saturday afternoon get-togethers and the women went to CWA — not that my husband went to the pub at all. He wasn't allowed to. But that was the reason for the Saturday afternoon meetings, and it remained that way for many years.

Originally CWA met in a shop front. I can't remember what the fellow who owned it did but we were able to rent one of the rooms. The kids all went. There was a group of us who'd had babies at about the same time and, after the children were walking and out of nappies, one of us would say, 'It's off to the toilet, troops', and we'd collect all the kids and cart them off, down the backyard, to go to the toilet. There was none of this flushing toilet bizzo.

Then I became a Branch secretary and later, secretary of the Dolling Group. There were about twenty-three Branches in the Dolling Group back then and we later acquired the other part of the building which we turned into two holiday cottages — the Dolling Group Flats. It worked very well for a long while. We had very keen and interested members who were extremely hard working, as always. But unfortunately the holiday flats became defunct many years ago. Situations change. You know, the usual story: the young ones have other things to do and the old ones get too old and drop off the end of the line. The Port Germein Branch is still functioning though it now meets in the United Church kindergarten hall. It'd be an exaggeration if I said there was a dozen members. But it remains active, well, as active as those few women can make it.

As for special memories of that time, I'd say that the trips through the Port Germein Gorge were a feature. We were in a very marginal rainfall area, twelve inches if we were lucky, so it was good to get out and see that sort of country. Of course, there was also the friendships and, because we all had very little spare money, no one was any better off than anyone else. But once life on the land went bad I went back to teaching and my affiliation with CWA stopped because, by then, they were meeting during the week.

Eventually we sold the farm and my husband became a professional bowling green keeper at one of the city clubs in Adelaide. So we came to town and I was State President of the Hand Knitters Guild. Then at one of our wool days the then CWA State President, Marie Lally, asked me to come along as a guest speaker. From that, Marie contacted me and wondered if we'd be interested in starting up a new Branch in Adelaide which, of course, is what we did. It's called the Dequetteville Branch because we meet at the state offices in Dequetteville Terrace. Actually, one of the names we considered was the Business Women's Branch because we had a land conveyancer, a librarian. We had certificated nurses, teachers. We now have a writer. So it's a very diverse group and because the majority worked during the day we decided to hold our meetings on a Monday night. Still do. And that was back in 1997, so we've just past our twentieth year.

I guess you could say that our Dequetteville Branch is a little bit unique in so far as, where most follow the old traditional

CWA ways, we tend not to. We don't take part in any table days. We don't have a handicraft group. We don't do floriculture as a group. But we have a lot of guest speakers and we always do a daylight saving tour to places like the West Terrace Cemetery and to North Road Cemetery. One Christmas we went on a tour of the Botanic Gardens. We've looked at how they have their Christmases in other lands. Our Branch is involved with the catering here at the CWA Club. I'm Catering Co-ordinator and I'll ring around and say, 'Look we're catering for forty next Saturday week, will you be there?' and they'll say, 'Yes, what time?'

So we are a bit unique in that respect, and it's working very well. We've got a steady trickle of new members, which is good, very good.

Janet Henderson
Nelson Bay, New South Wales

Actually, my family were pioneers on the Central Coast of New South Wales. In 1823 a great-great-grandfather was granted three hundred acres of land in the Port Stephens district; land which was later acquired by the government to build a naval base. But the naval base never eventuated. My father also grew up in the area. He died twelve months ago. He was ninety-eight and a half. I grew up there. My maiden name's Cromarty, and we have a lane named after us.

I'd always known about CWA and I had belonged to various organisations — Junior Farmers and such — but after I was first married I went and lived in Sydney for a number of years. Then I moved back here in 1979. At that stage the CWA was raising funds to build a hall and they had a stall in an arcade in Nelson Bay. Of course, coming from the district, I knew some of the ladies and they said, 'Oh, come along.'

However, at that stage, I had three sons at school and the Nelson Bay CWA meetings were held on a Monday morning. We have an Evening Branch as well but even that was a bit awkward because I was quite tied up with school activities. So I really had to wait until I could get away on a Monday to attend meets and that's how I first joined. But the Nelson Bay Branch itself was formed back in 1949. There weren't many competing activities in the district back then. CWA was basically it, and so the ladies decided that they'd meet every Monday. About five years ago it was mentioned, 'Do you still want to meet every Monday?' and we all said, 'Oh, yes.' So we have a main meeting once a month and we have other activities on the other Mondays. But these days, some of our ladies are getting into their eighties and nineties and, they've done a lot of work for CWA over the years and so they're happy to sit back a little now. Naturally, they still support CWA and, if they're able to, they come for morning tea.

Of course, CWA does take up a fair bit of your life. You look at your calendar and there's functions everywhere. We start with a Friendship Day in January. Then this year we had a Country and Western singer from Soldier's Point, called Rolly Manton. He came and sang. We got three new members from that because they enjoyed it so much. And that's what we need: to keep getting new members. That's the main thing. We need new members to keep us going.

After a lot of fundraising we eventually built our CWA Hall in 1984. It's just a little way out towards Shoal Bay, and that building has now been paid for, which was a big effort by the ladies. It's quite substantial, with a big kitchen. We have crockery and everything you'd need. They ran a camellia show for thirty-three years, which was quite an event though, unfortunately, we don't do that now. They also ran a ball for a number of years but we don't hold dances anymore either, and we've had to stop things like eighteenth and twenty-first birthdays because, with the liquor, they can get a bit out of hand. We don't allow people to use it at night now. Once upon a time it was all right but not now. But we've had various people hire it. The Salvation Army hired it until they found their own rooms, then we had a minister from the Baptist Church hiring it for a while. The JPs also used to hire it.

For a long time Port Stephens was a nice quiet spot. But everything's changed. The whole district has become more urban these days, with an enormous amount of clubs and things, so you're competing against everything else. Now we only have casual hires of the hall, like the Garden Club, and that helps with the costs of running the building and the upkeep. Of course, we have a lot of our own CWA functions there and we invite other Branches. We've done lots of things. We've had handicraft exhibitions. We've also had International Days and, even though many of our members can't travel too far these days, we still have good attendances.

Actually, we're quite well known for our International Days. That's a state-wide thing where the CWA chooses a country of study each year. We had one on Austria and, for our International Day, we had a hall full of people. We had morning tea and lunch and we had an Austrian person come and speak and we always try to dress and have some of the food of the country. Following the success of the Austrian International Day we decided to hold one on New Zealand. That's always been remembered. I must say, the lady who was our International Officer was really quite apprehensive about it all, but some of the Maoris in the district had already offered to do the cooking.

'We'll do the cooking in someone's backyard,' they said and they told us they were going to cook a hangi — which is the traditional way they do it, by cooking their food in a pit in the ground. There was a lot of excitement about that and about seventy-five people said they'd come along, including our State President. So they all came along. Our International Officer was still a little on edge about it all but the Maoris came down to let her know that everything was going fine.

'Thank goodness,' she said, and gave a sigh of relief.

So we had morning tea. Then at about half-past eleven, some of the Maoris came back and they said, 'We're running a little bit late. The meat's not quite done. It should only be another half an hour.'

Of course everybody's getting a bit hungry by this stage, but we had some bread rolls so we served them up, with a cup of tea. Then the Maoris came back again. 'Sorry but we have to delay it some more,' they said, 'and, oh, the lady who was going to make dessert has gone to a funeral.'

Straight away, our ladies said, 'Well, we'd better rush out and buy some pavlovas and fruit from the supermarket.'

We did that and when there was some other sort of other delay we decided to eat our dessert before the main course arrived. Then another Maori came back, 'It's all right, don't worry about dessert, we've organised another lady to do that.'

Anyway, this went on, and every half-hour they're coming back and announcing a further delay. All through this, the poor lady who was International Officer just sat there, absolutely stunned. But I think because the Maoris had been living in Australia for so long they weren't as practiced as they might have normally been and they hadn't lit the fire in the pit early enough to put the food in. Then the next time they come they said, 'It's still not quite ready so we're going to have to take the food out of the pit and take it to someone's home to fast-forward the cooking.'

Of course, by now everybody's starving. They'd already had their bread roll and a cup of tea and then they'd had their cake and when the Maori lady did finally turn up with dessert she only had two small plates to be shared amongst about seventy-five people. Everybody only got the tiniest of tastes, with a little dob of cream. Anyhow, by now it's about half-past one. Then two o'clock. And it got to about half-past two and they're still coming and saying, 'It wont be long. It wont be long.'

But some of our ladies had come all the way from Muswellbrook and Cessnock and Scone and places like that and so it got to the stage where they were all needing to go home, including the State President. Anyway, we had to give a few refunds and by three o'clock there were only about fifteen of us left and that's when all the Maoris arrived. 'Here we are,' they said, and they'd brought all this beautiful food. It was an absolute feast. Far, far, too much for the remaining fifteen of us. Oh, they had two or three lots of meat. They had big pots of potatoes, pumpkin and cabbages, and it's been a talking point ever since. Nelson Bay's International Day on New Zealand. People still say, 'Yes we remember that day.'

So that was one of our little debacles. However, we're still going. This year our country of study is Egypt and once again we'll have an International Day and we'll have our cultural days and a few outings. I'm not sure if we'll be having an Egyptian meal or not but, if we do, we're hoping all goes well.

Alma Herrmann
Murrami, New South Wales

My name is Alma Herrmann; that's Herrmann with a double 'r' and a double 'n'. I say, 'It's Herrmann with the lot.' This is my second term on the CWA Executive and I'm from Murrami, near Leeton, in the Murrumbidgee irrigation area of New South Wales. Murrami CWA was sixty years old in 2009. In the early days the meetings were held in people's homes. Now we have our own community hall. It looks really great. We have a microwave and a dishwasher and a fantastic electric stove that everyone envies.

The story I have to tell is that, back in 1949, when the Murrami Branch was first formed, my mother-in-law-to-be, Iris Herrmann, was the inaugural President and, as did the other CWA members, she always took her children to the meetings. Iris had three children: there was Ray — who many years later became my husband — then there was John and Margaret. Ray was taken to his first CWA meeting when he was two. Then, on my side of the family, both my mother and grandmother were also members of the Murrami Branch and as us kids got older, we used to go to the meetings after school and have afternoon tea. And then after Ray and I were married and we had children they were also taken along to CWA meetings and now both my daughter and my daughter-in-law are members and their children go to the meetings. So, currently, this is our fourth generation going to the Murrami CWA.

But with having been brought up in that environment, I find it hard when I hear people say, 'Oh, I wanted to join CWA but I was told that I couldn't bring my children', because it's my feeling that that's what community is all about. I've been President of the Branch and, at times, you have to say, 'Hey, we're here for a meeting, because the ladies are so involved watching some child or other take their first steps or draw something new. So I don't know what we'd do without the children, especially considering how CWA is looking for new members and, when you've got the chance for children to come along and growing up in the CWA environment, it'd only be a natural for them to get swept up into it all and think, Well, Grandma belonged and Mum belonged, so I may as well belong, too.

That's my feeling, anyway, and an example of that would be how, at the moment, one of our younger members has just done her certificate to teach aerobics and we've arranged it though CWA to encourage our members, plus anyone else in the community, to come along to stay fit. Of a Monday and Thursday morning, there'd be five or six women there, doing pilates, and there's three or four babies crawling around the floor and every now and then you'll hear a giggle because one of the mums is trying to lift her leg and she's got a little one hanging on to it. To me, that's what CWA is all about.

But these days, in the township of Murrami there'd only be about twenty houses, plus there's the wider farming community. Still, it's not near as big as it used to be and that's because of farming being the way it is nowadays. Ray used to employ four workers and now we don't have any. At the moment we'd normally have about one thousand acres of rice in, but we just can't get the water. Allocations have been cut. We started off with seven per cent at the beginning of the season. We're up to twenty-five per cent now but it's all too late for rice.

It's the same everywhere so thankfully we have a very strong community. Australia Day in Murrami is always a big occasion. This year we had a movie night in our hall, on the Friday night, and about a hundred and fifty people came in. That was for drought relief. Also, since 1988, CWA has been running an Australia Day breakfast and, though it's not really a fundraiser, we do have a container there that's marked 'donations', just to cover expenses. Mind you, we always get more than our expenses and all that goes to a good cause. It's very popular. We say that the breakfast is between 7.30 and 9 am and this year we had about a hundred and thirty people come along and some of them were still standing there, talking, at 10.45.

We also had a jumping castle for the children. Then at about 5 o'clock in the afternoon there's the challenge cricket match between Murrami and Gogeldrie. It's a shortened version. I think they play indoor cricket rules, outdoors, with a few of their own local rules thrown in for good measure. In all, we had over a hundred people turn up for that. Murrami won last year and they were that confident of winning again this year that they'd already had the plaque engraved with 'Murrami Winners 2009'. This was even before a ball had been bowled. Then three quarters of the way through the game all the Gogeldrie children up and walked on to the field. Of course, that caused a lot of confusion and so everyone's telling them, 'Get off. Get off.' But it was all a big ploy because, while all this distraction was going on, two of the Gogeldrie teenagers pinched the trophy and they hid it in someone's car and they've never given it back. So, even though Murrami went on to win the game, Gogeldrie have still got the trophy, somewhere.

Jennie Hill
Miles, Queensland

I grew up on the Central Coast of New South Wales, in the town of Gloucester. As for schooling, Gloucester went right through, from primary to Year 12. Following that I worked in a chemist shop. That was in Gloucester as well. Then I joined CWA when I was nineteen, and I became a member because the girl that I worked with had joined and, also, it was the sort of the thing that young working girls in places like Gloucester did. You basically joined to meet and make friends and to help out in the community. It's similar to the young men joining APEX in as much as it's a community-driven organisation.

Then after I married I went and lived on a property out of Gloucester. It had been dairy but it was beef by the time I got there. On the farm we had a flying fox. In the wet, this flying fox was our only access in and out of the property and one day, three months after I was married, we were going across it and the cable broke and I fell and I ended up with four spinal fractures. So that was a rude awakening from the honeymoon stage because I then spent the next five months in hospital and, fortunately, after my stint in hospital I was able to walk out on sticks and a calliper. I say 'fortunately' because it could have so easily been far worse.

And I'll ever be grateful to the CWA for helping me through. They've given me the support and confidence to go and actually put myself forward and achieve things and to be able to stand up in front of people, on the crutches, and say, 'Look, I may be disabled but I've got a brain and I can still do things.' And that's what CWA has done for me and that's the greatest thing I've got out of CWA. So, yes, at times it's been difficult — very difficult — but it's just, you know, how things go.

Then ten years ago we decided to move from Gloucester. Basically, we just wanted to get off the coast. Tamworth would've probably been the logical choice but the prices around that area were quite prohibitive. Anyhow, one of our sons was living in Queensland and so we decided to have a look up there and we ended up buying a property here at Miles. Miles is about three hundred kilometres westish of Brisbane. It's a beef property again. We've got an Angus stud and the first year we arrived we had a very good year. Then that's been followed by nine straight years of drought. Yes, reality hit. So we're just hoping that something comes out of this current lot of rain. Almost everywhere else in Queensland seems to have had decent falls but not us. We're just above the Condamine River and the Condamine still isn't running as yet. So maybe this is the change we're after.

But after we moved up here to Miles the first thing I did was go to their next CWA meeting. Basically, I walked in the door and the following meeting I became the Branch International Officer. Since then I've been the Division Vice-President and Division International Officer, Division President and I'm currently a State Vice-President of Queensland. So I haven't done too badly. I mean, it wasn't planned that way because, at times, I really didn't think I'd ever be able to do anything like this. But thanks to all the support I've had through CWA I have come a long way.

In all, I've been a member since I was nineteen and now I'm fifty-eight or something like that. I love everything that CWA does though I'm certainly not in it for the cooking and sewing because I'm not good at either of those things. I'm more in it for what we can put forward to government to try and fix all the different problems that exist. That's always been my interest within CWA. An example there would be: well, one of the main things that's occurred around this area in the last three years or so is all the coal-seam gas exploration. That's where they drill down into the coal seam to extract the gas. The only trouble is that, during the process, not only is methane gas released but also massive amounts of water come up with it and, currently, all the water's just being put into huge evaporation ponds. Of course, after it evaporates, then you're left with this massive amount of salt.

Now, we in CWA, along with others, are trying to get the government to do something with that water because it's a massive resource that is, basically, just being wasted. Plus, also, there's the problem of what to do with all the salt that's left behind. Everybody's worried that it could well end up in the watertable or in the streams or in places like that. So in the last couple of years, that's been one of the things I've personally been involved in through CWA. And you can only keep trying to get our governments to look at some of these environmental problems, can't you?

Pickles and Chutneys

Tomato Chutney
CWA NSW

6 lb ripe tomatoes
¼ lb ginger
3 lb dates
1 oz cayenne
3 oz garlic

¼ lb onions
1 lb brown sugar
2 oz salt
5 pints vinegar

Scald the tomatoes and peel them, bruise and tie ginger up in a muslin bag. Gently boil tomatoes, chopped dates, cayenne, chopped garlic, onions, brown sugar, salt and vinegar for 5 hours with bag of ginger. Bottle and cover down tightly.

Indian Chutney
CWA NSW

2½ lb green cooking apples
6 oz brown sugar
1 pint good vinegar
½ oz garlic
2 oz finely chopped onion

¼ lb cut up and finely pounded whole ginger
1 oz dried chillies
2 oz mustard seed
4 oz salt
¼ lb raisins, stoned

Peel, core and cut up the apples and put them in an earthenware jar. Dissolve the sugar in two tablespoonfuls of boiling water and add to the apples then pour the vinegar over. Stand in the jar in a moderate oven and bake until the apples are soft. Leave until cold then mix with the garlic, onion, the ginger, the chillies, mustard seed, salt and raisins. Mix all together until thoroughly blended. Fill bottles with the mixture, cork and seal securely. Leave for a month before use.

Green Tomato Sweet Pickles
CWA NSW

Slice 8 lb green tomatoes and sprinkle salt between layers. Allow to stand 12 hours then drain off liquor. Boil 1 quart of vinegar with a good tablespoon treacle, put ½ tablespoon of allspice, cloves, peppercorns in piece of muslin and add to vinegar. Place in basin, 1 tablespoon mustard, 1 dessertspoon ground ginger, ½ tablespoon curry powder, 2 cups brown sugar, ½ cup plain flour, 1 tablespoon tumeric powder, mix with some of the vinegar to a smooth paste and stir into boiling vinegar. Slice 2 lb onions and add with tomatoes and boil for about 20 minutes, stirring well to keep from burning. Cauliflower can be made up the same way.

To Pickle Onions
C. Ambery, Evandale, CWA Tas

Cover 8 lb onions with boiling water and when cool remove skins. Cover with 3 quarts of water and 2 cups salt and let stand overnight then drain. Just heat (do not boil) 2 quarts vinegar, ½ oz allspice, ½ oz peppercorns, 8 cloves, 2 or 3 pieces of mace and a few pieces of whole broken ginger and ½ cup sugar. Pour over the onions and tie down. Ready in three weeks.

Red Cabbage
E. Faulkner, CWA Tas

Strip the centre leaves off a red cabbage then cut it into quarters and remove the core. Shred the cabbage very finely and when placing it on a large dish, sprinkle each layer well with salt. Next day drain the cabbage thoroughly in a colander and lay in a coarse clean cloth before pressing lightly into jars. Fill the jars almost to the brim with cold vinegar, which has previously been boiled for 10 minutes with a teaspoonful of allspice and cayenne pepper to every quart of vinegar. Must be kept airtight in screw top or closely sealed jars, if not, it will lost its crispness and bright red colour. White vinegar for shows.

Joyce Hughes
West Hobart, Tasmania

I grew up at a little place called Kootingal, which is just out of Tamworth, in the northern tablelands area of New South Wales. My father was a farmer. It was a mixed farm and, oh, we had everything: poultry, sheep, wheat, lucerne, pigs. The lot. For my primary school education I went to Kootingal, then for high school we caught the bus into Tamworth. So I went to Tamworth High School for three years and I finished up there during the last year of the war and then I went back home and helped out on the farm. And mind you, I did 'work' on the farm and not in the house. That's just what you did in those days.

Then I stayed on the farm for two more years before I went and did my four years of nurse's training at Maitland. Maitland is just west of Newcastle, and after I'd finished there I decided to set off and see the world. For some reason I thought that Tasmania was as good of a starting point as any so that's what I did. I came to Tasmania and, lo-and-behold, I met my husband-to-be. But before we got married I did do a twelve-month midwifery training course in Melbourne and I spent six months over in Western Australia, at both Busselton and Carnarvon. Then I came back to Tasmania and I got married in May 1955. My husband wasn't a farmer. He was a bricklayer and after that he went into the building industry as a scaffolder, then his health broke down and he ended up working as a bailiff for the court. Unfortunately, he died three years ago.

But I'd known about CWA all of my life. My mother was a founding member of Tamworth CWA. Actually, they made her a Member of Honour. But I'll always remember, when I got married, my mother saying to me, 'When you go over to Tasmania, join CWA and Red Cross and you'll never be without friends.'

And I did that. I followed my mother's words, and she was right. I've never been without friends.

Gloria Hyatt
Glenreagh, New South Wales

I grew up in Glenreagh, which is on the north coast of New South Wales, between Grafton and Coffs Harbour. I was the fifth youngest of thirteen children and, at the age of eight, I lost my mum through breast cancer. We were on a farm so we all had to chip in and do our little bit and so, at the age of fifteen, I had to leave school to take my turn at looking after the family. At that stage there were still three young brothers and a young sister at home. The youngest was twenty months and when the next eldest one was ready to leave school and look after the family I went off to work. After that I married and we went and lived at Sherwood Creek, which is in a little valley, just six miles east of Glenreagh. That's where I still live. I've been there for, gosh, some forty-six years now. We have a reasonable-size property so I'm not looking forward to the time I might go to town. And I emphasise the word 'might'.

Glenreagh has a population of around five hundred people. It's just a small village with properties all around. There's not very much farming going on here now; just a bit of grazing, but no dairy farming and no cropping. We used to have about four or five timber mills here at one stage and the main north coast railway line still goes through. But our station has closed so, to get the train, you have to drive in to either Grafton or Coffs Harbour.

I was actually a junior member of CWA and I've been involved in other organisations such as the P&C [Parents and Citizens], with the school. Then, when my youngest daughter was ready for high school, I thought, Oh, I needed another outlet. So I decided I'd go back to the CWA and I've been here now for twenty-nine years. I suppose you could say I'm still only a relatively new member.

The positives of belonging to CWA would be the fellowship. That's very important, and being there for others and helping others. It's all to do with involvement. Glenreagh is not a big

Branch. We have about sixteen members and, like lots of other Branches, we have an aging group. But we're still very active. We have CWA rooms where we offer tea and scones and pikelets and, around the side, we have a little handicraft section where there's also the homemade jams and preserves.

We're also fairly well known for our catering. We cater for wakes, for weddings and parties. Unfortunately, the catering we did for the tourist coaches has eased off a little, recently. They came along the Coffs Harbour–Grafton route, then we might get coaches from the Gold Coast. It's an arrangement we have on a year to year basis where they call in and have morning tea or lunch. Then perhaps some interstate coaches may have heard about us and so they'll pull in and have a cuppa. Something that we haven't done for two or three years is that we used to cater for around about thirty-five police who came to do weapons training up and around the hills. They were mostly men and they'd spend the week down on the river, at the scout camp, and we'd serve them all their meals. We had quite a reputation with the boys. It was a big job but, honestly, they were magnificent. They were really good fun fellows. You'd quote x-amount of dollars to cover each person then, naturally, you added on a little bit for CWA.

We also give an annual prize to the local primary school's Dux of the Year. It's usually something that they may need next year in high school, such as pens and pencils and binders. Then sometimes the town may need a little support. Last year there was a campaign to build a brick memorial wall at the cemetery and we made a reasonable donation towards that. Of course, we do also support CWA's various state-wide and international projects. To date, I've been President, Secretary, Treasurer and Cookery Officer at both Group and State level and I've been the State Cookery Chairman. That entails running an annual cooking competition throughout the state. The *Land* newspaper sponsors us. There are twelve sections, with different categories in each section. To start with, members cook in their own Branches and, if they win at Branch level, they go on to their Group. The state of New South Wales is made up of thirty Groups so then the winners of each Group go on to the State for the finals contest.

Also, I'm now State Agriculture and Environmental Officer. I've only been in that position for just under twelve months. It's still quite a learning curve but I have a good committee of eight whom I can call upon to give me any information I may need because living on the coast, naturally, I don't have a great knowledge of the wheat or sheep areas. It's such a diverse area to cover. The committee members can bring forward any problems that might be out there with farmers, such as climate change. Recently we put in a submission to the state government as to why Lippia should be eradicated. Lippia's used in lawns but once it gets into water streams it becomes a big problem. A huge problem. Then, just pre-Christmas, in my capacity as State Agriculture and Environmental Officer, I went to a round-table forum with the NSW Department of Primary Industry. At the moment they're talking about closing down some of the CSIRO Research Centres, so they're trying to work out just what to do with the vacated CSIRO buildings. They're also amalgamating sections of the Rural Land Protection Board. I think they went from forty-nine down to about fourteen. Mind you, we're just one voice amongst many and so sometimes we hear back from them and sometimes we don't hear back from them. But at least we're contributing by making them aware.

So I guess I've achieved more than I ever set out to do within CWA and there are times when I think, My Lord, what am I doing? I need time for me. But I always say, 'The day I don't enjoy it is the day I'll stop doing it.' And I do enjoy it. I particularly like meeting new people and there's places I'd never have been to if not for the CWA. As far as any other highlights go: at last year's State Conference, at Tweed Heads, they held the cookery, the handicraft and a cultural competition and I was lucky enough to get first prize in the fruit cake. So in a tongue-in-cheek way you could say that there's very little more for me to achieve in CWA now, that is, apart from making the perfect sponge cake, and that may take some time yet.

Nicola Kelliher
Wandering, Western Australia

I'm from Wandering in Western Australia. Wandering's about an hour and a half south-east of Perth. It's spelt like as if you're wandering around. It's a lovely name, actually. But I've only lived in Australia for just over four years and I'm sure that my pathway into CWA is very different. Originally I'm from Wickford, in Essex, England, which is nowhere near a farm. But have you watched the film *Calendar Girls*? It's about an organisation known as the Women's Institute, which is the English version of the CWA. Well I always thought that if I ever got married and moved to the country that's the sort of thing I'd like do.

Then in early 2004 I saw an advertisement for girls who wanted to take part in an Australian television show called *Desperately Seeking Sheila*. It was about country bachelors, looking for wives. Some of the girls were to be Australian and twelve English girls were to be involved. In all, about four thousand girls applied. I got an audition, which was like a TV screen test, and the videos were then sent out to the bachelors in Australia and I was one of the girls chosen. It was filmed in April '04. I was twenty-five at that time and I was to be paired with a guy who was twenty. It seemed a bit young, actually, but I thought, Oh, you never know. Some twenty-year-olds are quite mature. Well he wasn't, and it didn't work out.

I was then paired with another bachelor who didn't like his girls when he met them. He came from Margaret River so I went down there and I had the most terrible time. That didn't work out either. But that was all right because it gave me the chance to travel. So I did the whole outback thing, then I went back to England and I started a business with my mum and my dad. But I still had an itch for Australia, Western Australia in particular.

For me it's 'west is best'. Then in October '04 they were having the premiere of *Desperately Seeking Sheila*, over here in Fremantle, and my dad said to me, 'Look, Nicola, we can't really afford it at the moment and we can't afford to have you away from the business but, what you really need to do is to just go over there and close the book on Australia. Go on, go to the premiere.'

Okay, so I flew out to Australia for the premiere and the producer said to me, 'Oh, Shane will be there.' Shane had been one of the bachelors in the show and things hadn't worked out for him either. I'd heard of him but I'd never actually met him. The producer showed me his picture. 'Oh, he looks really nice,' I said, 'but I don't think he'd be my type.'

Then on the Saturday night we had the party for the premiere. I met Shane at about half-past six and it was immediately obvious that he was my type. So after the party finished we went to the Left Bank Pub. It was just closing as we arrived and so we decided to go for a walk. We went up to the prison and down to the wharf and we just kept walking and talking, and I was thinking to myself, Well Nicola, he's such a nice genuine person that, if you don't want to marry him or even consider coming out to Australian and living in the country, it's pointless getting to know somebody like this because you're only leading yourself on and them on and that's not right. So it got to about one o'clock in the morning and, because I was wearing high-heeled boots, my feet were really hurting. I'm quite a small person, not even one metre fifty, and Shane's nearly six foot. Then he said, 'Oh, do you fancy going up to King's Park?'

I'd only been taken there briefly by the bachelor I went to Margaret River with and he just pulled up at King's Park and said, 'Look, there's the view. Get back in the car,' and off we went to Margaret River.

Yeah, so Shane and I, we went around King's Park. And it was just really pleasant to be able to talk to somebody and not have them want to maul you or anything. I felt so safe with him. Then he took me back to where I was staying at about three o'clock in the morning. So we met on the Saturday night and I went back to England on the Tuesday and we didn't see each other for another four months. We were in contact every day though, ringing and texting, and it wasn't just one-sided either. But it was all still such an unknown because you just can't tell if you're going to marry someone within four days. Then in March 2005, around my birthday, Shane came over but, because I was working and couldn't take any more time off, we only saw each other on the weekends. Then on the last week we still really liked each other and we went down to Devon, to where some of his family had run a farm many years ago, and that was fantastic.

So it was all getting very serious and so I came back out to Australia in the May for three weeks. That was the time when I really had to make a decision, because there's no point in coming out here and living on a farm and not being involved in farm life. And I had a blast. Shane would drag me out of the house at six in the morning and I went round and I learned to brand cows. I even castrated two bulls. It was brilliant and, also, during that time I met quite a few people — some of whom were CWA ladies — and I found everyone to be very warm and friendly.

That was in May, then Shane came back over to England in July to ask my dad if he could marry me, which was so romantic. July 7th was the day we got engaged, which was also the day of the London bombings. And if we would've gone into Harrods, to buy the ring, as we'd first planned, we would've been in the underground at that time the bombs went off. But on the morning we were going to go up to London I said, 'No, actually, I liked that ring I saw last night in the shopping centre.'

Then I came back out to Australia in the August and it was so wonderful. My sister-in-law-to-be, Kerry, hosted a kitchen tea party for me. I didn't know what a 'kitchen tea party' was all about. At first I just thought I was just going to have tea at Kerry's kitchen but then all these local women brought little gifts like recipes and someone gave me a little Wandering tea towel. It was just so personal and they made me feel so welcome. Then we got married in England on October 8th, 2005 and we got married on 16th October over here in Australia, and it was just fantastic.

But my first real connection with the CWA was a Christmas dinner in 2005, and that was really lovely. I remember dressing up and it was, 'Oh, you know, I'm going to the CWA.' Then I joined in March 2006, on my birthday. I was pregnant at the time and, with the CWA, they're so friendly and lovely. They're always there. Oh, I'm getting emotional even just thinking about it. Like, when my son, David, was little, it was a difficult time for me. I don't know if I had depression or whatever but, being without my mum and having moved over to Australia and everything else, some days it'd all get too much for me and I'd stand there and I'd cry and they'd hug me. It was just like having an extra group of aunties, and I'm really a homely, family person.

So having all these women there chatting away I felt so close to them. And you can tell them things honestly. Because they're not just people who have been parents, some are grandparents as well and you don't feel judged or anything. It's like words from the wise. They say, 'Oh, don't worry, that's happened to me many times.' They're so reassuring and kind and there's never any pressure from them to do anything.

It's so lovely just being here in Wandering and belonging to the CWA. At present I'm the Branch Treasurer. Some Branches organise their meetings to be quite formal and run to the minute whereas, at the Wandering meetings, we'll be talking about something and it's, 'Oh, did you see that on the telly,' and it goes off into a tangent. So now we have a lunch before our meeting and that helps to get the chat out of the way.

But there's such a feeling of community. I suppose it's part of the CWA's ethic to be wise with your resources and include everybody, so whenever we do an event we try to include every member of our community. We've started to do a Market Day three or four times a year where, for example, CWA can earn money and other different organisations can be involved too. And people come in off the farms so, during the dry, when the guys are waiting for rain, everybody's all there together. I'm also the president of the playgroup and they get involved too. It's a real community thing and that's really nice to see because, back in England, Wickford was obviously a community too but I was never a part of that sort of community. I was part of a family and part of a group of friends, whereas here I'm part of the whole community.

At the moment I'm the youngest member in Wandering Branch but I've never thought of it as being an old person's thing and I'd really like to promote CWA to a younger audience because, as I say, 'It's the young ones of today who are going to be the CWA members of tomorrow.' And actually, it's been approved by CWA State Council for me to go ahead and do a children's CWA cook book where the kids can make simple things and be all proud of themselves; even make a dinner so that Mum hasn't got to cook meals every night.

So that was my pathway into CWA, all the way from Wickford, in Essex, England, to Wandering, Western Australia, Australia.

Heather Kerr
Oaklands, New South Wales

I got into CWA very easily. In fact, I totally grew up with it. My mum was a founding member of Oaklands Branch, a tiny town, about sixty-five kilometres north of Corowa, which is on the Murray River. We owned a farm and back then, because there was very little else for women to get socially involved in around the area, when they first formed the Branch, just about every woman in the district joined. They had something like a hundred and fifty members. Then, because we owned a townhouse in Corowa, we used to go in there a lot and as a child I can remember going with Mum to CWA in Corowa. Interestingly enough, even though the township of Corowa is on the New South Wales side of the border, the Corowa CWA actually belonged to CWA Victoria, so I don't know how that works.

All our family were great needleworkers. My mum, my sister and myself, we're all artistic and we all sew. At an early age I was even making my own doll's clothes. My sister made a lot of my clothes then later on I started making them myself. Everything we had in our house was handmade. If Mum hadn't made it, my sister had made it and if my mum and my sister hadn't made it, I probably did, and if Mum, my sister or myself hadn't made it then our ironing lady had made it. That was yet another thing that inspired me: we had an ironing lady who made the most beautiful ensembles for my little dolls. So those were the influences that were around me and these days I'm a dressmaker by trade.

Oddly, with my mum, though she did embroidery before she married, she didn't afterwards. I don't know exactly why she stopped but she had some beautiful pieces. Though I imagine having six children and a large farmhouse to run, with at least six adults plus the children to cook for each day, may have had a lot to do with it. She was a remarkable woman. During the war, she was a lieutenant — a trained nursing sister and midwife — caring for the men returning from the Middle East and during the night shift she would catch a few minutes when it was nice and quiet to do her embroidery. She even used to pay my CWA Junior Membership and, during my teens, I remember how I'd do a piece of embroidery and she'd say, 'Oh that's great, we'll have that for the CWA exhibition.'

Then after I'd grown up, I left home and went to Sydney for a few years. Mum always had my membership paid up, so when my marriage failed, and I came back to Oaklands, I naturally fell into CWA. At that time, I was on my own with a fourteen-month-old boy and our lives centred around CWA. I just loved it. I'd go down there and work in their garden or I'd be at a meeting or be doing something. I built a house in town and stayed there for a long time before moving to Berrigan, then to Corowa. But I've always belonged to Oaklands Branch.

With the gardens, CWA shared a building with the local pre-school. There was a large outdoor area that we tried to keep nice for the children and we fenced it in so they'd have somewhere to play. Then there was the front garden. I'm a great gardener, as is my dad, and we re-landscaped all the front garden. Dad did all sorts of things. It was strictly a flower garden. My days were full of CWA and that's the way they've continued to be because there's something for everyone in CWA. I always say, 'Join CWA and see the world,' because I've been to heaps of places with them: Tasmania, down to Bendigo. I went to Perth just recently. Gundagai. I'm going to go to Jindabyne. Albury. All around the state. You just wouldn't have the opportunity otherwise. It just wouldn't happen.

So there. I'm afraid I don't have a really riveting CWA story, though there is something that I've always remembered: it was when I was very young, perhaps about ten or twelve, and I remember my mum taking me to a very elderly CWA member in

Albury. Her name was Mrs Morley and she had a house full of the most exquisite needlework. You name it, she did it: embroidery, the lot. Everybody knew Mrs Morley for her work.

Now, do you know what petit point is? It comes from the French words meaning 'small point' and it's one of the most versatile of stitches used in embroidery. It's a technique where you do double the amount of stitches per square inch, which makes for a finer effect. So when you're doing your normal tapestry you can highlight something, like skin or perhaps a flower. Anyhow, when we arrived at Mrs Morley's, there she was working on a little oval petit point. The subject would've only been about three or four inches. It was like a tapestry in miniature and she was doing it with the largest magnifying glass I'd ever seen. Just huge it was. But, oh, it was one of the most beautiful pieces of work I'd ever seen. I've never forgotten it.

Joan Kesson
Lucaston, Tasmania

I grew up in south-eastern Tasmania, in the Huon Valley region. My family owned an apple orchard and I've been in CWA for fifty years. The Branch I belong to is Lucaston Branch and even though I now live in Berridale, a northern suburb of Hobart, I still drive down to Huonville on the first Monday of each month for our meeting. On a fine day it takes three quarters of an hour, and then a bit longer if it's wet. Mind you, the road's not as bad as it used to be. Things have changed over the years, as does life. But we try not to stand still. We try to keep up with things.

I went to Lucaston Primary School though, in my day, it was known as a state school. We had about fifty pupils from Grade 1 to Grade 6 and we were all in the one room with the headmaster and a class monitor. Then, when they opened the Area School in Huonville, all those outlying small schools, like Lucaston, closed down and we all went to Huonville. Even our school building ended up at the Area School where it was used as an art building.

As for CWA, I grew up with it. Lucaston Branch was established back in 1949 and my mother joined in 1951 and she remained a staunch member until she passed away. Had she still been alive, she would've now been one hundred and four. As you may gather, my mother was very passionate about her CWA and I followed in her footsteps. I joined in 1960 and, back then, we all used to meet in people's homes. Then in the early 1980s I went to Canberra for ten years where I also remained involved and by the time I returned they were meeting at the CWA shop in Huonville.

In the 1960s, CWA had nearly six thousand members in Tasmania. There's a lot less now of course and, although I don't know the current official figure, just to give you some idea, when I first joined, CWA had twelve Branches in the Huon Valley Group.

But by the time I came back from Canberra, in the early 90s, many of those Branches were closing and the Huon Valley Group then combined with Kingsborough Group and became known as D'Entrecasteaux Group; D'Entrecasteaux being the Frenchman who sailed into the area when Tasmania was first settled. Anyway, with so many of the Branches closing, our Lucaston Branch now has gained some of those members from the other areas. There's some from the Grove Branch. Some come up from the aged care facility, Elder Care, and some joined us after the Geeveston Branch closed.

What makes CWA so special for me is all the great work it does. When I first joined we were basically considered to be just a 'tea and scones' association in the eyes of the general public. But what many don't realise is the huge amount of work that goes on in the background. We've always been involved in many community activities, like show societies. And we still are. At the Huon Agricultural Show, the CWA ladies act as judges and stewards in both the Women's and the School's Section. The Women's Section covers all the handicraft and the cooking. Then, with the School's Section, we invite students to display their work and we judge all that. There's also youth sections for cooking and handicrafts.

As well as that we support the local hospital and there's the Baby Box, which is run through our Tasmanian State Head Office. Baby Boxes are parcels of nappies and some of the other necessities that we make up for newborn babies and their mothers who are perhaps struggling. We also make tiny outfits for all the prem-babies that are born in Tasmania — yes, all — and we've made bunny rugs and things like that for the children's section of the hospital. As far as our international efforts go, we collect old school books and pens, pencils, rulers and other items to send over to the Pacific Islands to help with the children's education there.

Another of my passions is State Handicraft, and then there's Choral and Drama. With Choral and Drama, in the early days, we often used to hold concerts in the Huon Valley area. Both my mother and I were very involved in that. My mother did elocution at school and she also encouraged me in that area and we'd quite often go down to Elder Care and do little skits and recite poetry for the residents. My mother had a wonderful memory and when she'd recite things like 'The Sentimental Bloke' she'd hand me the book and say, 'Cue me if I need it.' But she never needed it. Ever. She was spot on. So those are some of the things we did back in the 1960s and 70s.

Then at a more personal level, unfortunately, I've been widowed twice and I must say that it's been the support of CWA, along with my involvement in the community and the church, that has really given me the strength to get on with my life. Because, sometimes, after something like that happens, people can find it extremely difficult to continue. And in my case, the first time I was widowed, I had four very young children — ranging from fifteen months to eight years old — and, mind you, back in those days there was not the government support and so forth that they have these days. I was still only young and I had to work to raise and support my children. As well as that, I continued with my CWA and church commitments, plus I was coaching six hockey teams for the school and two hockey teams after school.

Even so, through tragedy and all, I still consider that life's been very rewarding and a lot of that's due to the support of CWA and the care and friendship of its members. In fact, I'd venture to say, I've received far more than I've been able to give.

Maria Keys
Condamine-Arubial, Queensland

I actually grew up in Brisbane, so I'm a city girl. For my primary education I went to a little convent school at Ekibin, called St Elizabeth's. Then for high school I went to another Catholic girl's school called Our Lady's. That was at Annerley, which is a suburb on the south side of Brisbane. Following that I went to the Brisbane Kindergarten Teacher's College and became a teacher and from there I got a position as a Year 1–2 teacher at St Joseph's in Chinchilla. Chinchilla is about three-and-a-half hours west of Brisbane and it was while I was there that I met my husband-to-be, Paul.

Paul grew up on a property just south of Chinchilla, at Condamine, and after we were married that's where I shifted to. At that time we were growing wheat and we had sheep. But the seasons changed somewhat, so we got out of sheep and there also wasn't much profit to be made in cropping. We're mostly into cattle at the moment and we grow forage through winter and summer to help see them through. It's been a little hard of late. We've been in drought for the last three years and many of our dams have gone dry and, even though we've had nearly three inches in this past week, thanks to ex-cyclone Olga, we still haven't had that big storm rain to fill the dams.

Still, we're a bit fortunate in as much as there's been a couple of flows down the river and we do have rainwater tanks, here on the house and the sheds as well. But we mostly rely on bore water for the stock. Now I don't know if you know but this area is also sort of in the middle of a very prosperous coal-seam gas industry. What they do is they drill underground and pump the methane gas out but, as they do that, they also pump out a whole stack of underground water and it's become quite noticeable that the water pressure from our stock bores has diminished somewhat over the past few years. So that's where we're at and what we're up against at the moment.

Then, as to how I came to join CWA was that, when we married, Paul's parents were still living here on the farm and his mother was very involved and being very new to the district I didn't know too many Condamine people. Mind you, I was a little tentative because, back in my early twenties, when I was living in Chinchilla, I'd been involved in Rural Youth and some of the other young ladies had spoken about CWA in not too favourable terms. I really don't know why that was because I didn't know any CWA members myself, personally. Perhaps CWA was perceived to be an 'older person's' organisation by the younger ladies. Anyway, I went along to a few of their social gatherings with Paul's mother and I quite enjoyed it even though I didn't join, initially, because I had two littlies. But it did give me the opportunity to get to know some of the other women in the district and it wasn't until I was in my late twenties that I finally joined. At that time I was one of the youngest members in the Branch, then soon after I joined we were able to attract a few other mums with children, so that was really nice.

We're called the Condamine-Arubial Branch. It's a double-barrelled name. Where the Arubial came from was that Arubial was quite a large property in the district. It even had a school and a library and a School of Arts hall and there was a number of homes and cottages. It was the ladies of that property who initiated the Arubial CWA Branch and they used to meet in the School of Arts hall. Then later on, Condamine township set up a Branch as well and eventually the ladies from the Arubial Branch came in to Condamine.

When I joined, there were perhaps twenty or so members which over the years has dropped to as low as thirteen or fourteen. But in the last three years some younger ladies, with young families, have moved into the district and they've become members. We're quite a creative Branch. We do a lot of different and interesting things and so I think word just gets around. Then also, as the women move into the district, we invite them along so that they can meet some of the locals. We have lunches or craft days or different things and they join from there. So at present we're back to around twenty members, which is nice and comfortable, and we've got a good solid core group to call on if need be.

As for special moments, there's a few things I suppose but, personally, for me, CWA have a Country Woman of the Year competition and a couple of years ago I was very fortunate to be the state winner of that competition. There's a number of steps in the judging process. From Branch level we have a Divisional competition. Then the Division winners go on to the next stage, which is the Regional judging. We have three regions across Queensland — Northern, Central and Southern — and if you happen to be successful at the Regional judging you then go on to State judging. At all levels the judges are looking for people who have a broad knowledge of Queensland CWA. Plus there's the member's achievements within the organisation. How well we present ourselves. We're also judged on general knowledge, state politics, geography and on our practical knowledge. You know, we might get asked some way out question about how to get out of being bogged in a sand dune. That sort of thing. So being selected as a Queensland CWA's Country Woman of the Year, yes, that was certainly a highlight.

Then I'm also rather proud of some of the things we've done as a Branch. This last year we celebrated International Rural Women's Day, here at Condamine, and we were very fortunate to have the Queensland Governor, Penelope Wensley, attend, along with over a hundred ladies who came from all corners. That was a special day. We had a lunch where Penelope Wensley spoke about her travels and rural women worldwide. We had Jennie Hill who's our State Vice-President, Southern Region. She spoke about Queensland CWA. But basically it was a day to focus on rural women and some of things CWA does to help those less fortunate, not just here in Australia but also how we can help those women in underdeveloped countries as well. And for me in particular that was another highlight because I'd only been President of the Condamine-Arubial Branch for less than twelve months. So it was quite a big deal because I really don't think CWA promotes itself well enough and, if more women were made aware of just what we do and how many people we help, I'm sure we'd attract many, many more members.

Scones, Buns, Pikelets, Tea Cakes and Loaves

Baking Powder (homemade)
CWA NSW

8 oz cream of tartar
7 oz bicarbonate of soda
2 oz tartaric acid

Mix well, pass through a sieve 3 times. Use 2 teaspoonfuls to 1 lb flour.

Hot Cross Buns
Mrs E. J. Kay, Smithton, CWA Tas

1 oz compressed yeast
½ pint milk
2 oz sugar
1 lb plain flour
1 teaspoon salt
1 oz butter

3 oz sultanas
2 oz currants
2 oz chopped peel
1 egg
A little cinnamon

Crumble yeast finely, add milk (warmed to blood heat) with sugar, and add 1 teaspoon flour. Cover and stand in warm place for 15 minutes. Sift flour and salt, rub in butter, add balance of sugar and washed and dried fruit and peel. Beat the egg and mix with yeast and milk. Make a well in centre of dry ingredients. Pour in liquid, work dry ingredients in from the sides until all is absorbed and a soft dough has been formed. Knead well on a floured board, cover basin, and stand in a warm place for 1½ hours until well risen. Knead again, divide into 24 portions, mould each into bun shape and place on a warm greased tray, mark with a cross on top of each with a knife. Leave in a warm place for 15 minutes for further rising. Bake in hot (200°C) oven for 15–20 minutes. While still hot, glaze with hot milk and sugar, dust with cinnamon and return to oven for a few minutes.

Jubilee Loaf

Mrs T. O'Callaghan, St Leonards, CWA Tas

1½ cups self-raising flour

¼ teaspoon salt

1 teaspoon sugar

1 dessertspoon butter

1 egg

½ cup milk

1 cup sultanas and currants

Little lemon peel

Mix flour, salt and sugar and rub in butter. Beat egg and add with milk, add fruit last, mixing well. While still hot, pour on 2 tablespoons icing sugar mixed with milk and water and sprinkle with coconut.

Jumping Johnnies

CWA NSW

Whisk well together 3 eggs and 2 tablespoons sugar, add grated rind of lemon, ½ cup milk, 2½ cups self-raising flour. Fry teaspoonfuls in boiling fat, roll in icing sugar and eat hot or cold. Johnnies will turn themselves when cooked on one side if there is enough fat.

Nut and Raisin Loaf

Mrs D. Mathews, Longley, CWA Tas

1 cup raisins

1 cup sugar

1 cup water

2 oz butter

½ cup nuts

1 heaped teaspoon bicarb soda

2 tablespoons self-raising flour

2 cups plain flour

2 heaped teaspoons baking
    powder

Place raisins, sugar, water, butter and nuts in saucepan and bring to boil for 4 minutes. Stir in soda. Leave to cool then add flour and baking powder. Bake ½ hour in moderate (180°C) oven.

Pikelets

Mrs P. Cairns, Winnaleah, CWA Tas

Beat 2 eggs and 4 tablespoons sugar till very thick and creamy, add, alternately, 1 cup milk and 2 cups flour (sifted with 2 teaspoons cream tartar and 1 teaspoon bicarb soda). Blend well and drop small spoonfuls on hot griddle or electric hot plate. When bubbles begin to rise, turn with a knife and cook other side. A tablespoon melted honey added to mixture gives a nice flavour.

Potato Cakes
CWA NSW

1 lb mashed potatoes	1 oz butter
2 oz flour	Enough milk to mix into
Salt	smooth paste

Mix all ingredients together. Roll out ¾ inch thick, cut into circles and bake on a greased oven sheet for about 15 minutes, split open, butter and eat while hot.

Scone Making Hints
CWA NSW

1) Dough too dry produces tough looking scones.

2) Dough too wet causes scones to spread.

3) Liquid added slowly and not mixed evenly causes scones to be leathery.

4) Beware of baking too slowly (tough) or too quickly (inside soggy).

5) Place scones on cake cooler when cooked.

6) Do not cut with knife. This makes scones doughy.

7) Do not pack when hot.

Drop Scones and Flap Jacks
CWA NSW

1 egg	1½ oz sugar
½ cup milk	Pinch of salt
4 oz self-raising flour	

Beat egg well, add milk, mix in other ingredients. Bake on a griddle using about a dessertspoon for each scone. Place on dish when cooked and pile up.

Scones Plain
CWA NSW

1 lb flour
Salt
3 teaspoons baking powder
1 tablespoon butter
½ pint of half milk and half water

Sift dry ingredients together, rub in butter with the tips of the fingers. Mix with milk and water, lightly with a knife, to a smooth dough. Roll out dough ½ inch thick, cut into rounds, bake in a quick (200°C) oven 7–10 minutes.

Scones Savoury
Mrs H. E. Heard, Dysart, CWA Tas

Sift together 2 cups plain flour, 2 teaspoons baking powder, 1 teaspoon salt, ½ teaspoon cayenne pepper, 2 teaspoons powdered onion, 1 pinch of celery salt. Rub in 2 oz butter and a good tablespoon of grated cheese. Chop finely 2 tablespoons parsley and add to dry ingredients. Mix thoroughly with milk, not too stiff. Cut into shapes and bake in hot (200°C) oven for 10 minutes. Grated onion may be used if powdered onion is unprocurable.

Sultana Loaf
Mrs A. E. Burke, Parattah, CWA Tas

2 cups wholemeal self-raising flour
1½ tablespoons butter
¾ cup brown sugar
1 cup sultanas
1 tablespoon chopped peel
½ teaspoon cinnamon
1 teacup sour milk
1 egg

Sift flour, rub in butter, add fruit, peel, cinnamon and sugar and add milk to beaten egg. Mix to a light dough and bake in moderate (180°C) oven 40–45 minutes.

Tea Cakes
CWA NSW

1½ cups self-raising flour
½ cup sugar
Good lump butter
Pinch of salt
A few raisins, dates or walnuts
Enough milk to make a stiff dough

Rub butter into the flour, salt and the sugar. Press into tin. Put almonds or walnuts and sprinkle a little sugar on top. Bake in fairly hot oven, 20–25 minutes. Will keep a week.

White Bread (basic)
CWA NSW

1½ lb flour
¾ pint of tepid water
2 tablespoons of homemade yeast
2 teaspoons of sugar
1 teaspoon salt

Sift and warm 1 lb of flour and make a well in the centre, pour yeast and water beaten to a cream into the flour and stir to a moist dough, beat well. Cover and allow to stand in a warm place until the dough doubles its size. This will take several hours. Turn on to a board and knead in the extra ½ lb of four and salt until dough is of even texture and will not stick to the hand. Do not use too much extra flour to make dough workable. Shape into loaves, put into greased tins, allow to rise in a warm place. When risen to size, cook in hot oven for the first half-hour and cooler part of oven to finish — 40 minutes in all. When finished the bread should give a hollow sound when tapped on the bottom.

Jane Kidd
Croydon, Queensland

Originally I came from a small cattle property, out near Roma, in south-eastern Queensland, between Taroom and Wandoan. My parents owned the place. By 'small' I mean it was only six thousand acres whereas, up here at Croydon, the cattle station my husband and I are now on is 61,500 hectares or, in other words, around about 152,000 acres. So there's a big difference. There were four of us children in our family and we did our schooling at a one-teacher school, out in the middle of nowhere. It wasn't even an actual town. One of the property owners donated some of his land to the government for the purposes of a school and so that's where they put it — out in the middle of a paddock. At first there were no buses so we were driven to school. But then, when I was ten and a bus service came in, I used to drive the car the seven miles from our house, down to meet up with the bus.

So that's a bit about my background. I then went to an all-girls Presbyterian boarding school in Toowoomba, called Fairhome College. Going from a one-teacher school out in the middle of a paddock to Fairhome College, I must say, was a bit of an eye-opener. It was pretty strict, you know; you'd just get dumped at the start of the year and we weren't allowed to speak to our parents for a month and, of course, phone calls weren't as easy to make as they are these days, with all the kids having mobile phones and all that. So it was a bit different. But I survived. Then at the end of Year 12 my father died and I went back on the property to help Mum out and in between I did courses on governessing and nannying in Brisbane and I also worked in some pre-schools, just on a voluntary basis.

Then in 1988 I got a job as a governess, on a property in the south-west of Queensland, about eighty kilometres east of

Windorah. I went there for two years and taught two children and, while I was out there, that's where I met my husband, Tom. Tom was on a property that is family owned, just to the west of Windorah, near town. We met at the local pub or something. I mean, there wasn't too much else to do in Windorah. But there were a lot of young people there back in those days and so it was an enjoyable time. We got married in 1991 and now we've got five children — four boys and a girl. But that's it. I've called a full stop at five children.

So we married and we lived on the family property near Windorah, then in 1999, Tom, his father and his brother bought this place just twenty-five kilometres out of Croydon, up in the Gulf of Carpentaria, and so we'd moved up here by Christmas '99. As I said, it's 61,500 hectares and we've got probably around four thousand head of cattle here at the moment. We were flooded out last year, when that extreme weather went through the whole Gulf. That was an experience, that was. Even parts of the house went under, and everything.

As for the CWA, I did actually know about it when I was a kid because my grandmother, Marie Speed, was right up in the association. She was even a Queensland State President at one stage. She's dead now but she got an OBE because of all her work with CWA. And I still have family in CWA. But I didn't really get involved until four or five years after I got up here and that was only after I found out they were going to close the Croydon Branch down because they didn't have the members to keep going. So I basically joined to boost the numbers and, even now, there's only about five or six of us. So it's a bit of a struggle and we only meet a couple of times a year whereas your regular Branch might meet every month or so. So I guess we mightn't seem like we're the most with-it Branch. And, with only so few of us, we just manage to fill the committee positions of President, Secretary and Treasurer, then there's just a couple of extras. My good friend, who's from another property, and I are the youngest. We're in our forties and the others would be in their late fifties or in their sixties.

I mean, you mightn't think we do too much but we still do chook-wheels at the local pub every now and then and when the Poddy Dodgers Music Festival is on we do our usual coffee, tea and cakes and all that. We also have all the kids helping us, which is great. Like, our kitty's not very high but we do what we can and I do enjoy it when we do our fundraising, especially at the Poddy Dodgers Festival. Everyone loves coming into town for that. It's usually held in the September holidays so that all the children in the area, who are at boarding school, can come along.

The Poddy Dodgers started off as a big music festival but over the years it's become more of a local show where all the property owners and the ringers and the women and kids come in from off the stations and have a go at all the activities. Like, they have what's called the Stockman's Challenge. That's where you get in a team of four people and you contest different events: say, you might have to build a fence or roll some bales of hay or eat a cold pie and, if you're a man, drink a warm beer, and the kids drink a warm soft drink. There's also 'rolling the swag' competitions and 'boiling the Billy'. They're all timed events, and bands play music at night and you have a bit of a fete with stalls in the morning, which is when CWA does the morning tea or whatever.

So that's a real fun time and it gets the community together. But as I said, there's only a handful of us in the Croydon CWA and, just like some of our other members, I'm out here on the cattle station and, because it's a family business, we all have to pitch in. Then with the children being on Distance Education, I also teach the kids. Well I'm only teaching the one now because the other three boys are at boarding school and the little girl's not old enough yet. But even so, that takes up most of your day. So trying to do all that and fit in with everyone else, who's also busy doing all the things they have to do, well, to even organise a meeting it can become quite a big issue.

But I would like to see more younger people get involved in CWA and see more community stuff going on. Like, in Croydon, there's not many arts and crafts or those sorts of things happening. Yes, so that would be my wish: to try and make more people aware of CWA and to let them know that we do a lot more than just make tea and cook cakes and that you're able to put back into the community. So we're well and truly open for new members, especially now that one of our ladies, who's recently turned seventy, announced that she'd done her time and has decided to pull out.

Barbara Kregor
Wattle Hill, Tasmania

I was born in Sorell, in south-eastern Tasmania, and I live on a farm about twelve kilometres up the road at Wattle Hill. I come from the Gatehouse line and there's a bit of family history there because there were four brothers, George, Silas, William, and Clement Gatehouse. They were from Dorset, England, and George, who was the eldest, he was sent out to New South Wales as a convict where he somehow made some money. He may have been pardoned or whatever. Following that, he returned to England for a while before coming out to Tasmania where he did all sorts of things like buying a lot of property in Hobart and starting our state's first brewery. Then George's three brothers, Silas, William and Clement, they came out to Tasmania later on as free settlers.

My branch of the family came from Silas Gatehouse. Silas was my great-great-grandfather and he received a land grant at Wattle Hill in 1824. The fifty acres that I now live on was part of a much larger acreage that had belonged to Silas. I think the original allotment was only about two hundred and fifty acres but he kept on getting land grants until it eventually grew to about two thousand acres and he had about twenty or so tenant farmers working the property. Now, I'm not exactly sure how the tenant farmer business worked but I'd presume that Silas allowed them to farm a block of land in return for rent. There's actually a record of all the tenant farmers dated 1854 which was the year that Silas returned to England.

So there's a bit of a history lesson. Then I was born in at the cottage hospital at Sorell and I lived on the farm at Wattle Hill and I started primary school at a little place called Cherry Tree Opening. But when the Area School at Sorell opened in 1939, all those little schools closed down and we went in there. Following that, I went to Ogilvy High. At that stage Ogilvy was called a 'Commercial' school. There were three lines of schooling. If you wanted to do typing and office work and that sort of thing you went to a Commercial school. If you wanted to do the technical trades, you went to the Tech, and if you wanted to go to university you had to go to high school in Hobart. You could also transfer from one type of schooling to the other if you wanted to.

Then, when I was about sixteen or so, I started as an office worker with Optical Annex. This was during war time and Optical Annex was run by the Ministry of Munitions and they made things like prism lenses and prisms for range finders and camera lenses. Up until then, the only place that the Allies could get these special type of prisms and lenses was from Germany and, of course, that was now out of the question. So Professor McCauley, from the university in Tasmania, he said he'd be prepared to take it on. Originally the powers-that-be thought otherwise but Professor McCauley insisted — 'Yes, we can do it' — and so Optical Annex started up in Tasmania. It employed three hundred people and a lot of those were students who were doing science degrees and weren't yet old enough to join the forces. My husband served his apprenticeship there. Originally he wanted to join the navy but they wouldn't let him because the work he was doing at Optical Annex was considered to be an 'essential service' to the war effort. Other occupations were in the same boat; people like farmers and that. So there's some more history.

Now to my involvement in CWA. In a way, I grew up with it. My mother was a foundation member of the Sorell Branch, which was formed in 1936. CWA ran the library in the early days. Actually, a lot of the libraries were started by the CWA as a fundraiser. People would donate books and then you'd pay a penny or tuppence or whatever to borrow a book. Child Health was also run by CWA. Actually, when the Sorell Memorial Hall was built in 1954 they incorporated the CWA room and the Child Health

Clinic and the mums used to bring their children in to get them weighed and checked over. Of course, all that folded later when the government took over child health. But we've still got the room there. We paid for that years ago. Though, unfortunately, in 1967 the bushfires went through and we lost all our records between 1936 and, well, I've still got one minute book from about 1954. But we lost everything else and I'm currently trying to research some of that past history.

As for special moments, something that stands out was when a member of ours, a local doctor's wife, was a dancer and an actress who'd studied under Chekhov in Russia. She was actually Latvian and apparently she and her husband and their first two daughters had a horrific time getting out through Germany. Anyway, they first migrated to South Australia then eventually they came to Sorell through some sort of Commonwealth Government medical scheme.

I just forget her name at the moment. She was actually a member at Sorell before I joined and she'd started a CWA drama group. Then one time they were rehearsing a play and one of the women's husbands died and she had to drop out. So they came to me and said, 'Would you do it?' Oh, well, I thought, I suppose I'll give it a go. So I did and we ended up putting on little sketches and concerts and plays all over southern Tasmania. We used to go to a lot of nursing homes and, back then, Choral and Drama was a big part of CWA, so we'd enter CWA competitions. But, oh, she was absolutely marvellous. She was just so good at movement and at make-up and performance and all that. That's right, her name was Otilija (Leah) and he was Arturs. But, oh, they were wonderful, wonderful days.

Marie Lally AM
Lock, South Australia

I'm a country girl: born at Blythe, in South Australia, and reared at Hilltown — in the mid-north, between Clare and Spalding. For my early education I attended the one-teacher school at Hilltown. There were just the three others in my class and we went all the way through primary school together. I've always been on a farm. I've never lived anywhere else except for when I went to boarding school. That was at Loreto College in Adelaide and I lived down there for four years. I can't say I enjoyed the school curriculum side of it but I thoroughly enjoyed the company of the other kids and I also studied things that I much preferred like speech craft, dramatic art and music. Of course, in those days a woman was expected to go into nursing or work in an office. But really, my ambition was to go home and be a farmer with my father and, after I'd finished my education, even though I did go back to the city once a fortnight to continue my creative studies, that's what I did — I helped my father on the farm.

And I've never got away from it because, what did I do? I married a farmer, didn't I. My husband came from a district close by called Hill River. We had two daughters and after ten years we bought a semi-cleared bush block on central Eyre Peninsula, near Lock. And if you know the Clare area, there couldn't be anywhere more different. In fact, people were saying, 'So you're going pioneering are you?' and my reply was, 'No, we're going for a harder life,' and we've certainly had it.

Then after a year or so my husband said he'd like a bit more scrub to clear in the same area and we went and had a look at this 14,000 acre block, which we bought, and, with me on one tractor, my husband on another, and a chain strung out between us, we cleared four thousand acres. My husband, of course, had the stronger tractor so when I got stuck on a stump my tractor's front wheels would rear up into the air. So I was quite pleased when the state government put an end to the clearing of any more scrub.

As to my connections with CWA: my mother always wanted to be a CWA member and when she retired and moved into Clare, she was right into it. But she so much wanted me to be a member. 'Oh, Marie,' she'd say, 'you really should join CWA.'

We were still out on the farm near Clare at that stage and I'd say, 'Mum, I haven't got the time. I've got two little children and I'm busy milking cows and feeding pigs and doing all the things you have to do to try to make a living.'

In the end, I gave in and Mum paid my subscription for the first two years and I remember going along and the dear ladies, they welcomed me so much. Then after we'd decided to go over to the Eyre Peninsula, Mum looked up a map and she worked out that the closest CWA Branch to our bush block was just south of Lock, at Murdinga; Lock being the main town in the area. So she transferred my subscription over to the Murdinga Branch and after we'd arrived, the first lady to visit me was a neighbour. 'I've come to take you to CWA,' she said, and I saw that as the hand of friendship coming through the bush. So I went along. At that time they would've only had a dozen or so members. But Murdinga was just a small district, really. There was only a hall, tennis courts, silos, and that's about it, and we met in the little hall.

But with my children going to school in Lock and with the sport and everything it was getting more and more difficult to get to Murdinga for their CWA meetings and, after a couple of years, the Murdinga ladies transferred my membership to Lock. By then Mum was quite ill back over in Clare and I was spending a lot of time going from the Eyre Peninsula to Clare, which was no mean feat, I can tell you. It's a six-hour drive each way, there and back, and so I wasn't getting to CWA that often. Then there just happened to be a State CWA Oratory Competition coming up where you had to give a ten minute talk about a great Australian woman and the Branch President said to me, 'Would you go in the Oratory Competition?'

Anyway, because of the amount of money my parents had spend on educating me in speech craft and such, I though it'd make Mum happy so I said, 'Okay then, just as long as I can talk about Dawn Fraser.'

Well I won the Branch round because I was the only one in it. Then I went to Group level. I think there was fourteen in that and I came out the winner. Then I won the Divisional Section and I went to the State Conference for the final and came out the winner there. Little did I know that as soon as I walked off the stage I was a marked woman. 'Oh, you must be our Group President,' they said, which I did, then I went on to Divisional President, to State Officer. I was State President during the late 1990s. Then a great friend of mine said, 'Why don't you stand for National President?'

Anyway, I was nominated by the South Australian administration. That was supported at our State Conference level. In the end, two of us were vying for National President and I got the nod. It's a three-year term and you get to choose your Secretary and Treasurer and I ran the National Office of CWA from my farmhouse near Lock. It was a very big change because, to me, it hadn't seemed too long ago that I'd got up and spoke about Dawn Fraser at my little CWA Branch in Murdinga. Now I was speaking on behalf of 39,000 women members throughout Australia and representing CWA on national committees dealing with health and education issues and the ACCC [Australian Competition and Consumer Commission] and the Taxation Department. I was also dealing with federal ministers and, believe me, CWA is held in very, very high standing at federal level. There's no doubt about that.

I remember one of my first experiences as National President was when I went to a Continuum of Care Conference at Darwin where I was invited to speak to all the various health professionals, and here's me, a farmer from central Eyre Peninsula. So I just told them what I thought worked and what I thought didn't. I don't know whether it was what they wanted to hear or not but that's what they got. I was then asked to give a speech at the National Health Alliance Conference at Canberra. I polished that one up a bit and spoke on a topic very close to my heart because at Lock we just have the one medical centre which is run by a nursing sister. We have no hospital and the nearest doctor is fifty miles away at Cummins. Anyhow, my granddaughter, Donna, took really ill this particular day. Her vision was blurred so her mother, Caroline, took her to the nursing sister and the nursing sister said, 'I think she's got meningitis.' She said, 'Don't go home. Go straight to Cummins. I'll ring the doctor and tell him what I think and he'll be waiting for you.'

So that's what they did. They drove the fifty miles to Cummins and the doctor said, 'Yes, I think the nursing sister is right,' and he contacted the flying doctor who arrived not long after. In fact, it was only two and a half hours from when Caroline took Donna to the nursing sister at Lock to when she arrived at the Royal Children's Hospital in Adelaide. It all worked like clockwork. Perfectly. But when Donna got the children's hospital, she was left out in the corridor with a sign on her which said, 'Kid from the country with the flu', and she was ignored. So by about three-thirty in the morning she was on fire with fever and that's when a nurse decided to go above her superiors and she rang the doctor and said, 'If you don't get in here immediately this kid's going to die.'

The doctor arrived not long after and he was able to relieve the pressure on Donna's brain and, luckily, she lived. She's great now. But everything worked beautifully in the country, right up until she got to the city. So I told them that story and that sat them all up and got them thinking. Actually, one of the flying doctor people came up after and thanked me for what I'd said.

So that's just one little episode of what's happened in my time as National President and, for my service to rural women over the years, I've received the AM. But it's been a long, long journey and the friendships of our CWA members has always been top hole, as has the support from those woman who have fostered me throughout. And, just to think, I might not have achieved any of that if my mother hadn't originally paid my subscription and made me join. Still, you've got to take your opportunities as they arrive, don't you? And I must say that I couldn't have done what I have done without my husband's support, and that's been there all the way through.

Janette Mason
Tatura, Victoria

I live in Victoria but I grew up in Southport, on Queensland's Gold Coast, so you might say I'm a long way from what was once called home. How it all happened was that I was working for an accountant up there and I went on a P&O cruise with some of my girlfriends and that's where I met my husband-to-be, Tony. He was there with some of his mates. It sounds very romantic doesn't it? The only trouble was that Tony lived in Victoria. In those days it was too expensive to use the telephone so we wrote letters to each other and we married about nine months later.

I was nineteen by then and I moved to down here, to Tatura, in the Goulbourn Valley. Tony was a dairy farmer so to go from working in an accountant's office on the Gold Coast, to a family farm in Victoria, was a big eye-opener, to say the least. Everything was totally different — the culture, the weather — and to move somewhere where you hardly knew anyone and you had no special girlfriends, that was a huge thing, and that's where CWA came in. I'd heard of CWA before I moved to Tatura but I didn't know much about it. In Southport they had 'restrooms', as they were called in those days, where the older ladies could go and have a cup of tea and use the bathroom. I guess they also had their meetings there. But that's all I knew. Then, here, in Tatura, the CWA girls were my age so we were classified as 'the younger group'. We're known as the Rodney Branch. Rodney being the name of the shire before it amalgamated. We met once a month of an evening, and I've now been a member for thirty-one years. Not like some of the other Branches did, we decided not to take our children along because we wanted it to be our small 'escape', so to speak. As long as the baby was asleep, Tony didn't mind. It was our CWA girls' little couple of hours, once a month, and that was very important for us.

Within Rodney Branch I've held many positions: Minutes Secretary, Secretary — many times — President, Vice-President and Treasurer. From there I went on to become a Group President. We have ten Branches in our Goulbourn Valley West Group. We're on the western side of Shepparton, and Tatura would probably be the central point. You can get to any of the other Branches within a half hour's drive, which is really good. And now I'm one of the State Vice-Presidents. There are four of us with the same title of Vice-President and we all share the work load. Above us is the Deputy President, then the State President.

Friendship was definitely one of the important reasons why I joined CWA in the first place, and it still is. We still have some of the girls from back then and a few of those were members even before I joined. Rodney Branch is now forty-three years old. We have twenty-six members so we're still quite strong; because you do hear stories of Branches struggling to exist and attracting the younger ones and keeping them is one of our biggest concerns. As to how we're going to solve that, I don't know. We have had younger members but they tend to move on with their work and life. When I say 'younger' I mean if we could get some thirty-five-year-olds that would be wonderful. But the structure of family life has changed and now women don't stay at home as much as they used to. These days, because of the economic side of things, even if you live on a farm you still have to go out and find other work, which is what I do. I'm practice manager for a group of anaesthetists in Shepparton. Basically, a practice manager makes sure that everything's done and organised and the accounts are up-to-date. And even though our son's on the farm now and we've moved into town, Tony still goes out there every morning and doesn't come back until dark, every night. But that's dairy farming.

Then as for special moments: well, the absolute highlight for me, throughout the whole of my CWA career, was when I won the Book of Honour. That was in 2008, and it's an award for the winning State Secretary's Report of the year. Well, every Branch Secretary has to write a report of the year's activities and the best one at Group level is selected and then that goes on for judging at State level. The award is given to the Branch who best represents all for which CWA stands. We'd had a very busy year in 2008, with it being the first year of the drought in our area so, yes, winning the Book of Honour would definitely be my greatest achievement. In fact, it was wonderful.

Val Maynard
Cobden, Victoria

These days I live between Warrnambool and Colac, in a town called Cobden. It's not terribly far from Port Campbell, which is quite well known because there's a National Park there. So it's down in the south-western area of Victoria. I'm currently our Group President and in our Group we've got Branches like Camperdown, Terang, Mortlake, Simpson, the Warrnambool Clubs and, of course, Cobden.

I was born in Casterton, actually, but my father was a baker and he'd buy a bakery somewhere and we'd stay there for a few years and then he'd think, That's enough, and he'd sell that bakery and buy another one somewhere else and off we'd go. So we lived in lots of different places in Victoria: we went from Casterton, down to Gippsland, to a little place called Cowwarr. Then we went up to Inglewood, to a bakery up there, and finally Dad decided he needed a career change and it was Mum's turn to earn the living so we went over to a little place called Dingee, in the central north of Victoria, where they bought a post office. Dingee is near Bendigo and that's where I finished off my schooling, in Bendigo.

Then after I married I wanted to buy a post office of my own. But back then the banks wouldn't lend money to a woman so Mum and Dad backed us and they mortgaged their place and we bought a post office over at Calivil, which is up past Bendigo, on the Pyramid Hill line. Of course, even then, it had to be in my husband's name. A woman couldn't own anything back in those days.

Anyhow, that's what we did and I ran the post office. It was only a little country post office — basically just a telephone exchange, really — one of those where you pushed in the plugs to connect people and it ran twenty-four hours a day. Of course, with having already worked at Mum and Dad's telephone exchange it was all quite easy for me and also there was no mail delivery service or anything attached to the business. Oh, a bag of mail did come into the post office and people came and got their own mail or they dropped off their mail, but we didn't deliver anywhere. Someone from somewhere else did that.

I found it really interesting because, in small places like that, if anything happens, the post office is the first point of contact. It's like the hub of the community. I remember when Mum and Dad were at Dingee there was a very bad train accident and because my father was on the telephone exchange at the time he was just about the first person to hear about it. And, of course, with knowing everyone in the district, as soon as the news came through, he automatically rang the local doctor and a local nurse and someone who had first aid. So there's those sorts of things then, on the other hand, you also get to know all the wonderful things that happen too, like if somebody had a baby or if someone was going to get married.

The township of Calivil was even smaller than Dingee. Other than the post office, there was only a store and a hotel and that was about it really. Oh, there was a school, but when they built the big East Loddon Consolidated School and once that happened, of course, all the little country communities lost their schools. But with East Loddon, I think someone gave the land to the government and so they decided to build a big school out in the middle of nowhere and bus the students in from all the local towns. They also built some houses out there for the teachers but really, most of them lived in Bendigo anyway and then they just drove out each day.

Then as to how I got to join CWA: well I didn't grow up with it because we were travelling about so much but, when we did settle down in the post office at Dingee, that's when my mum joined CWA. Lots of mums did back in those days. Then I joined when I was twenty. That was when I was in the post office at

Calivil. I'd had my first child by then and so I'd take him along to the meetings with me. And it was so good because all the CWA ladies were like second mothers to him, as they were to all my children. Because, in those days I was a very shy young married lady who didn't particularly know all that much about cooking or looking after children or anything and here were these lovely CWA ladies, they'd just take over and they'd look after the children and they'd look after you and they'd share their experiences and they'd give you such helpful advice. It was just wonderful. And so my children were very welcome there, which was very much unlike another certain place I shifted to where I was told that I'd be better off going to an Evening Branch rather than the day Branch because they didn't like having children there.

But thankfully that didn't happen at Calivil and I very much appreciated that. It was just wonderful what they did and, in particular, the confidence that they gave me in the years to come. Because many years later I went back to Calivil as Group President. It was their sixtieth birthday and I stood up and I congratulated the ladies and I told them how much CWA had meant to me, and some of them who remembered me as a very shy young woman, with my first baby and then the three other babies, they couldn't believe how I could just get up and say what I did with such confidence. And, well really, when I first joined I never dreamt I'd be able to do anything like that either. So that's just one of the things CWA has done for me. It's given me confidence.

Joyce McDonald
Myrtleford, Victoria

I grew up in Beechworth, a town in north-eastern Victoria. It was a quiet little place back in the 1940s and 50s. Beechworth CWA is about seventy years old now and my mother was a founding member, so I knew about CWA from when I was very young. Then after my schooling I worked for the Victorian Forest Commission and that's when a few of us girls decided to start up what was known as the Beechworth CWA 'younger set'. With most of us working, we met at night while the 'older set' met during the day. I remember us knitting jumpers, mittens, socks and balaclavas and gloves for the servicemen in World War Two, and we also made things like macramé camouflage nets.

Then after the war, whenever the fire brigade or the football team held an event we'd help with the catering and when we ran a dance they'd help us. To make the dance floor suitable to dance on, the boys would first scrape candles over the floor, then they'd attach bags to the bottom of a wooden box and one of us girls would sit in the box and the boys would pull us over the floor to polish it. That's how we got the dance floor nice and slippery. It was a time-consuming job but well worth it. In those days everybody seemed willing to help everybody else and so when the older ladies wanted help, we'd help them out. If there was a wedding or something, the older set took care of the cooking and we younger girls would wait on the tables. That's what happened in country communities in those days.

It was a wonderful life, and we used to have so much fun. Have you heard of 'tin kettling'? Well, when a married couple came home from their honeymoon, we'd make a supper and we'd collect sticks and empty kerosene tins — whatever would make noise — and we'd wait until they'd gone to bed and we'd go around and belt the tins until they let us in and we'd all have supper together. It was like a welcome home to the newlyweds.

I remember the time that one of our CWA girls married a footballer and when they got back from their honeymoon some of us girls and some of the footballer's mates decided to tin kettle them. The girl's father owned the cafe in the main street of Beechworth and the couple were staying there overnight. So we made cakes for supper and the boys organised some sticks and tins and off we went. It was a clear frosty night, about eleven o'clock. There was no late night closing in those days and so everyone had gone to bed. It was dead quiet and then we started this tin kettling out in the street. Next thing, the girl's father opened the upstairs window and shouted, 'Get the so-'n'-so out of here.'

'Open your cafe,' we called back. 'We've got food and we've come to welcome home the newlyweds.'

'No,' he said. 'Go home.'

Then the butcher from next door, he opened his second-storey window. 'Get out of here, you've woken the baby,' he said.

Next, the man from across the road yelled out, 'You've woken everybody in the street. I've called the police.' Little did he know that his son and a daughter were with us. Then when the policeman arrived he sided with us. 'If you open the cafe,' he said to the father, 'these young people will go in and have supper with the newlyweds and then they'll go home.'

'No way,' said the father. So then the policeman, he joined in with us. Bang, bang, bang, clatter, clatter, clatter until finally the girl's father gave in. He threw open the window and said, 'Okay, anything to stop the racket,' and he let us in.

So we eventually had our supper, which was enjoyed by all, and then we went home. But we must've made quite a noise because, in the morning, the lady who lived away up the hill was heard to say, 'Did you hear the awful noise last night. I wonder where it came from?'

But tin kettling was just good country fun. No damage done. So that's when I first joined CWA. Then I married in 1953 and

I left Beechworth and went to live in Myrtleford and I've been living there ever since. Myrtleford was only eighteen miles from Beechworth but the thing was, in those days, married woman weren't allowed to work in a government job. So I had to give up my job with the Victorian Forest Commission and, with my husband being a dairy farmer, I also gave up CWA to help milk the cows. Then our three daughters arrived and I didn't return to CWA until 1990, and I've been a member ever since. That's with the Myrtleford Branch and I've been their Branch Secretary, Branch Treasurer and Branch International Officer. Then in 1995 I was elected President of North-Eastern Group. I also held that position in 2000, 2003, then again in 2008. I'm currently in my last year as their Group President and, to be honest, I'll miss the action even though I'll still be involved at Branch level and will carry on as the treasurer of four other organisations in town. So I'll still be quite busy. But I'll still miss it.

As for memorable moments, I'd just like to say how forever grateful I am for the many happy years I have spent with the Country Women's Association, not only for having the chance to assist so many people in need but also for the lifelong friendships I've made over the years. To that end I was also involved in the bushfire recovery work. Unfortunately, in our area, we had two fatalities in the fires and fifteen homes were burnt down plus thousands of acres of pasture and miles of fences burnt. But being Group President, on behalf of CWA, as soon as I was allowed to enter the bushfire area I went around to visit those who'd been affected and I gave them a set of CWA recipe books and a food voucher. The food vouchers were only worth about three hundred dollars but still, it helped them purchase food and other necessities. It was a simple gesture that showed that we cared about them.

Then later on I visited all the farms that had suffered the losses of fencing, pastures and other property. In conjunction with the Victorian State Government, CWA prepared a form for the farmers to fill in and, through our network, Group Presidents went around from farm to farm asking the farmers if they wanted to fill the form in. The way it worked was that they could get a certain amount of assistance to help them repair things like their fencing. By 'assistance' I mean that they had to tell us which firms they were dealing with and then we'd make the cheque out, directly, to that firm on behalf of the farmer. By doing it that way we were confident that the money was going to the right cause and it also helped assist the firms as well.

Many thousands of dollars were given away. Other than government aid, a lot of money came in from CWAs in other states. Also, people from all over Australia donated money straight to our Victorian CWA Fire Appeal. That received a great response and I think it was because people trusted us to dispense the funds and, of course, with us being a volunteer organisation, they knew that none of their money went into paying wages or got tied up in all the red tape.

But I spent many days visiting farmers. I didn't make appointments. I just began at the top of the valley and worked my way down to each farmer, each house, and, oh, it was a heartbreaking experience. Harrowing. Everything was burnt out and so it was all sooty with the ash. And the smell, dear me. The first place I went into I thought, I don't think I can do this. But then I realised that these poor folk were just so glad to have someone come and offer them some help that I was happy to carry on. I remember at one place, I went through what remained of a front gate and I headed to a house that stood in the middle of burnt-out paddocks and out of the corner of my eye I caught sight of a billy goat. 'Oh, it's you, Billy,' I said, and he came after me. Yes, he chased me. I was just lucky that he was on a long chain. Then when I got to the house, the lady asked me if I'd like to come in and have a cup of tea.

'That would be lovely,' I said and when I sat down she said, 'Oh, you're sitting on the cat's chair.' And sure enough the cat came in and it jumped up on my knee, and, oh, it was so black from the fires that it left sooty marks all over my clothes.

Then at the next house a small dog bailed me up at a burnt-out gate and it wouldn't let me in until the owner came out. 'Don't worry,' he said, 'the dog won't bite.' And when I told him that I was going to visit the farmers further on down the valley he asked if I'd made an appointment with the next man.

'No, I haven't,' I said.

'Well, just be careful,' he said, 'and don't go inside the house because he has a licence to keep snakes and he lets them crawl around everywhere.'

So when I arrived at the fellow's house and he asked me in, I was very quick to tell him I was very busy and didn't have time.

At another place, two men were cutting some burnt trees that had fallen across a pathway so I sat on the trailer of burnt wood while the owner filled in the forms and the other chap came up and said, 'I think I know you.'

For some reason I also thought I recognised him from somewhere, too. We were both really black from the soot and ash and our clothes were filthy and so we had to introduce ourselves and it turned out that he was the Anglican priest who was there helping out.

'Oh, of course,' I said, because I'd seen him at funerals and that.

Anyhow, I spent a week going up hill and down dale, visiting farmers and, oh, the landscape was just black from the bushfires. It was so eerie and the smell was terrible. It must have been dreadful having to live with it all because I've had grown men cry on my shoulder. That's how devastating it was. And because their livelihoods were gone, one feller looked at me and said, 'I'm finished. I'm done.'

I said, 'No, you'll be right.'

Then next feller said, 'I'm gonna fix this. No fire's gonna stop my farm.'

Yes, so in many cases the good old Aussie spirit showed through. But you couldn't even begin to imagine what some of those farmers went through, and what they're still going through.

I'm absolutely surprised that some of these poor people still haven't, as yet, been able to find their way through all the red tape and rebuild. It's terrible. After twelve months one young couple still couldn't get permission to replace a shed on their property so that they could return there to live. They're still having to pay rent in town and, of course, they now also have to pay storage on all the furniture that's been donated to them to replace all the furniture they'd lost in the fires. It's just lucky that people have been giving them food, just to keep them going. Oh, there's been some terrible, terrible stories of the heartbreaks and the stresses and strains. There's even been marriage break-ups.

So that's mainly the CWA work I did after the bushfires. But one funny thing: one day I got a ring from an underwear firm in Melbourne. CWA had given them my name and they wanted to donate underclothing so they asked if I'd go round to all the ladies who'd been burnt out and get the sizes of their bras and knickers. Now, it's a bit uncomfortable to just pop in and ask people that sort of personal information but, anyhow, off I went and I did it and later on the lady from Melbourne rang me and I gave her all the sizes. Then not long after that, I got a call from one of the ladies who'd been burnt out. She said, 'I got a parcel today.'

'Oh, yes,' I said.

She told me that she'd received six bras, four chemises — little singlety things — and eight pair of knickers and, 'Oh,' she said, 'I'm going to give you a pair of knickers as a present.'

'Oh, yes?' I said.

'It's an orange G-string.'

'Oh,' I said, 'no thanks.' I said, 'I don't think an orange G-string would be quite my style.'

Large Cakes

Brownie

(Has taken many prizes at Dubbo Show)
CWA NSW

1 cup good dripping
1 cup brown sugar
2 eggs
1 large cup milk
1 cup plain flour
2 cups self-raising flour

1 teaspoon ground nutmeg
1 teaspoon cinnamon
Pinch salt
2 cups currants and sultanas
   mixed
Peel

Beat the dripping and sugar together till creamy, then add eggs one at a time, well beaten. Gradually add the milk and flour with spices and salt sifted together, then lastly the fruit. A little cut up peel may be added if liked. Bake in a greased dish 1¼ hours in a fairly hot (200°C) oven.

Butterscotch Cake

Mrs J. Martin, Sandy Bay, CWA Tas

1 cup light brown sugar
4 oz butter
1 teaspoon vanilla
   essence
2 eggs, separated

½ cup milk
1¼ cups self-raising flour
1 tablespoon golden syrup
½ teaspoon cinnamon

Cream butter and sugar, add yolks separately, beaten between. Stir in syrup, milk and essence, then add the dry ingredients. Beat egg whites stiff and fold in lightly. Pour into tin. Bake 20 minutes.

ICING:
1 cup light brown sugar
3 tablespoons milk

1 teaspoon butter
Vanilla essence

Stir all together and bring to boil. Boil 5 minutes, take off and beat until it thickens. Ice when cake is not quite cold.

Chocolate Layer Cake
CWA NSW

Cream ⅓ cup butter with 1 cup sugar, add 1 beaten egg, 1 cup milk slowly and mix well. Add 1¾ cups flour, sifted with ¼ teaspoon salt and 4 small teaspoons baking powder. Mix in 1 teaspoon vanilla and bake in three greased layer cake tins in a moderate oven 15–20 minutes.

Put together with chocolate filling and icing made with 3 cups icing sugar, 2 tablespoons cocoa, 1 teaspoon vanilla, ½ teaspoon grated orange peel, sufficient boiling water to make a smooth paste and mix well. Put between layers and ice all over top and sides.

Christmas Cake
G. A. Turnbull, Smithton, CWA Tas

1 oz Jordan almonds	8 oz plain flour
6 oz raisins	6 oz margarine
5 oz currants	6 oz soft brown sugar
4 oz sultanas	Few drops almond
2 oz glace cherries	essence
1½ oz mixed peel	3 eggs
1½ level teaspoons	3 tablespoons milk
baking powder	3 dessertspoons of
1½ level teaspoons	rum, sherry or
mixed spice	whisky
¾ level teaspoon	¾ teaspoon cinnamon
ground ginger	¼ teaspoon salt

This quantity is for an 8 inch cake about 2½ inches deep when baked.

Prepare tin by lining with greased greaseproof paper. Blanch and chop almonds, clean fruit, chop cherries and the peel. Sieve all dry ingredients together. Beat margarine and sugar to a cream. Add almond essence and beat in eggs. Mix dry ingredients with fruit and stir in, moistening with milk and liquor. Place in tin and hollow out the centre slightly. Place on the second runner from the bottom of oven and bake at 325°F for 2½ hours. Leave in tin until cold.

Cinnamon Roll

CWA NSW

2 tablespoons butter

2 tablespoons sugar

1 egg

1 cup milk or more

2 cups self-raising flour

Cinnamon

Icing sugar

Beat butter and sugar to a cream, add egg, milk and flour. Bake in salt tins for an hour. Have mixture soft. When cooked, butter all over and roll in ground cinnamon and icing sugar. Sultanas or preserved ginger may also be added.

Coffee Cake (splendid)

CWA NSW

¾ lb flour

¼ oz baking powder
    (2 teaspoonsful)

½ lb butter

½ lb sugar

4 eggs

¼ pint milk or less

TOPPING:

1 oz sugar

1 oz butter

1½ oz flour

Good pinch nutmeg
    and cinnamon

Sift flour and baking powder together. Work up butter and sugar into a cream, add eggs one at a time, beat each egg in well. Add flour and milk. Bake one hour.

Topping: Rub ingredients well with hand until pliable. Rub through a sieve over the cake evenly. This goes on before baking. Cherries or fruit may be added to the cake.

Gingerbread

O. M. Thompson, Geeveston, CWA Tas

1 cup brown sugar

1 egg

4 oz butter

½ cup golden syrup

¾ cup milk

Pinch salt

2½ cups flour

1 teaspoon cinnamon

1 dessertspoon ginger

1 teaspoon bicarb soda

Beat sugar and egg. Melt butter, add golden syrup and milk. Mix together and add to sugar and egg mix. Add sifted flour and other dry ingredients, stir lightly until smooth, fold in balance of sifted ingredients, continue folding until smooth. Bake in a moderate (180°C) oven 35–40 minutes before turning out. Can be iced with lemon icing and sprinkled with coconut.

Sponge Roll with Raspberry Jam, Cream and Coconut

Mrs A. J. Barwick, Oatlands, CWA Tas

3 eggs
4 oz sugar
1 cup self-raising flour
2 tablespoons hot milk
Raspberry jam

Whipped sweetened cream, flavoured with vanilla essence
Desiccated coconut

Separate eggs whites and egg yolks. Beat egg whites till stiff and frothy, gradually add sugar, beat until dissolved and mixture will hold its shape. Add egg yolks, beat well. Fold in sifted flour then hot milk. Grease a Swiss roll tin and line the base with greased paper. Pour mixture in. Bake in moderate (180°C) oven 10–15 minutes. Turn out onto paper that is lightly coated with caster sugar. Quickly cut off crusts, ends and sides and roll up with the paper. Leave to cool on cake rack. Unroll carefully, remove paper, spread with jam and cream, re-roll. Cover the roll completely with cream, pipe or spoon diagonal strips of jam over roll. Sprinkle jam with coconut. To serve, cut in diagonal slices either parallel to jam strips or across them.

Sultana Cake

CWA NSW

½ lb butter
½ lb brown sugar
1 dessertspoonful treacle
½ cup fig jam
4 or 5 eggs
A little milk

1½ lb sultanas
¼ peel (lemon or orange)
½ lb flour
1 teaspoon baking powder
Pinch salt

Cream butter and sugar. Add treacle then add jam. Beat the eggs in one at a time, then the milk, the sultanas and peel and the flour sifted with baking powder and salt. Bake 3 or 4 hours.

Wendy Meyer
Kaniva, Victoria

I'm from the Victorian Wimmera town of Kaniva, which is right over near the South Australian border. It's a pretty place with a lot of history and we have a very strong community. For example, they were going to close our roadhouse one time and so everyone got together and put in money to save it and now we've got the Kaniva Community Roadhouse.

But I actually grew up in Melbourne. My father worked in the State Savings Bank and he was transferred to Kaniva, as the manager, when I was thirteen. Then when I was sixteen, he was transferred back to Melbourne. I was still at school at that stage so I went back to Melbourne and then I worked for a tiny bit in the State Savings Bank there. But I'd already fallen in love with a farmer from the Kaniva district, hadn't I? So when I was seventeen, I got married and returned to Kaniva and I went on the farm and I've been there ever since and we've got three children. The two boys are now helping out on the farm — they're thirty-five and thirty-three — and my daughter's in Melbourne and she's twenty-nine.

The property is half sheep and half grain: you know, wheat, barley, canola and peas. But we're still in drought. It's still dry and we haven't got any natural rivers or creeks or anything. Yes, we've got bore water but it's very salty so we only use that for flushing the toilets and for the garden. But luckily, we have got a big roof area and I've got enough rainwater tanks that we've never actually run out of water. Not yet, anyway. So we do catch a lot of water.

As for CWA: my mother came from around the Shepparton-Bendigo area and she was from a farming background family and her relatives were in CWA. So I sort of knew about the organisation before I went to live in Kaniva. Then when I got married, my mother-in-law was in CWA and so I became a member of the Kaniva Branch and have continued to do so. There were about twenty-five of us when I first joined and we're down to about fifteen now. I'm the youngest in our Branch and always have been.

But it's difficult to get younger members because, these days there are a lot of other farming-related community services that the younger women can get involved in, such as Women in Agriculture and organisations like that. I feel though, it's cyclical and there is a real interest swinging back toward the CWA. Just recently we held a CWA information evening and about forty women came along to that and twenty-five showed interest. So there's definitely an interest in the Kaniva and Nhill areas, especially for the night Branch style of CWA. I'm currently our Group President, yet again, and a night Branch has just started in Horsham. Night or Evening Branches are aimed more toward business women or mothers who can't attend meetings during the daytime for one reason or another. The way I see it is, whereas the older generation worked at home and CWA fulfilled their social activity, with my generation and the following one, a lot of us work off-farm so we only really have the time for meetings and other activities in the evenings. That's what I'm finding, anyway.

Take the drought for instance: in our area, unless they've got young children at home, ninety-nine per cent of farming wives would now be working off-farm to get an income to help the family survive. I do. I nanny for a family in Melbourne on weekends, which has very much helped with our survival for the last four-and-a-half years. I normally drive down from Kaniva on the Friday, nanny Friday night, Saturday, Saturday night and then drive back home on the Sunday. It's about a thousand kilometre round trip, when all is said and done, but it gives me the week back in Kaniva. It might sound a bit unusual but you'd be surprised what rural people do, not only to support each other, but just to enable themselves to survive.

With my week in Kaniva, I'm not only involved in the farm but I'm also a Guide Leader. Then there's my CWA commitments, of course. It's a very busy life. I love CWA. I love the fellowship. I love the type of work we do. Several years ago, with the drought, I was taking trailer loads of food around to all the farmers. It was just something that was very much needed and I felt that it was somewhere where I could do some good. That was with Food Bank, which is a Victorian Government set-up. They give food to the needy. That's not only to people who are struggling on the dole or whatever but also for those who have come upon hard times due to unusual circumstances like drought, as it was in our case. So they'd send the food up to Horsham by rail and I'd go and pick it up with the trailer and because all the farmers knew me and I knew them, I knew who was in trouble and so I'd drive around to all the different farms where the greatest need was.

I mean, it wasn't a lot. It was more of the tinned foods and packets of cereal and things like that. It wasn't going to save anyone from starving but it was more of an acknowledgement along the lines of, 'Yes, we are thinking of you,' which could well have been instrumental in saving their lives by simply letting them know that someone was actually caring about them. That's the theory I was working on anyway. And through doing that, the *Age* newspaper came up and took photos of me going out and distributing the food and, I think, if you Google my name it comes up with a picture of me handing out the food.

So that was probably about six or seven years ago now, when I was Group President the last time around and, as I said, I'm back as Group President, yet again. I guess it's another cyclical thing and as they all seem to say, 'If nobody else will do it, Wendy will.'

But no, I love it and I love that caring-for-the-community side of CWA as well. And because of the drought I also represented CWA on the Rural Counselling Service of Victoria and through that organisation I've been able to help organise counsellors for those who need them. Then there's all the filling out of the application forms and all the paperwork and the questionnaires that's required there. Oh, there's just so much paperwork to be done: questions, questions and more questions, almost down to what toilet paper everyone uses. But anyway, I've been on that committee, trying to help out there as well.

Then, do you know how, in CWA, we study a different country each year? Well two years ago Samoa was our country of study and we heard that they were in need of sewing materials. But when we tried to get these materials into Samoa they kept sending them back. We just could not get them in. Whether it was a government issue or what, I don't know, but there was some sort of blockage there somewhere and there was just no one that was coordinating it at their end. So my daughter and I — like you do — decided we'd fill our backpacks with sewing materials and take a little trip to a certain pacific island, didn't we?

So off we went with our backpacks absolutely stacked full of sewing materials: reels of cotton, lace and elastic and things, and I'd been warned that we may get stopped and questioned by the Samoan security, 'What are you doing with all this stuff?'

Anyway, luckily, no one stopped us and we got it all through okay. The next problem was that I didn't have a contact. The ones that I was given from Australia were not answering and so, from the Backpackers, where we were staying, I asked around and I found out that there was a group of nuns known as the Little Sisters of the Poor who sewed clothes for the elderly people and for the children and they also sold some of the clothes they made at the markets, to raise funds to help the needy. And I heard that they would very much appreciate any materials they could get their hands on. So I said, 'That's exactly what we're after,' and we delivered all the sewing materials there, to the Little Sisters of the Poor. So, you know, you just try to do what you can to help those who may benefit.

But there's so many facets in CWA. It's an extremely diverse organisation. There's also the craft side of it, which I love. I'm a sewer; a needleworker. Then we have our Fun Days and we have the Song and Costumes events. Those are where you entertain people, again trying to spread a little bit of happiness. And I enjoy that side of it as well because, even though I can't sing and I couldn't hold a note to save my life, I can still play a fool.

Mavis Mincherton
Wongan Hills, Western Australia

Now, so where do I start? I've belonged to CWA, in Western Australia, in total, for just over sixty years. The only time I had a break was when I left Cadoux to come in here to Wongan Hills and then it was nearly two years before I rejoined because I'd had enough to do with the then CWA President in at the Bowling Club and I thought, Well I'm not going into the CWA with her as well. So that's how that worked out.

Wongan Hills is a bit less than a hundred kilometres north of Northam. It's grown a lot in the last few years. There's somewhere between fifteen hundred and two thousand people here now. We retired in here about thirty years ago and I still belong the Wongan Hills Branch. During my time I've been the Divisional Secretary, which I enjoyed very much because you get out and about and meet people and talk to everybody over the phone and that sort of thing. It's been a wonderful experience, the CWA. It's like a big family. At present I'm Secretary of our Branch but I'm trying hard to get out of that because I reckon I've gone past my used-by date.

But I first joined CWA when I was in Salmon Gums. That was during the war. I would've been just over twenty-one back then. Salmon Gums is north of Esperance. My mum was one of the first members there when they started the Branch. Then, wherever I went from there, I went to CWA. I've been around a lot. Back in the early days, if you were going to move somewhere they'd send a letter of introduction to your nearest Branch. They don't bother these days. You just come and go. Things have relaxed a lot.

I've had some funny experiences too. Different ones alway say to me, 'Tell us about Mrs Barrett.' She was real character, was Mrs Barrett. Very sort of posh and uppity they used to say. She lived just near me in Ballidu, at the back of the shop. Ballidu is only about thirty kilometres from Wongan. This was back when my boys went into the bigger trucks and they were carting sheep and all that sort of thing and they'd arrive home at all times and say, 'Mum can you fuel the truck up while I have some tea.'

There was no actual mechanic in Ballidu and one of my boys, in particular, was always keen on fixing the trucks. So he'd get the truck manuals out and he'd start pulling the blooming thing to bits and it was: 'Mum, will you come and help me' or 'Mum, hang onto the torch and shine the light in here' or 'Pass me the spanner or the spark plug' or 'Do this, that or the other'.

At that time, Mrs Barrett was a CWA Divisional President. She was a funny woman, really. She took the job on and, oh, she loved it. But as different ones said, 'She only did it because she liked to be in the forefront.' Of course, with being the Divisional President, she'd be invited to all the little Branches away out in the sticks, places like Jibberding and Kalannie. Anyhow, Mrs Barrett had a little Volkswagen at that time and with the experience I'd had on the trucks with my sons, she thought I knew everything there was to know about vehicles and so I became her 'chief mechanic'.

'Oh, Mavis,' she'd say, 'I've got to go to Calingiri, can you come with me?' and I'd say, 'Yes,' and she'd say, 'Well that's good because if anything goes wrong with the car you'll know what to do with it.'

But, oh, she was a dreadful driver. She just whizzed around the place as if she didn't have a care in the world as far as driving the car went. Off we'd go and she'd be looking out into the paddocks to see what was going on and, before you'd know it, she'd be just about off the road and into the blooming paddock. And she'd turn a corner and she'd change down into a lower gear and then off she'd go and I'd often have to say to her, 'Mrs Barrett you'd better change up into the top gear.'

All that sort of thing, and she'd sing. Oh, and how she always loved to sing when she was driving, and she'd get so carried away with the singing that she'd start pumping the accelerator in rhythm with the song and you'd be going along the blooming road in leaps and bounds. Oh I tell you, and one day she took her cousin with us. We were going to Piawaning for some CWA do or something. Both the cousin and Mrs Barrett were big women. I'm not terribly big. This was in the middle of winter and it'd been pouring with rain and the road between Ballidu and Piawaning was an awful bit of ground, awfully slippery. Anyhow, I'd been invited along as chief mechanic as usual and Mrs Barrett's husband had said to her, 'Now go up around Miling and come back to Piawaning on the good road.'

Okay, so I'm in the back seat of the Volkswagen and away we went. Well, her husband hadn't realised that the Main Roads people had decided to dig a lot of the good road up and rebuild it, did he? So we got to this muddy section and I said, 'You'd better slow down, Mrs Barrett.'

But, no, she didn't worry about that. She didn't slow down. She just went flat out into it and the whole car was absolutely covered in mud. Of course, now she couldn't see properly, could she? And we soon came to a stop. Then she just passed me a cloth and she said, 'Mavis, could you get out and wipe the windscreen.'

So I had to get out in about eighteen inches of mud to wipe the blooming windscreen. And even after that she didn't slow down and, with all this mud everywhere, it wasn't long before she couldn't see properly again and so she said, 'Mavis, hang your head out the window and tell me if I'm in the middle of the road, will you?'

Oh, I tell you. You can almost picture it. It didn't mean a thing with her, so we had some quite hectic times, really. She's dead now. They've both gone now, her and her husband. But no, there's some funny things that went on during those old CWA days. Anyway, these things happen in the bush, don't they? It makes the bush, really, it does, so you just got to along with it all and try not to get too upset.

Heather Mitchell
Happy Valley, South Australia

Even though I grew up in the Adelaide suburb of Plympton I was very aware of CWA from an early age, because both my aunty and my grandmother were members, over on the Yorke Peninsula of South Australia. My aunty still belongs to the Port Victoria Branch and my grandmother was a member at Minlaton and, when I was a kid, I remember helping my grandmother make sandwiches for CWA, at the Minlaton stock sales. It was a good experience; that is, other than the dirt and the flies and the smell of the cattle and sheep. My sister was also a member, just south of Adelaide, at Happy Valley, but she had gone to Queensland by the time I joined.

I owned a delicatessen in Adelaide and after I married we moved down to Happy Valley and I got out of it. But I knew I'd miss the people contact because, in a deli, people are always coming and going and, with my husband working and my children at school, I had the need to meet people and do something worthwhile. So I joined the Happy Valley Branch of CWA in 1988 and I did a lot of the Branch things like being Craft Secretary and Secretary. But I liked it at state level so I joined what was called the Club Management Committee and we help keep things in order over in the accommodation part of CWA in Adelaide. Now I'm also secretary of the Show Cafe. It's a two-storey cafe where we sell food over the Adelaide Show period. It's our building. We had it built. We've been there for sixty-one years; not in that actual building but as an association.

We make the majority of the food upstairs on the premises. We make the scones, the cakes, the sandwiches and meat and salad plates. We make the desserts. It's very popular. Most days people are lined up, out the door, waiting to get in. We have good healthy food and, because all our workers are volunteers, we're very reasonably priced. It's a fantastic fundraiser. In fact, the Adelaide Show is perhaps our major fundraiser for the year, and we must be doing something right because our sales have jumped almost eighty per cent in the last four years. Of course, not having to pay staff helps with our overheads but we do give our volunteers a free entry ticket plus their meals at our cafe. But everyone in CWA stops for it. It's all hands on deck. We even try to encourage the children and the grandchildren of our members to come along and help because, as much as they'd like to, some of the older members can't do some of the things they used to do.

Actually, there's a lot of us involved in running the Show Cafe. We're there two weeks prior to the Show opening, to serve the judges and the members of the Agricultural Society and those who are setting up. Then we start, proper, on the day the show starts. And it's very busy. I'd say that, on a daily basis, including committee members, we'd probably have about fifty to sixty volunteers working in the cafe. We start preparing things at seven in the morning and they shut the doors around eight o'clock at night. We have two shifts for the committee members and several shifts for the volunteers. To give you some idea, over the nine days of the show we give out about four hundred and fifty free entry tickets to our volunteers plus there's the tickets for us committee members.

Just organising the volunteers and setting up the work roster is nearly a full-time job. I'm in charge of the cashier side of it. I get people who are experienced in cashier work or who I know can handle it. It's certainly not a job you can simply relax into because you're constantly ringing up the till. Some days you can't see the front door from 9.30 in the morning till about three in the afternoon, so we've had to buy double the crockery and cutlery so that the customers can get in and out quicker.

I don't know how many people we'd have come through over the Show period. An awful lot, I'd guess. Lorraine Greenfield, the Chairman of the Show Committee, makes all the scones at the

Show and she starts at seven in the morning and finishes around three in the afternoon. She'd make around nine thousand scones over the Show period, so that might give you some idea. And at times we've been so busy that the scones come piping hot, straight out of the oven, to cover our orders. We have a special oven for it. It's about three foot by two foot. We used to make all the scones by hand but since we've had the Laucke's CWA scone mix deal, Laucke's have lent us their scone mix making machine, and it's just marvellous. It saves the shoulders, the arms, everything.

Then there's the noise to cope with. That's deafening at times. Other than the people activity, the dishwasher starts up at around nine in the morning and it goes ... bump ... bump ... bump ... all day. It's incredible to see the dishwasher at work. The dumbwaiter's also fantastic. It brings the food down from upstairs via a pulley wheel. It's as old as the hills. I'm in charge of that too and we have an intercom system and I ring upstairs and say, 'I need more jam' or 'I need more cream'. Up and down. Up and down.

But it's constant the whole time. It's exhausting, I can tell you. Oh, and that's right: this year, on the last Friday of the Show, our dumbwaiter broke down. It's never broken down before. Something happened with the pulley wheel and it was so old they couldn't find a replacement. Apparently they didn't make them anymore, so we had our youngest volunteers scampering up and down the stairs. Every time someone came down they had to bring scones or jam or something with them and every time they went upstairs they had to take plates or whatever up with them. It was bedlam and I just shudder to think how we would've managed if it had broken down on the first Friday of the Show. Perhaps we would've had to have shut up shop. Anyhow, we've got a new pulley wheel now and so the dumbwaiter will be back in action next year, guaranteed.

Anne Morris
Mt Isa, Queensland

I grew up around Brisbane during the Depression years. That's when I was about five or six. I was the second eldest of ten children and we went to a lot of different schools because my father was always moving around, working from place to place. We even lived in a tent at one stage. That was back when there were only just the five of us children. That was around Cooroy. Then we finally settled at Richlands and Darra. They were suburbs of Brisbane, on the Ipswich railway line. But I remember them as happy times because there was no television or anything like that so all us kids, we just made our own fun. Also, being one of the eldest, I enjoyed watching the different ones grow up and that.

Then I started my working life as a nurse in a mental hospital at Goodna. I was seventeen by then and I stayed there for twelve months before I went down to the Gold Coast to nurse at a private hospital. I met my future husband there. He was from Tweed Heads and, after going steady for a few years, we married. I was twenty-seven by then and so we went and said goodbye to both our families and we came up to Mt Isa. We just came here on spec, actually. The idea was, if he could get some work, we'd stay in Mt Isa for a couple of years then we'd move on. And he got work, first as a truck driver for Thiess Brothers and then driving a loader. So we stayed on and that was fifty-seven years ago. We had three boys and one girl though, unfortunately, my husband got sick and he passed away in 1977.

But when I first came here I looked around at organisations where I could meet people and get involved in the community. Mt Isa CWA was only a young Branch in those days so I joined and I've been with it ever since. That was in 1960, which means that this is my fiftieth year as a member, and I've got a Good Service badge for all the various things I've done with CWA over my years. Of course, Mt Isa has grown a lot since the 60s and a lot of the people I knew back then, they aren't around anymore. But CWA grows on you, and it's been very good to me because I've had my sad times, as is the same with other people. But I'm quite happy now.

As for special moments, I've got a few. We've had several functions to celebrate different things. Each year we have a Country of Study for CWA and this year it's Ireland so we'll be having an Irish dinner or something. That's how it goes. And if we've ever had anyone come from overseas, like from the Associated Country Women of the World Organisation, we always do something special for that, too. Though, mind you, no one from overseas has come to Mt Isa for a few years now but it just goes to show you that CWA is part of a great worldwide community for women.

We have a nice hall here in Mt Isa and another function I got a certificate for was when Charles and Diana married. I was President of the Branch back then and to celebrate their marriage I organised a luncheon and we watched the wedding on television. It was like we were part of the whole celebration. People came from all round. Everyone got dressed up and different ones added a bit more to it. As with all our functions, men were also invited and, just for a bit of fun, one husband and wife even came dressed as a bride and bridegroom. Then we had some special guests — identities — who spoke about different things. It was a lovely day. We had a nice meal with cold meats and salads and sweets and fruit. Tea and coffee.

Last year another important event was that our Mt Isa Branch celebrated its eightieth birthday. That was also a special occasion so we had a luncheon in our hall and we had two guest speakers who talked about how CWA had originated. But things have changed over the years. As I said, I joined back in 1960 and, at times, during those earlier years we had up to a hundred members. It's dwindled, of course, and we're down to about ten now. All of us are over the age of sixty so we haven't done any stalls or anything for a couple of years now. Some of us are even in our eighties. I'll be eighty in June. These days we're more of a support group to other organisations. We have done catering but, with our ages, it's usually only left to two or three, so it's quite a struggle.

But I'm trying to keep it together. Just recently a few women have rang and said how they wanted to join CWA. But they had jobs so this year we decided to meet on the Saturday. We've had ten Saturday meetings so far and it looks like we might be getting some new members. So that's good. We just hope it keeps up.

Shirley Morrisby
Howrah, Tasmania

My parents originally lived at New Norfolk, which is up the Derwent Valley, in Tasmania. They had a mixed farm with sheep and cattle and they also grew a few different crops. Then, coming towards the war years, we left the farm and we moved down to the northern suburbs of Hobart, to Moonah. I was only a toddler then and that's where I did my schooling. Actually, I lived at Moonah right up until I got married, then I went to live at Sandford. Sandford's just south of Lauderdale, heading down Cremorne, South Arm, Opossum Bay way. My husband had a hobby farm there with a small apricot orchard and he also grew a few vegetables. I say 'hobby farm' because at the same time he was working for Ansett Air Freight and he continued to do so until, unfortunately, Ansett went under. We lived at Sandford for about twenty-four years but the ground was very limy and sandy and it used to irritate our son's skin so then we moved closer to Hobart, to Howrah, which is where we live at the moment.

My mother-in-law was the one who introduced me to CWA. She happened to be a South-Eastern Group Secretary — a position she held for many years. We lived next door to each other at Sandford and when I got married, she said, 'Shirley, you've got to join the CWA.' So I did. That was in 1972 and I'm still here and, currently, I'm in my second term as State President of CWA Tasmania. You may not realise it but here in Tasmania we have three-year terms whereas in other states I think they only have two-year terms. So that's a small difference though, like in other states, we still have to be renominated and re-elected each year.

As for special moments? Well, one highlight would definitely be the work we did in the drought. You just don't realise how hard it's been, not only on the farmers and their families, but also on the whole community. Anyway, we decided to do some, what we called, 'Birds in the Bush Days'. They were just our way of getting the wives off the farm for a day and to come into town and be pampered. Some of the money for that came from the Foundation for Regional and Rural Renewal, which was a Commonwealth Government initiative. Then we also got some money from a women's organisation in Devonport, Soroptimist International.

For our 'Birds in the Bush Days', what we did was, we'd pick a specific drought-affected area and we'd go out into the local hall and the women would come in and they'd get their hair done and their nails done and we'd have a special champagne lunch. Oh, that's right, we started the day off with a laughter therapy session, which was run through the councils. That really broke the ice. We all got dressed up in funny hats and glasses and that. Then we were very lucky because, in a lot of towns, people, like the local hairdressers, came along and they did cuts and blow-dries and they didn't charge a cent. We also had people from Centrelink and organisations like that come along and they gave the ladies shoulder massages and hand and foot massages which helped them relax while they talked about their experiences. We also had people who showed them how to make jewellery and little jewellery boxes. Another lady demonstrated flower arranging by using dried flowers and things out of the bush and they got to take their own flower arrangements home. Oh, the people that volunteered were absolutely wonderful and the appreciation from those drought-affected ladies was absolutely wonderful as well.

Another very special time was the work we did in Hobart with the African refugees. That all began when we found out from the Migrant Resource Centre that many of the refugees, from Somalia and Sierra Leone and places like that, were arriving here in Hobart and they had difficulty buying food at the supermarket because they couldn't read or speak English. In one case, one of the African mums was sending her son off to school with cornflakes in between two pieces of bread because there was a picture of a chicken on the front of the packet and so she thought she was putting dry chicken on her son's sandwiches.

Anyhow, we were approached by the Migrant Resource Centre to see if we could help with their shopping and cooking. That was fine by us so we went to their homes in Warrane and we all walked down to the supermarket at Eastlands. Two of their husbands could speak a little English so they came along as well, to interpret for us. We then explained what the different foods meant and we bought some food and we went back to their homes and we showed them how to cook the meals. And they were so enthusiastic. They wanted to get in and help cook everything. It was a wonderful experience. Absolutely marvellous.

Another thing we found out was that they didn't understand the money side of things. They thought Centrelink just handed out money and after you'd spent it you could go back for more, like it was an endless supply. They didn't realise that once the money was spent you didn't get any more for another two weeks. Anyhow, they were forever turning up at Centrelink asking for money. But an experience like that really makes you realise just how difficult it must be when you come to another country and you can't speak the language, especially people like them. I mean, they'd been living in refugee camps, under horrific conditions. They'd also been living in a completely different climate to Hobart and you'd see them, as cold as anything, walking around town just in cotton dresses. So CWA gave them beanies and scarves and we also provided blankets and cooking needs.

That was another wonderful experience and because of the work we'd done with the refugees, as the representative of CWA Tasmania, I went to Canberra and received a Harmony Day Award. That's a special Federal Government award given through the Immigration Department. So, yes, that was also really special.

Lynne Robinson
Wollar, New South Wales

We're one of the newer Branches of CWA. We only formed in 1995, at the small village of Wollar, a couple of hundred kilometres west of Newcastle, in central-eastern New South Wales. We're called the Munghorne Branch, the Munghorne being a geographical feature of the area. It's like a spur up the Great Dividing Range. I wasn't a foundation member but I joined a year later. They were actually struggling a bit and so I got lured in. But I got involved and I enjoyed it, and CWA was doing such a lot of good, and I've been a member ever since. At Branch level I've been President, Secretary, Treasurer plus whatever else is going. Then at Group level I've been President and Treasurer. Now I'm Group Representative, along with other things.

In Wollar village itself, there would've been about a hundred and fifty families living there at one stage. But now that the coal mine has moved in things have changed and we've whittled down a lot with many of the more established families having left the area, including ourselves. We were mainly wool-growers and we had a few cattle, then, with the effects of the drought and the mining, we just lost our water. It was like pulling the plug out of a bath. The artesian water virtually disappeared and the creeks dried up. Even our fattening paddock, along the creek, couldn't keep our cattle going. Where once you would've seen green year after year, there was no longer the green. That's coal mining, and that's why some of the families have gone. Then others have left due to the noise and that's because it's on the strata of the rock and, with the machinery going day and night, it rumbles. Rumbles all the time. Of course that was never looked into when they proposed the mine. On a clear night it's like the noise is going on just outside your window. So we moved too — about fifty kilometres to the south — and, actually, we're probably better off now. We've got close to forty acres just out of Mudgee and I've got a better house.

Anyway, all that's not really CWA. I think what's good about our little fifteen- or sixteen-member Branch is that we all get on well. There's a strong bond of friendship therefore, whatever we do, we seem to be successful at. The money we raise is put back into the various CWA areas of need and you'd be surprised at just how different those areas of need are. With our CWA ladies coming from all over the country we hear so many stories of how people have had to overcome adversity. Just at this moment there's floods in the north and down south there's those horrendous bushfires. We know what our sisters and their families are going through because they come to our local and state meetings and share their experiences, then we all get together and work out where best we can help. In that way, as a women's organisation, CWA is a great support network.

On the other hand, one of the things that is a bit disappointing is how we're struggling to attract new members and, unfortunately, as our member base diminishes so does our political power. Sometimes the younger women think we're a bit old hat, but the basic reasons behind why we were established, all those years ago, are still here. Things like the government still wanting to give second-rate services to the country areas and its people. It started years ago with the Health Department taking over Mother and Baby Health Care, which was something that CWA was strongly involved in. To me, these days the Health Department seems a bit second-rate. It's far too big and there's too many bureaucrats at the top. We, in CWA, have to lobby for a return to where people are treated as individuals. We need more people on the ground, better service and better services. An example there is of women having to travel all the way into Dubbo Hospital for maternity — obstetrics. And now you hear of people having to pull up and deliver babies beside the road. It's simply not good enough. So when are they going to wake up and provide those services out of the small country hospitals. It's all a numbers game.

Then we've also lost our air service into Mudgee. Since 21st December 2009 we've had no daily plane flights, which means we can't get the medical specialists from Sydney up here on a fly-in-fly-out basis. We know that it's about the shortage of pilots and our local government is lobbying very hard. In fact, they've said they'll even waive the landing fee. But we need to lobby, too.

Something else CWA was involved in was that we used to run a Girls Hostel in Mudgee. That was a two-storey house where the high school girls from outlying areas could stay. CWA ran it and did the cooking on a roster system, while a Matron was in charge. Then, when they started to bring in the school buses, there wasn't the need and so the hostel finished up in the late 1970s. It was sold and part of the money went into a pool, with some of it going to the Tender Loving Care Committee, which helps kids with special needs. It's only small token amounts but they're helped with their transport costs to Sydney or wherever, to visit a specialist. It's letting them know that someone cares. One of the Branches also had a big Christmas tree for them. Our members made them small gifts and, oh, you should've seen the kids. They just loved it. There were kids in wheelchairs, the lot. Many of them can't communicate and one of the boys got so stimulated that he even started to say a word or two and that makes it all worthwhile.

Then, on a more personal level, as I've gone around CWA and I've gone to the State Conference and things, I've always admired the women there who can get up and impart their great knowledge in a confident manner. I was a person who would've run a mile before I'd be game enough to speak in public. But I learned to — not perfectly by any means, mind you — and I've gained that confidence through CWA's supportive atmosphere, and that's a great thing.

Small Cakes

Brandy Horns
CWA Tas

4 oz plain flour
1 level teaspoon powdered ginger
4 oz butter
4 oz treacle or golden syrup
1 dessertspoon water
4 oz sugar
Sweetened whipped cream

Sift together the flour and ginger and rub in the butter. Combine the treacle, water and sugar and stir until well mixed. Make a well in the centre and add the liquid, stir the flour in from the side and mix well. Place pieces (walnut size) on a greased tray, leaving room to spread. Bake in upper half of moderate (180°C) oven 10–12 minutes. Cool slightly then roll quickly around handle of a wooded spoon or cream horn mould. Cool and fill with sweetened whipped cream

CWA Fluffs
Mrs F. J. Jensen, Winnaleah, CWA Tas

¼ lb butter
2 oz sugar
1 egg
2 oz ground rice
3 oz self-raising flour
1 teaspoon vanilla
Raspberry jam

Beat butter and sugar to a cream. Add unbeaten egg, beat well, then add ground rice, flour and vanilla. This mixture is rather stiff and should be so. After having put into patty pans, make a hole in the middle of each one and drop a little raspberry jam in. Bake in a quick (200°C) oven for 10 minutes.

Lamingtons
CWA NSW

5 oz butter
5 oz sugar
2 eggs
4 tablespoons milk
A few drops of vanilla
10 oz self-raising flour

Cream the butter and sugar, add beaten egg with milk and vanilla and lastly the sifted flour. Grease a lamington tray and pour mixture into it and bake 30 minutes in a moderate oven. Turn out into a rack and leave until next day then cut into squares and ice with the following icing — 3 oz butter, 1 tablespoon cocoa, 8 oz icing sugar and a few drops of vanilla.

Cream butter and icing sugar, add cocoa mixed with a little hot water and vanilla. Ice the cakes all over then roll them in desiccated coconut.

Melting Moments
CWA NSW

½ lb butter
2 tablespoons icing sugar
2 tablespoons cornflour
7 tablespoons flour

Beat butter until white, add sugar, beat well then add cornflour and lastly flour. Roll small pieces into a ball, press flat with a fork and bake in greased dish in slow (140°C) oven until pale brown. Put 2 together with jam or icing.

Meringue
M. Page, Lucaston, CWA Tas

Whites of 3 eggs and pinch of salt. Beat until stiff, add 2 tablespoons sugar and 2 tablespoons cold water, beat again and add 2 more tablespoons sugar and beat, add last 2 tablespoons sugar, 1 teaspoon vanilla and 1 teaspoon vinegar, beat again. Place a wet paper over an upturned cake tin, spread about ½ inch from edge. Bake in oven about 300 degrees for 1 hour. Turn oven off and allow to dry for easily another hour, the longer the better. Fill with cream and fruit.

Rock Cakes
CWA NSW

6 oz butter
1 lb flour
2 teaspoons baking powder
½ lb sugar
¼ lb currants or sultanas
Grated rind of lemon
Nutmeg or any spice
3 eggs

Rub butter into dry ingredients then add eggs, well beaten, and a little milk if desired. Drop on to hot tray in small pieces. Bake in moderate (180°C) oven.

Short Bread — varieties
Mrs A. Sharman, Kindred, CWA Tas

Beat 1 cup butter and 1 cup sugar to a cream, add 3 eggs one at a time. Beat well then add 3 cups flour to which has been added 2 teaspoons cream of tartar and one of bicarb soda. Blend well. Divide mixture into six portions.

Kisses: Roll out, cut into rounds and bake in moderate oven at 450°F. When cold stick together with raspberry jam and ice top.

Sunbeams: Roll very thinly, spread with apricot jam. Roll up, cut into slices, roll in coconut and bake in moderate (180°C) oven.

Batchelor Buttons: Roll into small balls, roll in coarse sugar and bake in moderate (180°C) oven.

Nut Fingers: Roll out, spread with icing sugar and whipped white of egg. Decorate with nuts, cut into fingers and bake in moderate (180°C) oven.

Date Cuddles: Roll thinly, cut into rounds. Place date in centre of round, moisten edges and press two rounds together. Bake in moderate (180°C) oven.

Jam or Apple Tarts: Roll out, cut into rounds and bake in patty pans in moderate (180°C) oven. When cold fill with jam, lemon butter or stewed apple and decorate with whipped cream.

Yvonne Scarrabelotti
Kyogle, New South Wales

One of the first CWA Branches in Australia was started at Horseshoe Creek, a little place fifteen kilometres out of Kyogle. The idea must've been previously discussed in parliament because it was at the suggestion of a parliamentarian from that area that the local women form the Branch so that he could get a better idea as to what was happening. So, while the men were out playing cricket, the women formed a CWA Branch under a great big gum tree.

Seeing how CWA had originally started up in 1922, this would've been a year or so later, in about 1923 or '24. Back then Horseshoe Creek was quite an isolated place but, along with the local community, CWA was soon involved in the building of a little school house. They were also instrumental in bringing in a teacher. Then later on, a hall was built. So from those small beginnings, CWA has grown and grown, both locally and nationally, and it still does a lot of the same good work for the country people, today, that it used to do back then.

How I got into CWA was that, I went to live at Kyogle after I was married. Originally, we ran a dairy farm then we changed to cattle. My husband and his brothers also used to collect the natural grass seed and process and sell that, of which a lot was sold to the overseas market. But anyway, there was an old lady who lived next door to us. She was wonderful at handicraft. She'd had four sons involved in the war and she'd lost three of them and I was in the throes of having seven children in ten years, so she half-helped me rear them. But it was she that introduced me to CWA and I never dreamed that I'd ever go any further up the ladder than our local Branch, but I have.

It's just a shame that we can't get the younger ones more involved in voluntary work and doing the things we do. This business about how they're too busy, working and raising children, to join the CWA, I believe, is all wrong. I had seven children and I still managed to be active in the community and CWA. Actually, they were the best years of my life while I reared those seven boys. Yes, seven boys and, believe it or not, I'm one of seven girls and I didn't ever feel demeaned or neglected or that I wanted to be doing something else.

I always did things to keep myself involved and interested in life: like there was a little Technical College at Kyogle in those days and so I went to that. I'd done dressmaking before I was married and so I went to the Tech and now I'm a milliner and I'm a tailoress. I can do anything at all. I played tennis. I ran the Plain and Fancy Store at the school fundraiser every year. I just think that the young women in our country need to sit down and have a real good look at where they're going, instead of thinking about themselves so much. You only get return out of life when you give of yourself and they don't seem to realise that giving opens up other worlds. As to how we're going to get them to understand that, I don't know, but it's got to happen.

It's very difficult to say what it is that actually draws you in to CWA. I suppose it could be that you're looking for friendship. Or perhaps there's something you need to fulfil within yourself and, mind you, CWA provides a lot of areas where you can do that. Then there's the business side of CWA. There's the international work. There's the handicraft. There's culture. Cooking — and please don't turn this book into Tea and Scones story, like they had on the television. Yes, cooking is a big part of CWA but we go far, far deeper than that. CWA allows you the chance to broaden yourself on a personal level.

So being involved in CWA opens up your horizons. It gives you the belief and opportunity that you can do things you never ever dreamed that you'd do. It's the 'I am able to do it' mentality. It gives you confidence and that confidence comes from the support of those around you. I was a rather shy little girl when I joined CWA and last year I was instrumental in running the Annual State Conference in Tweed Heads.

I can never understand people who want to look back all the time. Life's out here. It's for living, not to say, 'Oh well we did that forty years ago.' Go with it. Go forward. Enjoy it, and you can change it.

Geraldine Scott
Wrattonbully, South Australia

I was born in the mid-north of South Australia, at Burra, in Warne's country, Mrs Warne being the woman who started CWA in this state. My mother was also a founding member and that initial CWA meeting was held in my uncle's room, alongside his chemist shop in Burra. That was back in 1929. I was off a merino stud in the area, called Koonoona Station. I'm now ninety so I've been around for a long time. But Mum loved her tree planting and she loved her CWA and so when I was sixteen, I joined. It's the most wonderful organisation and it's done so much for country people.

Then, when I got married, we went to the south-east. That was in about 1942. We got a property down there, just over the border into Victoria. There were about six families in that district and those women never went out, except to go to church once a month. That's true. It was terrible so we had an old van and I took these women just over the border, back into South Australia, to Wrattonbully, where we helped start the CWA Branch there, and, well, the Headquarters people, here in Adelaide, they said, 'You can't do that. You're residents of Victoria. You've got to go to CWA in Victoria.'

'Well, I can't help that,' I said. 'I'm bringing six new members to CWA here and that's that,' and that was at Wrattonbully and we had our first meetings in an old hut and the women brought tea pots and cups and saucers. It was great and we gradually built it up. It's been a wonderful Branch. We started off with those six, along with the ones who already lived in South Australia, and a couple of years later, as one of our projects, we planted the most trees in the state. Actually, I've just been down there for my ninetieth birthday party. They're such wonderful loving people and they also had a great sense of humour because I remember we had two women members, one was Mrs Batty and the other one was Mrs Looney. Batty and Looney, and we thought that was really funny and, in fact, Mrs Looney was down there the other day for my birthday and she's the only remaining original member, other than me.

As for special memories: well, I suppose the most important thing is the friendships and, when our property was burnt out and we lost everything, the CWA women were the first to come to our aid. And that fire was so horrific that, when the sheep were burnt alive, they died standing up. Extraordinary. We had one paddock of lambs and the whole lot went. But you can live through things like that because your CWA friends are with you and that's what helps you to keep going. But I love the land and I think that the country people who don't belong to CWA are missing out on a lot. I've heard that some people, with their noses in the air, think that us CWA women 'aren't the social mob'. Well, too bad, I say. CWA is what glues country people together.

But I think that one sad part of CWA is that we've got a lot of older members these days and not enough younger members. I once saw a segment on television; it was a Branch meeting somewhere in New South Wales and there were no children there. I though it was so sad because even the grannies should have had their grandchildren there. I mean, if the children cry, so what. At Wrattonbully, one of our members had thirteen children and she used to bring them along to our meetings and she'd put them down on the floor, with some toys, and you did not hear a peep out of them. Not one peep. They were wonderfully brought up. So it's my thinking that if the children go along to CWA they'll more likely become members whereas, if the children grow up knowing that they aren't allowed to come to CWA they'll think we're stand-offish, so they won't want to join.

And you make such wonderful friendships through CWA. At one stage I was sent to a school at Mount Macedon, in Victoria, where you learned how to cater for a thousand people in a crisis.

I forget now how many loaves of bread it takes, but it was a lot. But we CWA ladies, we've done a lot together and I do like to remember the happy things. We didn't have much money when we started off and so we just had to make do, and one day one of my best friends said to me, 'Oh, Geraldine, that dress of your mother's still looks nice,' and I said, 'Yes, she always bought nice clothes.' So, no, I wasn't too proud to wear my mother's old clothes. That's just what you did in those days.

Then I moved up to Adelaide in 1985. I'm hardly a city-slicker and it was a contrast coming from a country Branch to a city Branch but they've got used of me now and they know I say what I think. It's my feeling that it's far better to get up and say what's on your mind rather than keep quiet and talk about it afterwards. And, also, because you're from CWA I feel that it makes you more friendly to people. If I see some of the new migrants walking towards me, whatever colour they are, I always make the point of giving them a smile and saying, 'Hello.' And that's very important. That's also a country thing, too. If you've got new neighbours you go over and see them. You welcome them. You don't stand back and wait.

Anyhow, perhaps that's just me. I'm only an ordinary person. I might've lived frugally and worn my mother's old clothes but I'm proud to be a member of CWA and I'm very proud of my Life Membership Badge. Look at it. It's very nice, isn't it. It means a great deal to me, Life Membership, because it's such a wonderful organisation. Thank you very much.

Ruth Shanks
Dubbo, New South Wales

I was born and bred in Dubbo, in central New South Wales, and that's where I did my schooling and where, at the age of eighteen, I met my husband, Greg, and where I was married at nineteen and where we had our three children — two boys and a girl — and we now have nine grandchildren. So you could say that my whole life has revolved around Dubbo.

Greg was off the land. It was a family property. He was a twin and they had a younger brother. Then, when all the three boys were married within twelve months, it was impossible for them to try and make three family incomes off the one family property. So Greg's twin brother started a business, building stock crates. You may have seen them on the road — Shanks Trailers — and Greg works as a delivery agent at the saleyards in Dubbo mainly, and also Coonamble, and the younger brother has the farm.

After I'd left school I worked in the Commonwealth Bank for a while and then I started my nursing training. But when I got married I decided to give that up and so it wasn't until after I'd had our children that I completed my nursing training. In actual fact I ended up finishing in the top two per cent in the state. I then worked in a medical practice for twenty-five years before I retired and took on the position of State President of CWA New South Wales. That was in 2001.

Oddly enough, when I was young I wasn't really aware of CWA and, basically, the only reason I joined was that my mother-in-law was President of the small Branch near the family property. That was the Terramungamine Branch. It was about fourteen miles out of Dubbo, on the Collie Road. Anyhow, she said, 'Well, Ruth, if you're marrying into this family and you're marrying into the country you may as well join CWA.' So I did and that was over forty years ago now. And that Terramungamine Branch is still going today, even though they now meet in Dubbo because most of the women have retired and come into town to live.

I'd left that Branch well before then and I'd helped form the Dubbo Evening Branch. We started that because there was a need for a local CWA Branch to cater for the women who were working. And that's gone from strength to strength. We've currently got a membership of about twenty and we're a happy little band of workers. It's gone through its various stages. We initially went through a stage where we were all working, then we all sort of retired and now we've got some new ones who are back working again. Oh, yes, the Dubbo Day Branch is still going too. They've got the large CWA rooms in Dubbo, near the RSL Club. They've got quite a few members as well, though they're having the same trouble that all the voluntary organisations are experiencing and that's the difficulty of getting new people to join. It's hard, really. Very hard.

As for a single special moment over my years with CWA, that's also a hard one but, probably — and this is going into the international side of my work — it was back in 1992 when I was a delegate for CWA New South Wales at a conference of the Associated Country Women of the World, at The Hague, in the Netherlands. And I remember we had a church service in this wonderful, wonderful old cathedral. It would've been hundreds of years old and there I was standing in this beautiful old cathedral singing the 'Song of Peace', which is the song we always sing at those conferences. And it suddenly struck me that I just couldn't believe how a once shy little person like myself, who'd spent all her years in Dubbo, was there, helping women to improve their lives throughout the world. And every time I hear that song I get goose bumps because it takes me back to the Netherlands, to the Hague, and to that beautiful old cathedral.

This is my song, O God of all Nations.
A song of peace for lands afar, and mine.
This is my home, the country where my heart is.
Here are my hopes, my dreams, my holy shrine.
But other hearts in other lands are beating
With hopes and dreams as true and high as mine.
My country's skies are bluer that the ocean
And sunlight beams on clover leaf and pine.
But other lands have sunlight too, and clover
And skies are everywhere as blue as mine;
O hear my song, O God of all Nations
A song of peace for their land and for mine.

Mary Shattock
Booborowie, South Australia

I was born at Clare, in the mid-north of South Australia, and that's where I attended school until I went down to Adelaide High School in 1950 to do a year of Leaving Honours. Leaving Honours was only offered in the city. After that I went to Teacher's College where I qualified as an infant teacher and was bonded to the Department of Education for three years and posted to Booborowie, just north of Clare. Back then, Booborowie was a two-teacher school, with around forty-five students. I say 'around' because numbers fluctuated. In those days there were a lot more farmhands and station hands coming and going. But I remember, before I went to Booborowie, somebody saying, 'Oh, you'll probably marry a farmer,' and I was adamant that I was not going to marry a farmer. But, famous last words — what did I do? I married a farmer, didn't I!

Those days, if you were a woman working in a government job and you got married, you had to resign. That was the rule back then. So I resigned and I moved to the farm and later, my children did their primary schooling at Booborowie before heading off to Burra and Clare for their matriculation. And I'm still there on the farm. It's mixed farming. We run sheep and grow wheat and oats. The oats are used as feed and we sell the wheat and the sheep and the wool — not that wool's worth much these days but good quality sheep are.

But people ask me, 'Why did you join CWA?' Well I then had a bit more free time, I suppose, but really, I didn't need a reason to join. I just did. My mother had been a CWA member in Clare and, I later found out, my grandmother had also been a member at Clare. Booborowie was only a new Branch at that stage. It started in 1953, and so I joined in 1955 and, since then, I've served most of the offices. I was our Branch Handicraft Officer at one stage;

Treasurer for a while; Branch President off and on. I was Group Handicraft Officer, which meant coming down to Adelaide once a year to learn three different crafts and take those skills back and teach them at Branch level. They're not necessarily new crafts. Sometimes they tend to be those older skills that can easily get lost if you don't keep them going.

In 1994 I became our Group President and later on Divisional President, but with falling membership a number of Branches closed. We've only got six Branches left in the Group now. Booborowie Branch closed in 2000 and with Clare being my hometown and the place I might, one day, go back to live, I decided to transfer to the Clare Branch, and I've been very happy there. So these days I travel the hundred and ten kilometre round trip on CWA meeting days.

Interspersed with all of that I've also been on various state committees such as the Evaluation Committee, dealing with our direction and how to get new members. Then I've been on the Finance Committee as well as the Social Issues Fact Finding Team or SIFFT, as it's called. SIFFT is the lobbying arm of the Association. An example of what we do there would be when they decided to get rid of the resident policeman at one place and just have the police do visits. Well that was all right while he's there but as what seems to happen, 'while the cat's away', the mice play', don't they? So along with the community we lobbied to have a resident policeman reinstated, and we got that. Another thing — and I wasn't involved in this one — was when they first started building new shopping centres there were no public toilets included, and it was due to our lobbying that toilets are now installed in shopping centres.

Then I was elected Deputy State President in 2003 and following that, South Australian State President. But fifteen months before I finished my term of office, my husband died quite suddenly and, really, I think what helped me cope with the loss was, with the responsibilities of that job, I just had to keep going. And so I did.

But, on a lighter note, probably one of the biggest achievements that happened while I was State President was the marketing of our CWA scone mix. That came about when the daughter of one of our Marketing and Promotion Working Party members bought some scone mix at a supermarket and the scones were awful. For years we'd been using the bulk bags of Laucke's Scone Mix in our cafe at the Adelaide Show. So we decided to approach Laucke's — a very reputable South Australian firm — and see if they'd like to market the mix as Country Women's Scone Mix, and we'd get something out of it. I then wrote to Mark Laucke outlining the idea, and he was just so enthusiastic. Laucke's then produced the 1.2 kg pack of Country Women's Scone Mix with the history of Laucke's on one panel and a bit about CWA on the other side, along with the contact numbers for each State CWA. Coles were the first to release it nationally, then Foodland and IGA. Now Woolworths has come on board, and the whole thing has just caught on. It's snowballed. It's been wonderful.

CWA gets forty cents for every packet sold. Out of that, twenty cents goes to help run our Association and the other twenty cents goes to our South Australian CWA Emergency Aid Fund, where the money is used help people in need. To instigate that, applications have to be made through a social worker, a minister of religion or a hospital. For instance, there was a woman who'd been living in a tent, south of Adelaide. It was summer, forty-degree temperatures, and she'd had a baby. The hospital wouldn't let her go back to the tent with the new baby so they found her accommodation. But she didn't have any clothes so we gave her what we call a Baby Parcel. It's basic baby clothes, about $150 worth, but they're done up so beautifully. Then another time there was a girl and the father of the baby got a bit nasty and took all the baby's clothes and she was left with nothing but a bassinet. So after the baby was born the social worker referred her to us and we were able to help.

But, you know, when you have a run of bad luck it just seems to keep going, doesn't it? The telephone bill might come in, then the electricity bill arrives, and you must have a telephone and electricity in this day and age. So CWA might pay the bill. Another case was when a woman was struggling. She got a job and we registered her car so that she could get to work, and hopefully that helped her get on her feet. And it's not only for women: one fellow was referred to us who had an interview for a job. He only had a pair of tatty old sneakers so we helped him buy two pairs of shoes, so he had a spare pair. And that just might've been the thing to set that fellow up. We don't give huge amounts but sometimes, just a little bit of help can make a world of difference in someone's life.

There's also been a number of other programs that CWA has been involved in. Through the Department of Agriculture, Fisheries and Forestry (DAFF), the previous government gave us some drought relief money and I had a number of meetings with the DAFF people to help set that up. Then one morning Michael Luscombe, the CEO of Woolworths, was wondering what he could do to help those affected by the drought. So he approached the CWA of Australia and, from that, Woolworths had their first Drought Action Day where one day of their profits was given to each CWA in that particular state who then distributed the money. A maximum of $2000 was made available to each family in need. Now, I've never been hungry, and nor have my children, but just try to imagine how you'd feel if your kids were saying, 'Mum, I'm hungry', and you didn't have the money to feed them.

So there's just a few of the things our association does and, keep in mind, we're all volunteers and as a member you make many, many friendships along the way.

Pam Simcoe
Lisarow-Ourimbah, New South Wales

My position in CWA? Well I hold lots of positions actually. Currently I'm President of the Lisarow-Ourimbah Branch of CWA. I'm the Northumberland Group Handicraft Officer. I'm also Northumberland Representative to Executive. That's enough I think. Oh, and I'm the Minutes Secretary of our Branch, though that's not a recognised position. Then I have other interests too. CWA is not the be-all and end-all. So I keep busy, you could say.

But I love CWA, otherwise I wouldn't have stayed in it since 1972. That's well over thirty-five years. I've seen a lot of changes. I first joined in the days when you wore hat and gloves and you got all dressed up, whether it be to go to a function or to go to a meeting. That's just the way it was back then. It's relaxed a lot now. Some of it's good. Some not so good, but we've got to move along with the times. And times are different. That's why a lot of the young women aren't joining. They've married. They've got a couple of kids. They're working to help pay off the mortgage. They get involved with their children's sporting clubs. Sport wasn't as structured in my day. Kids didn't go racing off to a Cricket Club, they played cricket in the backyard. I was on the P&C [Parents and Citizens] at Peats Ridge school and a couple of parents were always rostered to help on sport days. The girls played basketball or softball and the boys played cricket or ran around like mad fools. But they needed supervision, especially the boys. One time the boys went missing so I hunted around and I found them in the toilet block having a competition of their own, seeing how high they could pee up the wall.

But I've got a couple of funny things that have happened in the CWA. I shouldn't say names, should I? Okay, this was back when you wore a hat and gloves and you were 'fine ladies' and I'd go to some function or other with a particular lady who always dressed her best. What's more, she expected everyone else to dress their best, including me. The only trouble was that she didn't have the best of memories and so sometimes we'd arrive at a function that had either been and gone or it wasn't on until the next week. But she was very 'environmentally inclined', I guess you could say, and she never wasted the moment because on our way back home she'd have us out on the side of the road picking up litter and what-have-you, all dressed up in our best clothes.

Another time, another friend — a different one to the one who always dressed up — well, her and I were coming back from a CWA function and we found a litter of puppies that had been abandoned on the side of the old Express Way. No sign of Mum. Sad really but, oh, they were so cute. Kelpie crosses they were. So we wrapped them up in old towels and we took them home and we kept them warm in an electric fry pan, that was turned down low. We even gave them names: one was called Sinbad, after Sinbad the Sailor, and we found homes for them all. So that was a good outcome.

That same lady and I raised five rooster chicks in a dish with a bedside light. You normally have the proper lamp but we used an old bedside light, one of those you can bend around. Anyhow, we brought them home and we put them in a round bowl and put a shelf from a fridge on the top, so they couldn't escape, and we set up this bedside light to shine down on them. They said it couldn't be done with a bedside light. But we did it. Then those same roosters, after they'd grown up, they turned around and they attacked us, spurs and all. Oh, they're pretty vicious.

Do you want to hear some more? Well, another time CWA set up a little stall in the main street of Gosford. This was back in about '72 or '73; back in the gloves, dresses and hats era. I was one of the younger ones then. It was outside the Women's Centre. CWA had a wheel-out stall, like a cart. It was about two metres long and a bit less than a metre wide. You used to see them in Martin Place, in Sydney. Same sort of thing and, when you finished, you just pushed it back against the wall. So we were there, in the main street of Gosford, and we'd set up our stall. Coming from a farming area we were selling fruit and vegetables, jams, pickles, honey, lemon butter and some handicraft. Just a little bit. All donated. We also ran a raffle which always consisted of a fruit and vegetable hamper plus, sometimes, a bottle of homemade wine from one of the Italians or Greeks who farmed up on the mountain. It was pretty potent stuff, too. I'll tell you a story about that later.

So we'd sold all these raffle tickets and we'd pulled all the butts apart and we'd put them in an ice-cream container. We then put the lid on the ice-cream container and, after we shook all the loose butts up, we chose someone from the public to come and pick out the winning ticket. The only trouble was that, when we took the lid off the ice cream container so that the person could take out the winning ticket, a strong gust of wind came along and it blew all the butts down the main street. So there were all us ladies, dressed up to the nines, crawling around the street on our hands and knees, picking up the loose raffle tickets. And we got them all, too.

Now, back to what I said about the farmers up on the mountain. At Peats Ridge, the Italians and Greeks had been peasant farmers in their own country so they knew how to grow things. They really did, and they still do, and so coming to Australia was absolute heaven to them. It was mainly citrus, but they also grew vegies and they still have stands at the markets in Sydney. They also put down their own wine and their own olives. Make salami. That still goes on. That's tradition. But they're the most generous people, you know. If you said, 'CWA Stall,' the stuff's right there for you. Those farmers didn't hesitate and they still don't.

I can tell you, every Christmas, we used to drive around and collect money and things so that all the local children got a gift from under the community tree. If you couldn't afford to donate anything, your child was still included. Nobody felt bad and you took a plate of food on the night. So we'd go collecting around the area and we'd visit all the friendly, ethnic people; namely Greeks and Italians. But we had to be very, very careful of their hospitality or else, by the end of the day, it could easily have ended up with one of us steering while the other one was changing the gears.

Then it was always my job to pick up Santa and to ferry him to the Christmas tree and, one time, we had him perched up in the back of our ute, on one of those real old vinyl chairs. It was all decorated up and everything but, apparently, I went around a corner a bit too fast, didn't I? Because, when I looked in the rear-vision mirror, it was, 'Where's Santa?'

As to how I came to join the CWA? Well I almost didn't, actually. My mother-in-law lived out at place near Dubbo. She was a CWA member out there and I went along with her one time and, whenever I opened my mouth, the other CWA ladies would say, 'Oh, we don't do it like that.' So I thought, Well I don't care if I ever see CWA again.

Then when I moved down on the coast, the lady I was telling you about — the one with the litter of puppies — she kept calling on me, saying, 'Please come and join us. We'd love to have you,' and, as an excuse, I'd organise friends to visit me on the day of the CWA meeting, which, of course, meant that I couldn't make it to the meeting. Well eventually I ran out of people to come and visit me, didn't I? So I gave in and said, 'Oh, all right I'll come.'

It was an evening meeting back then and I went and, I tell you, they made me feel so welcome that I paid my membership fees on the spot. They were totally different to the ladies I'd run into out near Dubbo, that time. The ones with my mother-in-law, they were nice ladies, yes, but they were the 'old school' and I suppose I was still only quite young. These ones at Peats Ridge were a real mix. Mothers could bring their babies. You could bring your toddler. You could bring your school children and during the school holidays the CWA meetings were always structured around the kids. We'd go on picnics. We'd go to a local swimming hole. Go on a ferry ride. The children were always involved. It was fantastic, and I think we need to be even more tolerant of that.

Local CWA is all to do with community. It's a silent worker. If, for any reason, a family is in need of clothes or food, the CWA always arrives on the doorstep with clothes and some food. It's the same with a fire. I absolutely take my hat off to the volunteer fire brigade. It's a horrible job, it really is. In the past, the CWA has gone and worked alongside the Salvation Army, and anyone else, to make sandwiches, coffee, tea; anything that's required by the 'firies'. If somebody died, you alway cooked something and arrived on the people's doorstep with the food so they didn't have to think about what they were going to eat. They've got enough on their mind. That still happens. It's just the thing to do. The Mangrove Adult Day Care for the oldies is unique because just about every volunteer who works there is from the Mangrove Area CWA. Again, it's the community getting together. I teach handicraft. Once or twice a month CWA members do the cooking, to give the cook a break. We also take the oldies on outings.

It's all fun. That's the way I look at it. One time a friend and I decided to liven up a Peats Ridge CWA Branch meeting and so we got dressed up as Dave and Mabel. I was Dave. She was Mabel. She had her hair done up with a big bow on the top and wore this big floral dress and her husband's work boots, which she painted with silver frost. I had bib and brace overalls, an old straw hat, a big chequered shirt, gumboots, blacked out my front teeth. Then, as was written on the invitation — Please bring a plate — we arrive with a plate each. Mine had nothing on it. We knocked on the door and we said, 'Is this the CWA? We understand that we had to bring a plate.'

Well, they didn't even recognise us, did they? They didn't even know who we were. Not a clue. It was as simple as that. Anyway we carried on a bit but it backfired because it turned out that there was this very important lady visiting. If she wasn't the State Vice-President or Vice-President then she was definitely someone very high up. So perhaps they just didn't want to recognise us. What do you think? Well, we had fun anyway.

Vera Stephenson
Spalding, South Australia

I grew up in South Australia, on a farm midway between Clare and Spalding. I milked cows with Mum until I was into my teenage years and we used to go to Clare for shopping and various things like that. The school I went to was at a place called Euromina. It was only a little tiny primary school with about fifteen children in it. That was at the end of the war and so I never went on any further with my education than that. My mum was a CWA member but I never worried about joining at that early stage.

I met my husband, we married in July 1951, and I went on another farm to live. My parents-in-law lived next door to my husband and I and my mother-in-law belonged to CWA in Spalding. She'd never learned to drive so, after our honeymoon, in the August or September I think it was, one day my father-in-law said, 'Vera, I'm busy on the farm, would you mind driving your mother-in-law into town for the CWA meeting.'

'Okay,' I said and when we got to Spalding I thought, Well there's not much to do in town, I may as well tag along. So I went to the meeting, then at the next meeting they put me in as a member. From there my CWA life began and that's almost sixty years ago now and even when I had the two children I took them to most of the meetings. I'd just put them on the floor and they'd play. A couple of members used to say that you shouldn't bring children but my daughter never used to open her mouth, though, I must say, my son was a bit of a different proposition at times. But my thinking was that, if they wanted members, they'd just have to accept it. And they did.

Anyway I got interested in handicrafts and before I knew it I was on the handicraft committee. In those days we made a lot of coverings for stools with linen thread. I was a bit keen on doing it that way and I've still got three of the stools I made away back then. We also crocheted and we knitted and we made things to sell at our CWA fundraising stalls.

Then in the 1960s, I got landed with the job as Secretary of the Spalding Branch and I held that position for a few years even though I didn't really think I was cut out for it. Actually, the Spalding Branch was the second oldest in the state. Burra was the oldest, we were next, then a Branch was formed in Adelaide. Mary Warne started CWA in Burra and then she came to Spalding and started Spalding. So I've got that history with both my mum and mother-in-law being in CWA long before I existed. Then one day, someone happened to say, 'Oh Vera, why don't you be our President.' So I became President of Spalding Branch and, on and off, I was President of the Branch for something like twenty-one years in all.

Spalding was a wonderful Branch actually. In my early days, in the 1950s, we had up to sixty members. But then it fell away and in 2000 I was elected again as Branch President. I had a Secretary, Joyce, who had been our Secretary for ten years, on and off. Joyce had Parkinson's by then and she couldn't drive so I was driving her around. Then our Treasurer, Beryl, she was a very solid Treasurer. She knew the works but when the money side of things shifted to our Head Office in Adelaide, Beryl wouldn't do the Treasurer's job any more. So there I was, landed with the job of President, and nobody would take on the Treasurer's job and poor old Joyce couldn't do it so, in 2001, I said, 'Right, I can't do every job and nobody else is prepared to so I'm going to Clare CWA.'

There were about ten at that meeting and they all went, 'Oohh.'

Anyway, we decided to close our Spalding Branch, which I was very upset about because of our history, and a month later I lined up with a car and I drove a load of women the thirty-nine kilometres down to Clare CWA. The funny thing was, I knew most of the Clare girls because I'd been their Group and Divisional President, and the first day we went to the Clare Branch they said, 'Oh Vera, can you be our Treasurer?'

So I came home as their Treasurer and I'm still Treasurer of Clare Branch, aren't I ? and every month I drive from Spalding to Clare to go to CWA, with a car load of girls. And I'm still taking two of the original members that came with me on that first day. While I'm going they'll all come. But I also know that if I stop tomorrow nobody will go. It's a shame, but the Clare Branch has benefited and we now have a membership of around thirty-one. We're a very happy and active Branch and we've got one young girl, Emily, who is dead keen. Emily's the chemist's wife and she has two children and we're encouraging her all the way as it's just wonderful to see young ones coming in like that.

As for special moments with CWA: I guess there's been many. One great experience was, when I was both our Group and Divisional President, being able to attend the various National Conferences throughout Australia. Another would be when I was at the end of my term as Divisional President and I held a rally at Riverton Hall and about two hundred women attended and we raised a lot of money for CWA State Objective. On that same day my Spalding Branch presented me with a Life Membership of the Association. Not only was that a great surprise and a shock but it was a great honour and I'm just so proud to wear the CWA Life Membership Badge.

Of course, there have also been the more difficult times. In those early days, CWA was a part of everyday life in places like Spalding and I remember a time when cancer seemed to hit the town all of a sudden. First of all, a little girl got leukaemia, though after treatment she, thankfully, went into remission. Then a twelve-year-old boy died suddenly, and that was tragic.

We felt so much for the parents of the young boy that we set up a trading table in the main street and we made $350, just over the Friday afternoon. That was to help the family. And I think that things like that are very important in small communities like ours. He was a young twelve-year-old. Cancer, he had. It's cruel, it is. As a parent, to lose a child would be one of the worst things because that's not how life is supposed to work. I lost my husband with cancer three-and-a-half years ago and I realise now something of what those parents must have gone through. Yet I accepted the fact that my husband died because I couldn't bear to see him suffer any longer and, at least, we'd had fifty-six years of good married life. We'd had our golden wedding anniversary and all that. But to see a young kid go out of the town, it just breaks your heart. I worked very hard for that stall that day. We all did. We canvassed the town to get people to support it, and they did. We sold cakes, plants, sewing, handicrafts — whatever people donated. And with just a population of about three hundred overall we made $350 in just that afternoon. Every bit helps. And the parents were battling. They were battling, like anyone would in their situation.

So that's about it really. Thank you for listening to my story. Compared to some of the others it might not be that exciting or wonderful but I'd just like to finish by saying that, through my involvement with CWA, I've received and benefited so much by the experience, in particular through the kindness shown to me by members and the many friendships I've made along the way.

Biscuits and Cookies

Coffee Creams
Mrs Piesse, Bridgewater, CWA Tas

¼ lb cup butter
1 cup sugar
1 egg

2 tablespoons coffee
essence
2 cups self-raising flour

Melt butter and sugar and beat to a cream. Add beaten egg and then the essence. Add flour. Mix to a very stiff paste. Put in teaspoonfuls on a cold tray. Bake 15 minutes in moderate (180°C) oven. When cold, join two biscuits together with coffee icing.

Cornflake Biscuits
CWA NSW

½ cup sugar
1 cup butter
1 egg

½ cup desiccated coconut
½ cup chopped walnuts
5 cups cornflakes

Cream butter and sugar, add well-beaten egg, the walnuts and coconut, then mix the cornflakes in lightly. Bake in paper cases, allowing about 1 dessertspoon of mixture to each case. Allow twenty minutes in a slow (160°C) oven for cooking. Store biscuits in an airtight tin.

Date Slices
CWA NSW

1 tablespoon caster sugar
6 oz self-raising flour
Pinch salt
3 oz butter

1 egg
Lemon juice and water
Dates

Sift sugar, flour and salt together. Rub the butter in the flour till fine like breadcrumbs. Beat the egg, add 3 tablespoons cold water and 1 of lemon juice. Mix into flour with blade of knife. Roll out and divide into two. Place one half of the paste into a dish 8 inches x 10 inches and cover with dates then cover that with the other half of the paste and cook in moderate (180°C) oven for 20 minutes. When cold, ice with icing — 1 cup icing sugar, 1 tablespoon melted butter, passionfruit and little hot water.

Makes about 2 dozen fingers.

Ginger Biscuits (delicious)

Mrs A. Bovis, Exeter, CWA Tas

3 oz margarine	3 oz sugar
4 oz golden syrup	¼ teaspoon bicarb soda
6 oz self-raising flour	½ teaspoon ginger

Melt margarine and syrup in saucepan. Allow to cool then sift in remaining ingredients. Mix well. Then between floured palms of hands form balls the size of a walnut. Place on greased tray allowing space to spread. Bake in a moderate (180°C) oven until golden brown. Allow to cool on slab tin.

Monte Carlos

CWA NSW

¼ lb butter	½ teaspoon baking
½ cup sugar	powder
1 egg	2 cups flour
½ cup desiccated coconut	Raspberry jam
2 teaspoons golden syrup	Soft icing

Mix in order given (not jam). Break small pieces off with fork. Bake on greased trays in moderate (180°C) oven. When cooked, fasten two biscuits together with raspberry jam and soft icing.

Nut Bars

E. A. French, Whitemore, CWA Tas

1½ tablespoons butter	¾ teaspoon cream of
2 tablespoons sugar	tartar
1 egg	Pinch salt
¼ cup golden syrup	1 cup chopped raisins
1 teaspoon bicarb soda	1 cup chopped nuts
2 cups plain flour	

Cream butter and sugar and beaten egg. Beat in syrup, add the carb soda that's been dissolved in a little milk. Add flour, salt and cream of tartar, sifted together. Mix in raisins and nuts. Roll out thinly. Place on greased tray. Bake in a moderate (180°C) oven. Cut into bars while warm.

Oatmeal and Raisin Cookies
CWA NSW

1¾ cups rolled oats
½ cup butter or shortening
1 cup sugar
1 egg
¾ cup raisins
1½ cups flour

2 teaspoons baking powder
½ teaspoon salt
¾ teaspoon cinnamon
½ teaspoon ground cloves
½ teaspoon allspice
½ cup milk

Put rolled oats through food chopper. Cream butter and sugar, add well-beaten egg, raisins and rolled oats. Mix thoroughly. Sift flour, baking powder, salt and spices together and add to egg mixture alternately with the milk. Roll out on to slightly floured board. Cut with cookie cutter and bake in a moderate (180°C) oven for 15–20 minutes.

This makes about 30 cookies.

Shortbread
CWA NSW

1 lb butter
7½ oz caster sugar
12 oz self-raising flour
12 oz ground rice

Cream butter and sugar slightly. Add the flour and ground rice, well sifted. Cut into squares ½ inch thick, pinch edges and cook for 20 minutes in a moderate (180°C) oven.

June Thiedeke
Goovigen, Queensland

The towns of Jambin and Goovigen are only seven-and-a-half miles apart and, even though I've been living in Jambin for almost thirty years, I've always belonged to the Goovigen Branch of Queensland CWA. To give you some idea as to where we are, we're about an hour or an hour and a half south-west of Rockhampton, and I've been told that Goovigen, in the Aboriginal language, means 'Box tree', whereas Jambin is meant to be 'echidna'.

I actually grew up in south-eastern Queensland, at Toowoomba, then, when I married, we lived about twenty miles out of Millmerran, at a little place called Bringalily. My husband won the block there back in the early 1930s after the government opened it up to a ballot. It was sandy sort of soil, with brigalow and quite a lot of Cyprus pine, and it had lots and lots of prickly pear on it. Lots. So we started clearing it and then the research people found a little insect — the cactoblastis — and that just about wiped the prickly pear out. We had a little dairy property, with just a few cattle, and we also grew oats, wheat, barley and linseed and, in the summer, we grew sorghum.

Then I got into CWA through handicraft. They had a CWA Branch at Bringalily and they asked if I'd like to come to handicraft lessons, which was something I'd always wanted to do. That would've been about fifty-six years ago now and, with handicrafts, in those days we mostly did cane work, like making baskets, and we also did crafts like tapestry. Then I could always knit but I'd never learned to crochet and so I learned that too. But really, no matter what it was, I'd have a go at it. That's my problem. I've got too many interests. Too many interests to fill a lifetime anyway, because I like gardening and, a couple of years ago, I got myself a computer, which I'm yet to master. But I'll get there.

As time went by, I got more into the Branch side of CWA and, for me, since I've belonged to Goovigen Branch, one of the very special memories I have would be of when I was Divisional President of Capricornia and we held a State Conference at Rockhampton. That was in 1999 and I've been led to believe it was one of the best country conferences Queensland CWA has ever had. So I'm quite proud of that and more so how all the members within the Division really got into it with me. Whatever I asked of them to do, they came across and did it and that was also special.

On the other hand I'd really like to see more young ones coming along to meetings because they'd bring fresh ideas. But unfortunately, many of the Branches aren't getting in new members. I think that's because, these days, a lot of the younger ones are working and whilst they may be interested in CWA they're not prepared to step in and give their time to it whereas, us older ones, we just get in and we do it, no matter what. I also think our modern way of living has a bit to do with it, too. Still, it's really hard to define because I know that some of the Branches are getting the younger ones in and they're proving to be really good members.

In actual fact, talking about good young members, something that may be of interest is that, in our Branch, we do have one young member, Michelle. Michelle's now in her thirties and she's a third-generation member. At the moment she's our Secretary and her mother is our Treasurer. Her grandmother used to be with us too, but she's passed on. So that's rather unique, and you have to foster it because, before I came back as President again, Michelle did a stint as President and she did quite a good job. Still, in general, these days we just don't seem to be getting many new members. It's unfortunate but you just have to soldier on, don't you? At the moment we have only the six members in our Goovigen Branch and we've just got one who's on transfer. She grew up in this area. She'd been up in Cairns and she lost her husband and she came back down here to live. So we've actually got seven members and we mostly get about four or five to our meetings.

Something else that may be quite unique to our Branch is that we've been running bingo, as a fundraiser, for the past twenty-one years. How that came about was that, when a new publican came to Goovigen, he had the right licence or whatever it was, to be able to run bingo. Anyway, he asked the local progress association if they'd like to do it but they weren't interested. Then of course, who do they always ask when nobody else is interested — they ask the good old CWA, don't they? I was our Branch President at that time as well and I'd never been to bingo in my life and so I needed to be sure that we were doing the right thing because I'd heard that one of our Branches had got into problems with their permits or whatever.

So I asked around and I managed to find out that, if we took no more than $500 at a game, we could run bingo on an ordinary permit. So that's how we got into running the bingo and, I'd say, we'd probably have at least fifteen or so come along each time. We hold it in the daytime, in the lounge, at the local hotel in Goovigen and it's been quite good for us. We start at 10.30 of a morning, every second Thursday. Then we have a break over the Christmas period, thank the good Lord, because I reckon it's the most frustrating game you can play. Just when you need one more number, somebody jumps in before you and calls out, 'Bingo!'

As I said, we've now been doing that for the last twenty-one years and, believe it or not, but out of everyone that's been going along to bingo all those years, I'm the only one who's never won a jackpot. No, never. Oh, I've won a couple of consolations but that's it; never a jackpot. But anyway, you don't let those little things worry you, do you? I just thank the good Lord for what He's given me. I make the most of each day and that's what we have to do, isn't it? With so many dreadful things happening in this world you just have to count your blessings and be positive. That's what I think, anyway.

Pam Vallett
Fairfield, New South Wales

I belong to a city Branch of CWA: Fairfield Branch, which is in the Nepean Group. Yes, we do have city Branches of CWA. It's not only just a rural association. In New South Wales our closest Branch to Sydney would be Granville, then we extend out to Ingleburn, up to Blacktown, Kurrajong, Wilberforce, Windsor, Galston, Castle Hill plus there's nine other Branches in between. Unfortunately we've lost a number of our Branches over the years but we're trying to address that in different ways. We're fighting back and now some of the younger women are joining, which is good. It's happening, and it will continue to happen.

I was actually born in the country but my mum moved down to Sydney during the war. Then when Dad came back from Malaya in 1944 we moved out to Fairfield, and that's where I've been ever since. And as to how I came to join CWA: well, after giving birth to my first child in 1966, I was visiting the Baby Health Centre in Fairfield and, when I came over a bit weak and wobbly, I was told, 'Go next door. The Country Women's Association are there. They'll give you a cup of tea and look after you,' which they did, and that, as they say, was that.

But in the early 1950s, when the Fairfield Branch was first formed, there were still a lot of farms in the area: vegetable farms, some dairies, flowers, grapes, large poultry holdings. Back then the CWA was somewhere for the mothers to go when they were in town. We've never owned our own building here, as such. That's been given to us, gratis, by our Fairfield Council, and they've been absolutely wonderful. They really look after us. In the early days they gave us the use of a cottage which had a nice backyard with a swing and a slippery dip and CWA had a lady living on the premises, permanently. That used to happen quite a lot. In the history of CWA of New South Wales, where they had cottages, they often had people in them as caretakers; someone who was well known and trustworthy and who was in need of somewhere to live.

There was also a lot of immigration back then, in the 1950s. In Fairfield, alone, we were surrounded by four migrant camps and so many of our early members were from families who had come to our shores from all over the world. You could say that we were a multicultural organisation long before it became the 'in' thing. We've also had members go into the homes of those new settlers and teach them English. All volunteers. With CWA, anytime we're called upon to do anything for anybody, we do. We've also done a lot of catering in the past. With the Naturalisation Ceremonies, as they were called, we provided the supper when the new settlers took their oath of allegiance, and over the years we would've done that for thousands of people.

Actually, Fairfield Council now holds the Citizenship Ceremonies at our beautiful Fairfield City Farm. Why they describe it as a farm is because it's an actual working property within our city of Fairfield. It's a place where children can pat the animals or go for rides on tractors or they can see cows being milked. These days it's amazing just how many children don't even realise that milk comes out of a cow. So an experience like that really brings it home in a practical sense. Then on the occasions when the Farm has hosted special days for handicapped people and those with difficulties, our CWA Branch members have been there to help with their care. So we do quite a lot for our own local city community as well as our work for those outside our area.

To that end we also raise funds to help our sisters in the country. We collect food. We send Pamper Packs out to the women who live in small towns and communities that may be suffering badly through drought or fire or flood. Pamper Packs are a bit more personal. They're packs that contain lipstick, shampoo, tissues; things that a lot of our country sisters might consider as luxuries and so, when times get hard, they stop buying them. Our Fairfield members and friends recently sent Pamper Packs out to Wilcannia, through a lady who's connected to Rotary. So we always try to let our country sisters know that we appreciate what they're going through and that they have the support and thoughts of others, and I think it's important that people who may be going through difficult times know that others care.

As far as other fundraising goes, some may knit garments or make goods or just send in cash. At Fairfield I organise a monthly day-bus trip where we take women to different places. That's now our major fundraiser. It's something that these people can afford. We've been to various markets. We take them to see some of the beautiful old colonial homes in the area or go out past Windsor to Ebenezer to visit the historic old sandstone church with its very old tombstones. It's a beautiful drive and the ladies get to see the rivers and the countryside. It gets them out of their homes — out from behind their four walls — and to do something different. We also enjoy a cruise day each year. That's a lovely day. We look after them very well and they very much look forward to it. And that's what everybody needs. If you're lonely, or if you are alone, being able to look forward to something is a great help.

Then we also raise funds for the Careflight Helicopter, the Diabetes Foundation and the Cancer Council. For many years we bought food for the Salvation Army, which their Welfare Officer would then allocate to those who were in the greatest need. We also sponsor a child to go to Asthma Camp every year. That's a wonderful thing because quite often, due to their parents being anxious about them, sometimes these children are a little smothered. So around Christmas, the doctors, the nurses and the carers give of their holiday time and they go out on these camps and they teach the children that, yes, they are able to swim and that, yes, they can be archers and that they're able to play games outside, even though they have asthma. Camps like these also give the medical staff the opportunity to monitor the way the children are self-medicating and, if necessary, correct any problems. So we do all that and, of course, we always raise funds for whatever CWA's Medical Research Project is for that particular year plus anything else we're asked to support by the CWA of New South Wales.

People may not realise that there's just so many things we do. We also visit nursing homes, just as a friendly face; someone to say hello to. I remember, years ago, we were visiting one particular nursing home and they had a piano downstairs that this lovely gentleman used to come in and play. He was a retired policeman. Then, when we went upstairs to say hello to the patients up there, we realised they couldn't hear the piano being played. So our Fairfield CWA members made a special effort and we raised some funds and we bought a portable keyboard. We gave it to the nursing home and they took it upstairs so that the patients up there could get to hear the piano being played. Then later on we were talking to the people from the nursing home and they said that some of those patients hadn't talked for years and yet, when they heard the music on the keyboard, they started singing. Yes, they started singing along with the songs they remembered from years and years ago. You know, just a simple thing like that, and the people from the nursing home couldn't get over it because these people hadn't talked for years and here they were, smiling and singing away. So it doesn't take a fortune to help people. You just have to have the will and find out where the need is and do what you can. And that's what we try to do in CWA.

Yes, they all started to sing. Wonderful, isn't it?

Dorothy Walker
Eromanga, Queensland

I grew up on a cane farm in the Innisfail area of north Queensland. That was back during the Second World War when the Menzies government declared what was called the Brisbane Line. The Brisbane Line was an imaginary line that was drawn across the country with the idea being that, just in the case of a Japanese invasion, the northern part of Australia would be automatically surrendered to the Japanese and we'd defend the south. With that in mind all the women and children to the north of the Brisbane Line were sent to safer areas and because we had relations down south in Brisbane, we went and stayed with our relations there.

We were away for most of 1942 and we returned to Innisfail at the beginning of 1943. I was six by then and I'd only done a bit of kindergarten in Brisbane and that was all. So, really, my schooling started at a place called Eastern Goondi. Goondi was just a little settlement that had grown up around the sugar mill. I was at the school there for about eighteen months then, after we sold the cane farm, we moved into Innisfail where I went to school at East Innisfail then onto Innisfail before I went away to an all-girl's boarding school. That was at St Hilda's, in Southport, near Surfers Paradise. It was a long way away from Innisfail, I know, but it was the family's idea that the climate would be better. And it was and it was also a beautiful spot though it was quite tucked away because, I remember that, the only way you could see the ocean was to stand on one bed, on the verandah, and you'd get just a tiny glimpse of the water. After St Hilda's I went back and worked in Innisfail for a year before going down to Sydney to do my nurse's training. That was at the Children's Hospital there and then I returned to Queensland

and spent a further year in Brisbane, doing midwifery as it was called back then.

Anyway, a friend and I intended to travel to England and my mother said, 'You must have enough money for your return fare before you go.' So I went out nursing to Quilpie to save money for the trip to England and I met my husband-to-be, Robert, and that was the end of the story and I still haven't been to England yet. Instead, we married and I came out farming near Eromanga and we've been here for forty-something years. It's a sheep and cattle farm. It's only a fairly small place in comparison to some of the other properties and, unfortunately, we've been through a very bad drought. But, just in the past few days, we've had all this marvellous rain. So we're smiling now.

As to how I got into the CWA: my mother wasn't involved in Innisfail. She was more Red Cross and the RSL Women's Auxiliary. But when I came out to Eromanga there were quite a few of us young women out here who'd married at about the same time and we had little children and one of the neighbours knew about CWA and she said, 'We should start our own Branch as a means of getting out of the house and meeting each other plus also all the children can play together.' That's how it started in Eromanga, and that was in 1966.

Back then there were quite a few families in the district but, in those early stages, we had no single meeting place and so we'd been going for a while and Australian Estates had a flying doctor's clinic building, in there at Eromanga, and they gave us the use of that building providing we maintained it for the Royal Flying Doctor Service. And we're still there and we still maintain the clinic, to this very day. As far as membership goes, the station properties don't employ so many people these days and so we're down to only about twelve members now. But something very special about our Branch is that, many of the children who used to meet up, when we first began CWA at Eromanga, have remained good friends and some of them are even involved in CWA. In fact, my daughter, who was a baby when we started, she's now our Branch Treasurer.

As for memories, well, the formation of the Branch is, of course, a very fond one to me because it was the beginning of something that's survived all these years. We've also been involved in many memorable shows in Eromanga and along with other organisations, we cater for things like, if the Department of Primary Industries have a special day or the State Emergency Service might have a day. So we cater for events like that and some of our money goes into maintaining the RFDS clinic in Eromanga. The flying doctor comes to visit once or twice a month, depending on the number of people they have to see. Then we support things like 'Safe Water' for our international work. Safe Water is where we help people put down wells in the countries where they have no fresh water, like in some of the islands in the Pacific. So we support that and that's a state-wide CWA objective. It's just not us at Eromanga.

I'm also involved at Divisional level in CWA. Currently I'm both Branch Secretary and Division Secretary. The Division takes in Tambo, Augathella, Charleville, Morven, Quilpie and Eromanga. So there's quite a few towns. It's about a three hundred kilometre drive from here to Charleville, then Tambo would be two hours north of Charleville. Morven is about an hour east of Charleville. So it's a big enough area. The Divisions get together four times a year and once a year at State Conference. This year's Conference is in Brisbane. Next year it's going to be held up at Charters Towers. So that'll be an exciting one.

But, really, it's the friendships. For me that's the one thing that stands out and that's pretty much why we started CWA off in Eromanga in the first place. So that's carried right on, through those years, since 1966. And having been a member from the start, I should know a few of the ropes by now, shouldn't I? But to put it in a sentence, I'd say our main objective is that we look after the welfare of all the women and the children. That's a big part of CWA as far as I'm concerned. And, you never know, I still might just get that trip into England.

Helen Wall
Caniambo, Victoria

I'm from a dry area sheep, cattle and cropping farm, near Shepparton, in central-northern Victoria. I went to primary school at East Shepparton. Following that I went to high school at Shepparton, then on to teacher's college at Bendigo, before going teaching. Then I got married. Even though we knew each other we hadn't gone to school together or anything. Our families lived on opposite sides of the Broken River and so I'd seen him around and we'd meet up at different things. But that was all. Then we met up again through Young Farmers and that was it.

I didn't join CWA until after I was married and, because my mother-in-law didn't drive, it was my job to take her to CWA. This is back in 1974, and the month after I married they had a flower competition — a best bloom or something — so off we went and I've been going ever since. That was with the Branch at Caniambo. There's not much there these days, just a hall and a fire truck shed. There used to be a church and a school but they closed down a fair while ago. When I first joined, we had around twenty-five members and we've got about nineteen now, which isn't too bad. But with CWA, your original Branch always seems to have the greatest attraction and, even though some of our members have retired or whatever and have moved into Shepparton, they still come back out to Caniambo for meetings. When you've been friends for so long, it's a good way of keeping in touch.

The Caniambo Branch first started in 1946. Prior to that, during the war, the women belonged to what was known as 'the Comforts Fund', which was run through the Red Cross. That's where groups of women got together, once a month, to make pyjamas and socks and things for the war effort. I've actually got the minutes of their meetings, which is quite interesting. Then after the war they said, 'Gee, we'll miss not getting together,' and so they formed a CWA Branch. It's virtually the same thing, really. We still work for the common good, plus we maintained the all-important camaraderie.

As for special memories: well, I've been involved at State level for the last eleven years and I've just finished a term as Victorian State President and, oh, it certainly takes you right out of your comfort zone at times. So when that happens I just take a deep breath and say a little prayer and sail on in, in the hope I get through it. But there's been so many memorable experiences. During my time as State President, one would definitely be when we celebrated CWA Victoria's eightieth birthday in 2008 and we had a wonderful party on the lawns of Government House. Then there's the occasional challenge where a Branch might be having problems and you have to step in to try and sort things out. There's also the ever-present dealing with people and their individual personalities. Unfortunately, I didn't have an administrative background. I just had to learn along the way. As I said, just take a deep breath, say a prayer and off you go.

Of course, then there's been the drought and the bushfires. That was a huge challenge because we were dealing with large amounts of government and other funding. I suppose, over my time, we wrote cheques out for something like five million dollars, just in Victoria alone. We also made up the pamper packs. They're packs that contained things like hair shampoo, deodorant, soaps; things that we take for granted and, through our committees, members went out and dropped the packs off to the women and their families. We also used to use milk tanker drivers or whoever and, when they went out on their runs, they'd put a pack in the mail box. We didn't want any great recognition. We just put a little note in the packs to say they were from CWA, and we've handed out thousands of those. They're just to let people know that someone cares.

Then, with the government money: both state and federal governments have a huge respect for CWA, so they approached us and asked if we'd distribute the money. Yes, they came to us. They said, 'We've got this money. You've got your contacts in all the affected areas. Can we work together to work out a form so that the people can apply for relief.' So we did that and we distributed the first lot of relief money, then they came back with more. They trusted us and they knew we had the network and, being a volunteer organisation, they also knew we'd be able to get the money out into those communities without a lot of red tape and expense. Mind you, we did take a little bit for administration. That was just to cover phone calls and postage and that. So a lot of reporting and recording was done because we did get audited by the government people. Then we've also dealt with funding through the Woolworths Drought Relief days.

We did the same after the bushfires and, oh, we were inundated with donated goods. The head office car port, here in Toorak, was full, so were a couple of bedrooms. The craft room was also full. We made up lots of packs with just the basics, you know, a towel with a face washer, some soap; things like that. Then other than the government money there were the financial donations. That not only came in from other states; people were even walking in off the street and saying, 'Here's a donation.' One lady from South Australia rang up and said, 'I'll send you a thousand dollars.' Then I was at a meeting out at Essendon one time and a lady walked in off the street — she wasn't CWA — and she said, 'We've had a morning tea and I've collected these goods and I've also collected money, can you distribute it all?'

Plus, there's also the fun things we do. For the last five years we've put a team in the Red Cross Murray River Marathon. That's a canoe race. You start at Yarrawonga and paddle down to Swan Hill, and that helps raise the reputation and image of CWA. We did it as a relay — one leg at a time. That's also a fundraiser, though it's not for CWA. It was originally for the Red Cross and to enter a team you've got to raise something like $3000. But we don't mind helping other organisations, just as long as it's for a good cause. We do that a lot. We work with Drought Relief. There's the Chernobyl disaster. There's Vic Relief Food Bank and there's the hospitals. So with things like that, we work with other organisations and it helps everyone.

But the Murray Marathon is good fun. As I said, it projects a different image of CWA and, in turn, it helps attract new members. Husbands and families come as well and daughters of members who can row. Some camp. I kid my husband to come along and we take a caravan and he acts as one of the land crew. A few of us have done it for the whole five years that it's been going. We have a seventy-six-year-old who has done the marathon every year, and also a seventy-four-year-old. And it's incredible: the oldest lady, she can't swim, she's a bit afraid of water and she's also got two bung knees. But she just gets in there and she paddles. And that's the character of the CWA, isn't it? Two bung knees. Can't swim. Is afraid of the water. Jumps in a kayak. Takes a deep breath. Says a little prayer, and away she goes. That's the attitude.

Joan Wallwork
Hamilton, Victoria

I live at Branxholme, which is in the western district of Victoria, between Hamilton and Portland. It's almost twenty-six k's from Hamilton, on the Portland Road. I belong to the Hamilton Branch of CWA which is in the Henty Group. There are nine Branches in the actual Group. We go from the South Australian border, down to the coast, almost to Warrnambool, then up to Glenthompson, along the highway to Hamilton and straight on to the Victorian–South Australian border near Penola. So, as a Group, we do a lot of travelling to get together.

Though, actually I'm not originally from Victoria. My father's parents were from Mangrove Mountain, which is out of Gosford, on the Central Coast of New South Wales, and my mother's parents were from Mangrove Creek, which is up the Freshwater end of the Hawkesbury River. Dad's family were mainly dairy and citrus people and Mum's were beef cattle and citrus. I'd say it'd be about approximately fifty miles between Mangrove Creek and Mangrove Mountain but Mum's parents had the tennis courts and so everyone in the district would come and play tennis there or if they had dances or had functions, the communities would all come together. And that's how my parents met.

After my parents were married they moved out of that area and so I was born in Sydney and I grew up in Wollongong. From school I went to Sydney University and I did science and also music at the Sydney Conservatory. At that stage Sydney didn't have a degree in music so I transferred to Melbourne where I did a Music degree and an Arts degree, then my Dip Ed. Teaching's been my life really. I've taught in many secondary schools throughout Victoria: places like Richmond High which, back then, was pre-fabs in the old Brighton Street State School grounds. From there I went to Camberwell High. While I was at Camberwell High I met and married my husband. He came from England. He's actually an engineer by training and he worked with the Environment Protection Authority, or EPA as it was known, here in Victoria. He's the feller that did the original Land Waste Management Policy, back in the 90s. So then, after Camberwell, I was at Ringwood, temporarily, then at another place, I just forget for the moment. Following that, I taught at Yarra Valley before moving up to Hamilton College in the late 1990s.

Oddly enough, though, I was unaware of CWA until we moved to Branxholm, and the neighbours, who were members, invited me to a picnic. As I'd only been there a couple of days I didn't want to offend them, so I went along and that's when I joined CWA. You could say that I was conscripted or whatever, but I never resented it. Never regretted it. That was with the Wallacedale Branch. Wallacedale was a small Branch near Branxholm and I stayed with them until I finished as Group President of Henty Group then I transferred to the much bigger Hamilton Branch. That made things easier for me because at that stage I was teaching in Hamilton.

When I was first came here, in 1999, there used to be fifteen CWA Branches in the Henty Group, then the Blue Gums People moved in. The Blue Gums People were the blue gum tree plantation people and they bought a lot of land off the sheep farmers and when that happened a lot of those farmers just moved on. Take Dergholm for instance, the Blue Gums People virtually bought the whole town out and so a lot of those smaller CWA Branches either closed or amalgamated. Though I'd say, overall, we've not really lost that many members, other than to death. Currently there's probably about two hundred and seventy members within the Group but, as I said, with less Branches.

Branxholm was too small to have a Branch of its own and so Wallacedale took in that area. By 'too small' I mean, in the Branxholm area there's only ninety-one people. They call it a town but it's basically just a tiny village with a shop and a hotel, plus a school. School numbers vary. Before the Blue Gums People came in there were about fifty students. Then, when the Blue Gums People moved in, it went up to about sixty-two children. But after the plantation had been established their numbers decreased because there was no more work there, so now the school's back to about thirty students. It comes and goes. Then for their secondary education the children go into Hamilton.

With CWA, I've been on various committees at both Branch and State level. In particular I've enjoyed my time at state level where I've been Chairman of Performing Arts, Chairman of Social Issues and then a State Vice-President. After that I had a year off from working at state level and I'm just getting back into it now, again as Henty Group President. But with the year I had off, although I was busy in my Branch, I did really miss the contact at state level; of coming down here to Melbourne on regular basis, where you're right in the thick of it. And you make such good friends, from all over. They say that, if you're with CWA, wherever you go, someone will find you through the CWA network. It's just amazing who you'll meet. Some people have even met relatives that they've forgotten about or didn't realise they ever had.

It happened to me: with me having come from New South Wales, three out of the four of my immediate grandparents were direct descendents of the First Fleet. So the Wallworks have been out here for that long. Then some years back we were at a CWA function up at Myrtleford, in the central north-east of Victoria and we went to a winery and the wife of one of the owners was a Wallwork. And it turned out that we were third or fourth cousins, from back a time in England. So as I say, through the CWA network, you never know who you'll meet.

But, of course, like everywhere, a lot of our members are getting on a bit in age. In Victoria we currently have one member who is one hundred and three. Then there's a couple of members who are a hundred and two and several that are a hundred and one. In fact, in our Hamilton Branch, one of our members will be one hundred and two in June and she still comes to meetings. Not every time, mind you, but she still comes along. Her mind is still very active but, unfortunately, her sight's not quite as good as it used to be. These days, other than getting the CWA magazine in print form, she also gets it as a tape recording and she'll sit with the magazine and listen to the tape, which she thoroughly enjoys. Though, unfortunately, she is getting a little frail because, a while back, she fell over her daughter's dog and broke her hip, and at that age the doctors tend to say, 'The shock of it all will probably be the end of you.' But no, she was two or three months in hospital and now she's back and walking around. She has a walking stick. That's all she needs and, as I said, whenever she's able she still gets along to our meetings.

Janette Williams
Trundle, New South Wales

Some very strange things can happen in some of these small country towns. The term could probably described as 're-birthing' or 'evolving', and it's when a misfortune turns into an opportunity. You might not be able to see it as you pass through those tiny dusty places, with their burnt-out weeds and small populations, but it's there, and it is happening.

For instance, take our town of Trundle in central New South Wales. We once had a blacksmith but, with the advent of cars, blacksmiths became redundant and his shop became vacant. The local pre-school was looking for a home so then, even though it was a little small for their needs, they moved into the old blacksmith's shop. The next misfortune — or fortune, if you will — was when the bowling club went broke and it had to vacate. Of course, the pre-school seized on this opportunity and so it moves out of the old blacksmith's shop and down to the bowling club. It's a wonderful pre-school with a beautifully flat playing area. They're good and settled. It's exactly what they want.

Then with the old blacksmith's shop becoming vacant once more, the library moves out of its cramped room in the Memorial Hall and it sets itself up in the old blacksmith's shop. Now we have a lovely library which has a Community Technological Centre and so it has banks of computers for us all to use. We used to get poor satellite reception and the Community Technological Centre was set up when government wanted everyone to learn how to use the 'new media' and all those sorts of things. That's been very successful and so we can now print all the necessary invitations and so forth, as we have a lot of funerals in Trundle plus there's also the occasional wedding and birth. Best of all is that the library has found a good home.

While all this is going on, the Masonic Lodge strikes hard times. They run out of sufficient numbers to maintain a Chapter in the area and so their large brick building becomes vacant. But because the community had built the building it had to be returned to the community and so they started looking at various bodies around the town that might find the building useful. And here was an opportunity for CWA. My belief was that we should have the building because we were used to running the administration of buildings and so we knew the traps to look out for. To that end it was agreed that, for the minuscule sum of $5,000, CWA would become the owners of the Masonic building. It was a bargain because the place was worth at least $220,000 on the open market.

So we become the proud owners of this magnificent old Masonic building. But then, misfortune strikes again. There's another twist to the tale. Because, I don't know if you know much about the Masonic Lodge or not but, it's a males-only organisation and so when we moved into the building, there were only male toilets. There was nothing for the women. So at the cost of $11,000 we had to build new toilets down the back and that was just for the digging out and putting toilets in and, as yet, we're still to get a proper sewerage system.

And that notion of 're-birthing' or 'evolving', that I spoke about earlier, encapsulates many of our country towns. Where there is a vacant building there's always someone willing to move into it, and that's what keeps the town evolving. Though, mind you, the ladies' toilet is still down the back of the old Masonic Lodge building, which is misfortunate. I'm Branch President at the moment and I won't go down there. I'm not fond of outside toilets, good, bad or different. You never know what's in them: spiders, snakes. There could be anything. We'll have to sort that out next meeting.

So that's my small contribution.

Confectionery and Homemade Sweets

Barley Sugar
Mrs E. Faulkner, Ravenswood, CWA Tas

1 lb loaf sugar
1 gill water
Pinch of cream of tartar

Juice and rind of half
lemon

Put sugar and water in a saucepan and when sugar is dissolved, add cream of tartar and strips of lemon rind. Boil mixture to 240°F. Remove from fire, add lemon juice, boil to 310°F. Remove rind and pour on to a slightly oiled slab. Cool slightly then fold sides to middle. Pull into strips and twist. Store in air-tight bottles.

Butterscotch
CWA NSW

¾ cup butter
3 cups sugar
1 cup boiling water

½ teaspoon essence of
vanilla

Combine the butter, sugar and boiling water and boil until a little that is tried in cold water is brittle. This takes about 45 minutes. Add vanilla and pour into a butterscotch pan, making mixture not more than ¼ inch deep. When nearly cold, mark into small squares with a buttered knife. Cover the butterscotch, if liked, with some chopped nuts.

Coconut Ice
CWA NSW

1 lb sieved icing sugar
Pinch of cream of tartar
Eggwhite

3 tablespoons condensed
milk
¼ lb desiccated coconut

Mix ½ lb icing sugar and desiccated coconut with cream of tartar. Slightly beat the white of egg and add it, also the milk. Work together till quite smooth, gradually adding sufficient of remainder of icing sugar to make a stiff mass. Dust the board and rolling pin with icing sugar and roll out mixture ½ inch thick. Repeat ingredients as above and when mixing add a little carmine to make a soft pink. Roll out mixture as before, brush over white layer with white of egg. Press the pink layer on top then cut coconut slice into bars or squares and leave to dry.

Marshmallows

C. Blackwell, Campbell Town, CWA Tas

2 oz gelatine	2 lb sugar
2½ cups water	Colours and flavours

Place gelatine in a basin, add one cup of the water. Place the remainder of the water, with the sugar, in a saucepan and bring to boiling stage. Add soaked gelatine and boil for 20 minutes. Pour into two basins. Allow to cool slightly. Flavour one with vanilla and colour the other pink and also flavour. Beat each mixture until thick. Pour into tins which have been greased and sprinkled with cornflour. When set, cut into squares and roll in icing sugar and cornflour.

Nougat

CWA Tas

1 lb sugar	4 oz blanched and roughly
6 oz glucose	chopped almonds
2 teaspoons honey	1 oz crystallised cherries
½ teaspoon of vanilla	If you like, a little chopped
2 eggwhites	angelica

Dissolve sugar, glucose and honey into ¼ pint water and boil to brittle stage. Stand pan in a bowl of boiling water. Beat till the temperature is below boiling point. Add stiffly beaten eggwhites and ½ teaspoon of vanilla. Beat till white and add heated nuts and fruit. When thick, pour into a narrow tin that is lined with wax paper. Leave to set in cool place for four days. Cut up and wrap in wax paper after rolling in icing sugar and cornflour.

Peanut Brittle

CWA NSW

6 oz sugar

3 tablespoons hot
  water

4 oz glucose

1 dessertspoon butter

4 oz peanuts, blanched
  and chopped or split

½ teaspoon bicarbonate
  of soda

¼ teaspoon salt

Boil sugar and water with the glucose. Add butter and peanuts and boil, stirring until the peanuts are cooked — 10 minutes should be sufficient. Remove from the fire and add bicarbonate of soda and salt, which has been dissolved in a teaspoon of water. Stir well and then pour out on a large buttered tray. Pull brittle out till very thin.

Snowballs

CWA NSW

FILLING:

½ oz gelatine

½ pint water

1 lb sugar

1 dessertspoon maize
  syrup or glucose

1 eggwhite

Few drops of vanilla
  essence

COATING:

2 oz sweetened chocolate

2 oz unsweetened
  chocolate

2 oz desiccated coconut

Few drops vanilla essence

Hot water

Soak gelatine in ¼ pint water. Stir water, sugar and glucose in saucepan over moderate heat till dissolved. Boil with lid on saucepan for a few minutes to steam sides. Remove lid. Wipe the side of the saucepan with a brush that is dipped in cold water to prevent sugar graining. Boil to 240°F. Stir in the water and dissolved gelatine and boil again. Beat eggwhite and add strained syrup gradually, adding a few drops of vanilla essence, and beat till thick and stiff. Shape into small balls or pour into small buttered moulds. Leave till firmly set before coating.

Stir chocolate over hot water till melted and evenly blended. Add a few drops vanilla essence. (Chocolate must not be more than blood heat). Dip each ball separately and toss in coconut. If preferred, the coconut may be mixed with the chocolate before dipping the balls. Dry in a cool place before storing in air-tight containers.

Toffee

CWA Tas

1 lb white sugar
¼ pint water
1 tablespoon vinegar
1 oz butter

Add all ingredients to saucepan and after the sugar is completely dissolved, boil, without stirring, to the brittle stage and pour into a buttered tin.

Turkish Delight (genuine)

CWA NSW

2 lb white sugar
2 egg whites
1 lemon
¼ lb maizena or cornflour
2½ pints water
Rose or lemon essence

Make syrup of 1 quart water and the sugar and clear it with the juice of the lemon and the whites of the eggs. Dissolve the maizena (or cornflour) in ½ pint cold water, strain and add it to the syrup when boiling. Boil until the mixture is stringy and thick then flavour it with rose or lemon essence. Have 2 dishes ready — one oiled and the other covered with sifted sugar then turn the oiled dish over on to the sugared one. Soak up any oil that remains. Cut into squares and cover with sugar so that when put away the squares will not stick together.

Evelyn Wilson
Darwin, Northern Territory

I'm originally from Western Australia. I was born in the wheat belt area, out at Southern Cross. Then, when I was young, my parents moved to Dardanup, just out of Bunbury, which is where all the cattle sales were. So it wasn't until the early 60s that I came to Darwin and I met my husband-to-be, Ted, up here. He was originally from Queensland, and so we met and then I went away on my travels and he went away on his travels. We corresponded — letter writing — then in 1966 we got married and we've been here ever since, and we love it.

But I think that, in many ways, to live in a place like the Territory you have to be different. You have to have a certain toughness about you and I believe that that strength comes from having a strong heritage. Because after the war, when my father returned to England, having served over in France and elsewhere, there was no work, so he volunteered to be a ten-pound Pom. Then, when he arrived out here, he was given ten pounds and he bought a tent and a shovel and a frying pan and whatever and he went out into the wheat belt to work for a farmer. As it turned out the neighbours were ten-pound Poms as well. They were a family of fourteen and Mum was one of them.

So my parents met up and they got married and they lived in homemade bough sheds, made from tree trunks and branches, and the walls were lined with painted wheat bags to keep out the weather — the scorching heat and the freezing cold and the rain — and they made their own furniture out of kerosene boxes, and Mum was a marvellous cook. All the women were, out that way. They could make a meal out of very little and they swapped their eggs and vegies and other produce. Dad was good at growing vegies and Mum was a real green thumb. Oh, she had a beautiful garden with masses of flowers. People even asked her for flowers for funerals and things and, of course, everything was always simply 'given' or 'donated', no matter how scarce money was.

My parents worked hard and through trying conditions and after living through all that the locusts came and ate them out. Then the next year prices fell and so the banks came in and they took over everything. After that, my parents shifted to Dardanup where Dad worked for a dairy farmer and he was also involved in the Veteran Defence Service. Dairy farming was something totally different from what he was used to and with me being a real little 'farmer' I also helped with the cows.

Then the government started selling fifty-acre blocks of land, at cheap interest rates, so they bought one of those. We were three miles out of Dardanup. It was all gravel roads and if Mum wanted to go into town she had to walk. More or less, the only time Dad drove her in was if he also had something to do in town or if she had cakes or anything like that to take to a CWA meeting. And as a five-year-old I remember how we'd ride our pushbikes over those bumpy gravel roads to go to school, and I continued to do that until I left there, after high school and work. So I think that sort of upbringing is what helps you do well in the Territory. You have to be strong to live up here. You know, if you'd been mollycoddled as a child I don't think you would've stayed in the Territory, especially not in the early days. So I think that's why I enjoy living up here. Oh, and I must add, what also helps is the positive support from your partner and with having Ted as my husband, I'm thankful of having plenty of that.

I'd known about CWA most of my life because of my mother being a member of the Dardanup Branch and I'd go along to the saleyards with her and Dad, during the school holidays, and Mum and the CWA ladies, they'd sell scones and cups of tea to the cattle men. And I remember listening to the auctioneers, auctioning the cattle. 'Hep. Hep. Hep,' they'd go and I just loved it. I also remember my mum making yummy cakes and toffee and marshmallows and lollies for fundraisers. So you could say that

CWA has always been in my life, as has Red Cross, because my mother was a member of both those organisations in Dardanup. In Western Australia, lots of towns end in 'up', like Gelorup, Boyanup, Manjimup and so forth. Lots.

Then, as far as my belonging to CWA, actually, I've only just joined in the last year. I used to patronise the little CWA shop in Knuckey Street, Darwin, when it was there, but after Ted and I shifted out to the Tiwi Village — the Masonic retirement village for the over-55s — I was still working then and because CWA always met of a daytime I never joined. Also, like my mother, I'm a mad gardener. I grow orchids, and that was like a disease, you know — an addiction would be a good word for it. I'm a Foundation Member of the Nightcliff Orchid Society. That was a night-time thing so it was easier for me to go along to that. But now I'm older and Ted finds it difficult to drive at night-time, because of cataracts and things, I've stopped going to anything of a night-time. Anyhow, I knew Nancy Fuchs, who is a past president and a keen CWA member and I also knew Maude Ellis, another keen CWA member — Maude also belonged to the Orchid Society — and I wanted a new interest and so last year I joined CWA because, with holding their meetings of a daytime, it just seemed the natural thing to do.

Though I must say that, when I first went along, I felt a bit like a fish out of water. Well, in my younger days, my mother taught me to sew and I sewed just about everything. Then when I got married, I bought a you-beaut, expensive Elna sewing machine and everything was sewn. But in Darwin, now, with all these places like Kmart and Big W and other big shops coming along, why would you want to sew? I also used to make craft cards and do floral art but all that stopped when I concentrated on gardening and my volunteer work. So I had put all those skills aside.

But I must say that all the members have made me feel very, very welcome — very welcome, indeed — and they get me involved and so now I'm very much enjoying being in CWA.

The only problem is that they set out all these lovely cakes and scones and sandwiches and things and here's me, trying to lose weight. That's why I bring along cuts of vegetables to meetings — like carrots and celery and capsicum — to nibble on, to try and distract me. Though, for some reason, that doesn't always work because I still somehow end up getting into the cakes.

Dawn Worrall
Para Hills, South Australia

In many ways I've led a sheltered life, especially when I was young. My ancestors were on a mixed farm of sheep and crops up at Yongala, which is up in, sort of, the mid-north of South Australia, near Peterborough. From there we shifted down to Long Plains, on the Adelaide Plains, and I went to Long Plains School. It was just a tiny school, with one teacher. For some reason I didn't enjoy school so my education didn't go that far. I was okay with the lady teacher but not with the men teachers. I think it was because my mother had left me when I was a little baby and I was always sort of looking for a mother image. My grandma brought me up and, oh, she was such a very strict and disciplined woman. I could go to church, yes, but I wasn't allowed to play any sport or go to dances. I had two older brothers and, when my mother left, they had to go to other places to live so our family was not kept together. Now, I've just lost my second brother. He was eighty-one and, because we hadn't been as close as I wanted us to be, I really felt that. All that missed time, lost. It's sad.

My grandma wasn't in CWA. Nobody in my family was and, even though I was living in the country, I'd never even heard of CWA. After Long Plains I married and we moved to suburbia and we lived at Magill and I had a son and two daughters. I was always involved with the church and Sunday School. Then, I'm afraid my marriage did split up. That was sad, but I kept my children. They're all mature people these days. But I did keep them together when my marriage dissolved and that was the main thing.

Then I looked after my father for his last ten years. He had nobody and, by then, my children were all teenagers. It was a big responsibility and I had to work as well. I got a school cleaning contract. Then after about eight years of being single I met a friend and we married and, after my father passed on, we shifted down to Para Hills West. I gradually got to know a few people there and there was a really lovely lady that went to the church and one day she said, 'Come along to CWA.' So I did. And that was it. That was back in 1990 and because I only knew family and work, I was so very shy for the first twelve months. But some very special ladies took me under their wing. So it was all right though, unfortunately, those ladies are not with us any more. Para Hills CWA was a big group of nearly forty. A real happy group they were, too, and we still are.

At first I just thought I'd go and learn handicrafts. Right from my childhood I was able to sew and knit but I wanted to learn more, but then I thought, Oh, that sounds so mean, just going to learn handicrafts. I've got to give something, not just take. So when they asked me to be Handicraft Officer I said, 'Yes,' and, oh, that was so hard. It was scary. Anyway I did do it. I don't say I was very talented. But with being Handicraft Officer I had to come to town and learn three crafts each year, which you then took back and taught to your Branch members. I specially loved Battenburg lace. That's a lacy tape. You buy it by the metre. It's about a centimetre wide and there's a thread in it that you pull in and gather and you bring it around to make leaves and flowers. You can decorate collars or make table centres or decorate table cloths. I don't think it's around at the moment. Fashion goes around in circles. But I loved it.

We also did all kinds of net darning and embroidery. Net darning is a special net you darn to make flower designs or borders. We also made felt animals, which were put in Baby Parcels and given to the needy women who'd just had a baby or as Christmas gifts for the underprivileged. I remember, once, I made a mummy mouse, a daddy mouse and a baby mouse. My stitching wasn't very good in those days and so when I entered them in a competition they only accepted one mouse. Anyway,

I didn't worry too much because after the competition my set of mice went to underprivileged children, which was good. Then during one of our wool campaigns we knitted woollen toys. We did a demonstration in at John Martins — that's when the John Martins store was there — and I sat in with the ladies and we knitted woollen toys.

Then when it was my turn to back out as Branch Handicraft Officer, somebody better came along and I ended up as Branch Secretary and later on Branch President. Now I'm back as Secretary again. It's been recycle, recycle. But it's all been wonderful. I've been in CWA for over eighteen years now and what I get out of it is the friendships and knowing that we're raising money for those who suffer through things like bush fires or floods or the drought. And coming from the country I can understand all that. It's all right to have land but you've got to have a bit of cash to live, don't you, especially when things go bad.

But CWA has been a big part of my life. We've got twenty-six members in our Para Hills Branch and, because we haven't got our own rooms, we hire the church hall. I'm also still strongly linked with the church, even more strongly now that my second husband is very ill. Yes, unfortunately, he's very ill. I think God had it in His plan that I've always needed to look after somebody and through CWA I've received a lot of moral support. It also keeps my brain active and I've learned to type. You see, I never went to high school and so, when one of our members brought along her electric typewriter and said, 'Here, can you use this?' I said, 'Oh, yes, please.'

So I taught myself how to type and now I type the minutes of our meetings. I'm also a keen gardener and for the last few years I've been pruning the roses in the garden at the South Australian CWA State Offices. There's a hundred and twenty roses, or so I've been told, because I lose count. And now that I've got a friend helping me, we look after the whole garden; everything except for the lawn mowing. We spend one day a week there — summer and winter — to keep it under control. Then I've got my own garden at home. It's a wonderfully colourful garden. A happy garden. I do everything there, even mow the lawn. I just love the outdoors and I'm so busy out there that I'm usually too tired, after gardening all day, to do any handicraft. Plus there's my husband to look after and I've also got to keep the Branch bookwork up. But gardening is a very big part of my life. Like CWA, gardening's a giving thing and it's one I get a lot of pleasure out of.

Gloria Wright
Cloncurry, Queensland

Well, what would you like to know? I came over to Australia in 1987, on the 15th of March. I came from the Philippines. I married Benjamin Wright from Cloncurry. Since then I stay here and I'm still here. The Wright family were pioneers of this area. My husband, he was born in Cloncurry but his father was from Staffordshire, in England, and his mum was from County Cork, in Ireland. They came here in the late 1880s. First they went mining. That's when mining was good in Cloncurry and then they moved a little farther out of Cloncurry and they bought the hotel — the Quamby Pub. Then they also bought the farm, Buffalo Plains. That was in a partnership and when they sold the property and the pub, sometime in the early part of the 1950s, they came back into Cloncurry to settle down.

When I married Benjamin we lived an hour's drive from Cloncurry, at Arrolla Station. It was isolated and I had no neighbours but I had to socialise somehow so I decided to go to the CWA. At first I didn't join, I just came into Cloncurry to be with the CWA ladies. I only decided to join in 1990, when I had my daughter, Maria. The main reason I joined was to be able to get together with the ladies and also so that the children could all play together. The CWA women used to come out on the weekends to visit me, with their kids and their families and we had fun. We would go on picnics at the billabong, whenever there was water. But most of the time we didn't have water anyway. Then, when my husband died fifteen years ago, it was too much for me to drive my daughter, Maria, to and fro into town for her to go to school so we moved in to town, into Cloncurry, and I've been in here for fifteen years now.

Other than my involvement with CWA I teach religious

education at the local Cloncurry State School and I teach arts and crafts during school holidays for the kids. It's very good because I have more than a hundred kids coming over to attend the arts and crafts, and with their mothers as well. We do knitting, crocheting and painting and sometimes we all pitch in. When there is a school holiday, sometimes Sister Lyn from the St Joseph Convent helps teach painting for the kids. Always somebody is waiting to do knitting because I have a knitting machine. Now I teach mostly crocheting and my daughter, Maria, teaches other crafts because there are a lot of kids, all with different ages. I handle the bigger ones and Maria handles the younger kids.

But in areas like this, isolation is a big problem and so I like to get together with the other CWA women. When we go to someone else's house we bring a plate of food. It's good to meet at different places and see what's happening in their area. We do our knitting and we exchange ideas and do some gossiping and we talk about what the news of the day is. It's really the friendship that's very prominent in our area. And all that is very uplifting for our spirit because, in the dry season, when you see that everything is brown and dying around you, it gets so depressing. So we help one another and we give advice, which is an important thing up here because in this area, which is very remote, suicide is a problem.

One of our member's husbands committed suicide, March of last year. That was very bad. It was over in the Normanton area. It was so dry; just brown and dry, everywhere. No water. No rain at all. We even had to get water in on the train at Cloncurry and it was delivered to our houses by the fire truck. But there was no water on the property where the husband was working and so things were very bad and all his stock were dying because there was no water. He found it too hard so he shot himself. His wife was a member of CWA and so we were able to be a great support to her and her kids. But, at the beginning, because of the remote property where they were, the flying padre was the only person that could get straight in to see her because he has a small Cessna aeroplane and he can move anywhere. So to start with we just sent whatever we could with the flying padre, to comfort that poor woman and her kids.

Yes, so the isolation is a big problem in our area and that's where CWA is so important in being able to help. But the irony of all that was that the husband committed the suicide because he couldn't cope when things were so dry and three weeks later the rain came. In some places it even flooded.

Robyn Wright
Moruya, New South Wales

I'm from the Moruya Branch of CWA. Moruya being on the south coast of New South Wales. As to how I came to join CWA? Well I was actually 'nagged' — I guess is the word — by a close friend. It was something that I was always intending to do but just didn't ever get around to doing it. Then, finally, when I did go to a meeting, I came home as Branch Secretary. So it was a rapid and steep learning curve. But it proved to be really good because, with having to go here and there and listen to everyone talk about 'Branch' and 'Group' and 'State' and so forth, I learned very quickly. Well I had to really, didn't I? At that time there was only about twenty members at Moruya, though not too many were what you'd call 'active members'. We'd probably only get about eight ladies to a meeting. Mind you, that was thirty-something years ago and we've grown significantly since then.

Now, as far as stories: I guess there's one I often laugh about and that happened a long time ago. It was when Pat, one of our past Group Presidents had the New South Wales State President on tour with her. As you may imagine, when you've got your State President attending functions, it's a very big thing so people really get dressed up. Anyhow, on this occasion it was raining and Pat and the State President were walking out the back of the CWA Hall and the person behind them kindly put up an umbrella to shield them from the rain. Always being a person who so well presented herself, for this big occasion Pat had a wig on but, unfortunately, as the umbrella went up it caught on to Pat's wig and up went the wig as well and it ended up on top of the umbrella. When Pat retrieved the wig, it was a bit wet and limp, but she put it back on and soldiered on in true CWA manner.

That's just one little story. Then, as far as my interests lie, at the moment I'm Branch Secretary and Catering Officer and my interests are international work, handicraft and cooking. Basically, all that CWA does I'm interested and involved in. But one of our greatest achievements is that our Moruya Branch has its own tea rooms in Queen Street and that's just one of six tea rooms still existing in New South Wales. We purchased the land in the early 70s and built on that. Then later on we extended the driveway area to house the Baby Health Centre and a dentist. That was at a cost of $75,000 dollars and I think within something like five years we had that repaid.

Then two years ago we put in a $50,000 refurbished commercial stainless steel kitchen and now that the dentist and the Baby Health Centre have relocated, we've converted those rooms into a little shop and that's also doing extremely well. In the shop we sell the home fair, the pickles, the chutneys, the jams and baby clothes. The baby clothes sell really well and we just can't keep up the supply of homemade and craft items. Just last Saturday, through the shop and the tea rooms, we took $186 and that doesn't include the $100 dollars or more we took on the Thursday prior.

So our Branch has done well. We have a great building. We have a lovely hall, which is rented out a lot. Parquetry floors. And because there's only one other place in the town that's available for community use, it's a great provision. The tea rooms, they're a real little social gathering place. People come in for their cup of tea and sandwich and sometimes an hour or so later they're still sitting there, talking. It's all at a very reasonable cost too: $4 for a sandwich, a slice of cake and a cup of tea or coffee. You couldn't beat that, could you? We had seven ladies come in last Thursday, along with a lady who'd just turned eighty. That was their morning outing and they sat around and they chatted for about an hour or so. It was just lovely. Men are also welcome. It's not only for women. A lot of single fellows come in and they have a little bit of a chat with the ladies in the shop and the tea rooms.

It's all word of mouth. All run by volunteers. It has a wonderful community feel about it and it's absolutely safe.

Moruya Branch is now seventy-six years old. We've got a strong foundation of history from the days of penny-slot toilets and boiling our water in 4-gallon drums to having a great building where we now boil water within the confines of a stainless steel commercial kitchen. That's how much our Branch has grown and the ladies have been very active and happy. So CWA certainly keeps you busy, and in a positive way. And, oh, we also cater for functions. A lot of functions. Moruya has a retirement place out at Broulee and we do a lot of catering out there for birthdays and wakes. It just makes it easier for people to, sort of, hand it all over to CWA and then they don't have to worry about anything.

So I'd say that, in the last couple of years, our little Branch has come ahead in leaps and bounds. It's always done well, but it now has a feel of 'rejuvenation' about it. Unfortunately we're not overrun with new members but they're dribbling in and they have fresh ideas. Just recently we had two new memberships and they'll be active ladies, which is wonderful. Like all Branches, due to age and other difficulties, we do have a lot of members who are not active within the Branch these days, but they're still very supportive members.

Then the money we make, our main priority at the moment is to get our loan for the kitchen paid off and we're very proud to say that we now only owe $8,000. Of course we also support the New South Wales CWA Association Fund and all funds that CWA stands for. Then locally we support six schools who do a project on whatever our CWA country of study is, and they also join in with us on our International Day. We acknowledge the school and, for their Speech Night, there's $30 given to each school to provide a book or whatever prize the school allocates.

On top of all that, we provide every new-born baby at the local hospital with a pair of hand-knitted booties and a little bonnet. I was a midwife at the hospital for many years and that's been a CWA tradition in Moruya for more than thirty-two years, that

I'm aware of. And now, since the Bateman's Bay Maternity Unit has been relocated to Moruya, we deliver up to three hundred pairs of booties and bonnets per year. They're all individually wrapped, with a little label — made by CWA — on them. So you pack your little trolley and off you go and you present the booties and bonnets to all the new mums. It's very personal and they appreciate it so much.